MW00397671

The Light
of Other Days

The Light of Other Days

Caroline Couper Lovell

Introductions by Hugh Stiles Golson
& LeeAnn Whites

Mercer University Press
Macon, Georgia

ISBN 0-86554-465-4

The Light of Other Days
by Caroline Couper Lovell

The paper used in this publication meets the minimum requirements
of American National Standards for Information sciences—
Permanence of Paper for printed Library Materials,
ANSI Z39.48-1984.

Library of Congress Cataloging-in-Publication Data

Lovell, Caroline Couper
    The Light of Other Days/ Caroline Couper Lovell
        xxxiv + 16pp. of photographs + 183pp.   6x9"
    ISBN 0-86554-465-4
    1. Lovell, Caroline Couper, 1862–1947.

Mercer University Press would like to thank Betty Anglin Smith for
permission to reproduce her oil on canvas painting "Barrier Island" on the
front cover of *The Light of Other Days*. For more information about the work
of this Southern artist, please contact the Wells Gallery, 103 Broad Street,
Charleston, South Carolina 29401/ (803) 853-3233.

Contents

Other Days

Illustrations and family photographs between chapters 9 and 10

The Light of Other Days is published in association with THE NATIONAL SOCIETY OF THE COLONIAL DAMES OF AMERICA IN THE STATE OF GEORGIA. As stated in its constitution, "The objects of this society shall be: to collect and preserve manuscripts, traditions, relics, and mementos of bygone days; to preserve and restore buildings connected with the early history of our country; to educate our fellow citizens and ourselves in our country's history and thus diffuse healthful and intelligent information concerning the past; to create a popular interest in our Colonial history; to stimulate a spirit of true patriotism and a genuine love of country; and to impress upon the young the sacred obligation of honoring the memory of those heroic ancestors whose ability, valor, sufferings and achievements are beyond all praise." For additional information about its mission and activities, please write the society at the Andrew Low House, 329 Abercorn Street, Savannah, Georgia 31401.

Introduction
by Hugh Stiles Golson

llow me to introduce a most fascinating lady whom you
will find to be observant, perceptive, witty, and charm-
ing. She was a product of the values and morals of antebellum Georgia society, but was honed by the turmoil of
the Civil War and Reconstruction. She was a resident of
the boom and bustle of Birmingham, Alabama, and the
New South, but yet she was an artist and author whose passion and talent
ushered culture into that city's developing society. She was known in her
own day for her 1932 history of the Georgia barrier islands, *The Golden
Isles of Georgia*, which saw strong sales with Little, Brown of Boston
and quickly became a regional classic. She is known today through Eu-
genia Price's *Savannah* quartet, which tells of the Stiles of Savannah and
Cass/Bartow County. She is Caroline Couper Stiles Lovell, and this is her
haunting memoir of her childhood in the postwar era.

The War Between The States and the Reconstruction era provided
grist for the writing of numerous Southern memoirs; here the testimonies
of noble service and the resulting injustices could be presented before a
jury of posterity. The bitterness of defeat, death, and fall from grace are
the major themes of such writings, and along with their veiled call for
justice, are also found litanies of names, statistics, and events, which col-
lectively serve as an elaborate communication within a family that heeds
the very Southern admonition, "Lest we forget." The final products can
prove to be a difficult jumble of skewed facts, sentimentality, and venom
seasoned with overwhelming family data. Usually these memoirs were
written by the elderly, and their styles are far from smooth or polished.

Indeed, memoirs as a whole are some of the worst histories ever written. Most authors are amateurs writing long after the fact. Their primary
purpose is to put down in a permanent fashion the many embroidered
stories they have been reciting for years. The results are mostly disjoined

efforts that are nostalgic in perception and whose historic facts are blurred by the myopia of time.

Caroline Couper Lovell's *The Light of Other Days* stands in contrast to the average memoir. On the surface it seems to fit that mold—written sixty years after the fact, heavy on war and its aftermath, and filled with family stories and data—but from behind the variables of this genre emerges a complex narrative with valuable insight crafted by a talented author. Caroline Couper Lovell is not hung up on the bitterness of the past, nor does she bask long in the glow of nostalgia. She is a guide in the galleries of events of her unique childhood and youth. *The Light of Other Days* evolves as an unusual narrative, more akin to the Victorian autobiography than the Civil War memoir. It offers new insight into Southern cultural history and postwar sociology; it showcases individuals of regional and national historical prominence; it gives detailed descriptions of postwar Savannah, Bartow County, Georgia, and Sewanee, Tennessee; and it is served up in a completely original style.

CAROLINE COUPER STILES was born on 7 May 1862, as the world that her parents had known was coming to an end. Her father, Robert Mackay Stiles, was a twenty-six-year-old civil engineer working in Savannah and was about to receive the commission of lieutenant in the Confederate engineer corps. He and his wife Maggie and their two-year-old son Mackay occupied rooms in the house of his maternal grandmother, Mrs. Robert Mackay, on Broughton Street just off Abercorn. The Union Navy's blockade of Savannah and their recent attack on Hilton Head Island gave credence to the rumors of an attempt on Savannah itself. Robert's father, Colonel William Henry Stiles, was stationed with his 60th Georgia Regiment on Skidaway Island, and he would have been privy to inside speculation about the Union gunboats he regularly observed in Wassaw and Green Island Sounds as the gunboats menaced the outside ring of defense batteries. Colonel Stiles knew what this enemy could do, as he had been part of the force that repulsed the Hilton Head attack. In March of that year, Fort Pulaski, Savannah's river defense, had been surrendered to the Union forces after they smashed through its southeastern exposure with a new rifled cannon. Clearly, Savannah was no place for a pregnant woman and a small child. Maggie's parents, the James Hamilton Coupers, were equally vulnerable at Cannon's Point on St. Simons Island and at Hopeton plantation on the Altamaha River.

Maggie and her young son Mackay ultimately moved to Colonel Stiles's large estate, Etowah Cliffs, in North Georgia. Certainly, this inland location would never see a Yankee attack. William Henry Stiles had started this impressive home when the Cherokee country was opened to settlement and his political career found the Savannah field a bit crowded. His home began modestly as a simple clapboard structure done in the Savannah side-hall plan. With time and prosperity, it was enlarged and improved. Stiles had served a term in the U.S. Congress with James K. Polk, and when that son of Tennessee was elected president, he appointed Stiles as U.S. minister to the Hapsburg throne. His family joined him in Vienna for this stay that climaxed in the revolutions of 1848. After his European sojourn, Stiles made an ambitious enlargement of Etowah Cliffs with an extensive scored stucco Italianate section based loosely on the designs of Palladio. From the Etowah River, the house loomed high on a rocky rise at a bend. Its double-galleried verandahs, called piazzas by the family, stretched across the river side of the house, broken only by a pedimented gable that shifted the central section forward a few feet. Those guests who arrived by road were taken through an English-style park that led to a carriage circle. Here was the formal entry, flanked by two-story bays. These separate facades were united in a design more akin to the coast or to the West Indies—a formal entry with side galleries facing the water.

At Etowah Cliffs in the spring of 1862 the concerns were for safety of loved ones and of shortages in providing for the servants and hands. Elizabeth (Eliza) Mackay Stiles and an overseer were managing the affairs in the absence of her husband, and, all things considered, their fortunes were at their highest when Caroline was born. Within two years of that date though, the Union army would occupy her birthplace. Brigadier General Milo S. Hascall, commander of the Second Division of the U.S. 23rd Army Corps, would write from his headquarters at Etowah Cliffs:

> I consider it my duty to call the attention of the Major General commanding the Corps to the terrible state of things that exist in different parts of the Grand Army under General Major Sherman, so far as the wanton destruction of private property and works of art are concerned.

Within days of the general's withdraw, less honorable members of the Union army stabled horses in the house, busted out stained glass windows and the French doors to the piazzas, and pulled up the flooring.

Colonel Stiles's library was scattered across the fields. One neighbor complained that the wives of Union officers were plying the countryside in wagons, entering the abandoned homes, and taking what they liked. By this time, Caroline and her mother had taken refuge in Savannah and were awaiting Sherman's advancing army. Her father, now Captain Robert Mackay Stiles of the Confederate engineers assigned to General William J. Hardee, was one of the last Confederates to leave Savannah on 21 December 1864. He cut loose the pontoon bridges he had created to move Hardee's evacuating army out of the city so that it could be declared "open" and not subject to attack.

Here *The Light of Other Days* picks up. Caroline fills in the rich but tragic details of the years following. Toward end of the war, in 1865, her grandfather Stiles died from exhaustion trying to open new lands in South Georgia. The war years brought other deaths to the family before the colonel's: in 1862 Mrs. Robert Mackay of Savannah died as did her daughter Mrs. Benjamin Edward Stiles, and the colonel's only daughter, Mary Couper Stiles, the wife of Andrew Low, died during childbirth in 1863. Colonel Stiles's estate was in shambles and debt, but after the war his two sons—Caroline's Uncle Henry and her father Robert—decided to return to Etowah Cliffs, farm the land, and pay off the creditors. More sadness followed in 1866 as the families of William Henry Stiles, Jr. and Robert Mackay Stiles both lost children, and Maggie Stiles lost her father, James Hamilton Couper. Eliza Mackay Stiles was not content without her beloved husband, and she died in 1867 on the second anniversary of the colonel's death.

Within a few years the two growing families needed more space, so the land was divided, and the Robert Mackay Stiles family built a home on a rise in a nearby field. Financed by the spinster Mackay aunts Kate and Sarah, sisters of Eliza Mackay Stiles, who wisely turned over their assets to Andrew Low before the war, the new home was named Malbone after a Mackay cousin, the famous eighteenth-century miniaturist Edward Green Malbone. The house was based on a design drawn by Maggie's father and was patterned on his Hopeton plantation dower house, Altama. Christ Episcopal Church in Savannah is the only other extant example of James Hamilton Couper's architecture.

The 1870s brought more pain to the Stiles families. In 1874 William Henry Stiles, Jr. lost two children to diphtheria, and Caroline's father, Robert Mackay Stiles, died in a carriage mishap in nearby Cartersville. In 1876 Aunt Sarah Mackay died, and in 1878 Uncle William Henry

Stiles, Jr. was gored by his bull "Baltimore." This violence opened his old injury from the Battle of Fredericksburg, and he died from the wound. In the following year, Aunt Kate Mackay passed away. With their husbands Henry and Bob dead, the strong widows Eliza C. Stiles and Margaret W. Stiles were left to run their households alone; for several decades, they cast long shadows across the land and their families.

Caroline's memoir ends with her marriage at Malbone to William Storrow Lovell in 1884. This promising young man, the product of a prominent Mississippi family, would be the center of Caroline's universe as she was to his. Though their sixty-year marriage was childless, there was an open affection and tenderness between them that they carried to their graves. "Tod," as he was called by his family, took his bride to Rosedale, a family plantation on Palmyra Island in the Mississippi River near Natchez. Here they lived for three years as Tod helped to manage the family holdings on that desolate isle. Working with his querulous father proved taxing, so the young couple made a decision to relocate to the town of Birmingham in 1888. Here Tod invested in business opportunities. Caroline later wrote of these years:

> It was eminently a young man's town, for what counted most in Birmingham was neither wealth nor family, but ability. With a fine climate and mineral resources that were unsurpassed—iron ore, coal and lime lying in the closest proximity known—it was destined to become the greatest industrial city of the South, and it was a fine thing to grow up with it. Birmingham . . . had nothing of the bitterness of war, and its people, coming from the north, south, east and west, have here become devoted friends. With none of the restrictions of petrified conventions, everyone can lead his own delightfully independent life.

The Lovells found their niche in this protean town. Tod was joined in business by his brother-in-law, Hamilton Stiles, and Edward Wilkerson of Chicago as partners in the Western Grain Company, a venture that was profitable. This success allowed Tod to found a company three years later that contracted labor for coal mining. Caroline became a civic and cultural leader, active in the Music Studio Club, the Little Gallery, the Drama League, the Nineteenth Century Club, and the Cadmean Circle. She was also a founder of St. Mary's Episcopal Church and a Red Cross chapter. In 1894 the Lovells built an impressive home at 2207 Ridge Park Avenue only to see it and most of their possessions burnt up in the following year. They rebuilt their home, and this structure served as their primary residence for the remainder of their lives.

Caroline's calling in life was her art, and her life in Birmingham allowed her to pursue drawing and painting. There was a high degree of artistic talent within the Robert Mackay Stiles family, and Caroline, as well as her sisters Belle and Margie, were accomplished artists. For several years Margie Stiles served as art instructor at the Hartridge School in Plainfield, New Jersey, and was later a curator at the Telfair Academy of Arts and Science in Savannah. Caroline, however, proved to be the more prolific. Her art instruction began at Madame Lefebvres's boarding school in Baltimore, where she received instruction from Mrs. Cuyler, a Savannahian. The Lovells' relocation to Birmingham also opened the opportunity for further study. As Tod's time in their first year in Birmingham was monopolized by his business venture, it was decided that Caroline would attend the Art League in New York City. In 1896 Caroline furthered her studies in Paris and commenced work on her primary area of expertise, the painting of miniatures. Although she made a name for herself in this field, it was not without its costs. Within a decade she would have to put down her brushes, the victim of ruined vision from painting in such a small medium. She did not dwell long on this loss, and instead she threw herself into serving the arts in Birmingham. Almost every exhibit, lecture, and dramatic performance in that city before the First World War was supported or assisted by her capable efforts and generosity.

Tod's mining enterprise was showing profit, but the incapacitation and death of his father forced him to take on the management of Lovell properties in Mississippi. Palmyra Island was proving more susceptible to seasonal flooding, a condition that Tod rightfully concluded was the outcome of the federal government's policy of building upstream levees to protect cities and towns. As Palmyra had developed into more of a cattle ranch, the regular evacuation of herds and tenants from the island was proving to be less than feasible. In 1906 Tod ended the Lovells' active farming interests on the isle.

Mining, however, was never better, and in 1912 Tod had accumulated the capital to purchase the Montevallo Mine in Aldrich, Alabama. The looming clouds of war and the need to fuel mighty navies created a lucrative market, but profits were unwisely invested back into the operation. In 1922 Tod found himself in an unfortunate financial pinch. The postwar glut of coal and a warm winter dropped demand considerably.

With this decline in sales, Montevallo Mine was not able to make payments on its convict-labor contract with the state of Alabama. Governor Thomas I. Kilby refused to release Montevallo from its financial obligations under the contract, and the company was forced into bankruptcy. The mine was operated in receivership under poor management, and in 1924 an embarrassing incident occurred when the recently abused convicts staged a highly publicized mutiny that culminated in those desperate men blowing up the mine.

As a result of the business failure, the Lovells leased out their home in Birmingham in 1923 and moved to Malbone, which had been recently vacated after the death of Caroline's brother Hamilton. They lived a meager existence trying to raise chickens and turkeys and bartering for their needs. Malbone lacked all modern conveniences and was in dilapidated shape. Affairs were just as grim across the fields at Etowah Cliffs, where Caroline's cousin Gulie Stiles, in failing health, was sharing responsibility of her invalid mother with her maverick brother Henry. Aunt Eliza, age eighty-six, was in a period of long decline with few lucid moments. To witness her beloved aunt in such a condition and to observe the physical and emotional strain placed on Gulie was difficult for Caroline.

To fill the long hours of rural isolation, she took to keeping a daily journal starting 1 January 1924 and continuing through 20 August 1925. This candid account reflects the sadness of the sixty-one-year-old author who was far from accustomed to deprivations and was resigned "to come back to my days where I began them." Prominently displayed in the front of this large standard diary is a flattering article about her taken from the Birmingham newspaper of 20 September 1923, entitled "Her Absence Felt In Music, Art And Club Circles." Caroline tagged this clipping with the terse commentary: "My Obituary." The journal itself carries throughout it the morose nature of her exile, but yet among the stark details of her routines emerge a candid nature of wit, charm, and endearment. Although Caroline probably began this journal for personal therapy, it soon became an excellent recording of the numerous comings and goings of the extended Stiles family. To accommodate the wishes of relations interested in her family diary, Caroline provided a typed, edited, and partially expunged version for perusal. Though this diary is properly titled "Journal Kept by Caroline C. Lovell," family members have always called the 370-page labor by a more familiar name, "Tannie's Journal." Caroline's sister Kate took to calling her "Tannie," and thus she has been known to the later generations of Stiles.

The journal ends with an optimistic tone as Caroline announces that Tod received an appointment as a clerk-of-court in Birmingham. Good friends had looked out for the Lovells, and the court salary would provide them with a modest but comfortable income. Tannie's ecstasy over returning to the city rings out on every page. Although she did not maintain her journal writing in Birmingham, an old pleasure had been revived. As a child, Caroline enjoyed writing poems, plays, and stories, and throughout the years she continued to write short pieces, and some were published in literary magazines.

Caroline had encouraged her maternal great-uncle, Charles Spaudling Wylly of Darien, Georgia, to write his memoirs. Captain Wylly's efforts were published in 1910 as *Memories, The Annals of Glynn*, and *The Seed That Was Sown*, but these editions were limited in number. After Wylly's death in 1923, Caroline decided to work on their second edition, and this labor grew into an idea of incorporating Captain Wylly's writings into a larger project that would also draw from memoirs, letters, and papers of the coastal families of Conrad, Spaudling, Dent, Gould, and Cater. This work occupied most of her time after returning to Birmingham, and Little, Brown of Boston published it in 1932 as *The Golden Isles of Georgia*. Not only did *The Golden Isles* enjoy a brisk sale, it also established Caroline as a gifted and smooth storyteller. This volume claimed a position as the premier general history of the islands, and, though modern efforts have tried to capture its following, Tannie's style cements the stories with adhesion the others do not have. Recent demand for *The Golden Isles* brought about a reprint issuance by Cherokee Publishing Company of Atlanta in 1981, and this edition is still in stock in bookstores across the state.

Working with her uncle's papers as well as those of the other families signaled a need to collect and catalogue the numerous papers of the Stiles, Mackay, and Couper families. This concern was also shared by Caroline's sister Bessie, Mrs. Franklin Buchanan Screven, whose leadership in the Georgia Society of the Colonial Dames of America was making her more aware of the need, in the words of the organization's constitution, "to collect and preserve manuscripts, traditions, relics and mementos of bygone days." In 1936, after a dozen years of collecting them through quiet diplomacy and persuasion, Bessie Screven and her cousin Miss Phoebe Elliott donated hundreds of eighteenth- and nineteenth-century papers of the Mackay, McQueen, and Couper families to the Colonial Dames. Two publications grew out of this gift. In 1943 the

Colonial Dames published *The Letters of Don Juan McQueen to His Family*, and in 1949 the University of Georgia Press published *The Letters of Robert Mackay to His Wife* under the auspices of the Colonial Dames. How appropriate that now in 1995 the Colonial Dames are sponsoring the publication of Caroline Lovell's *The Light of Other Days* with Mercer University Press. In addition to her donation to the Colonial Dames, seven linear feet of manuscripts were donated to Southern Historical Collection at the University of North Carolina at Chapel Hill by Bessie Screven; the Stiles-Mackay Collection, consisting largely of correspondence and business documents, was given to the Wilson Library because it was one of the few modern and fireproof archives in the South.

Another project that Caroline undertook to write about was her childhood. One member of her extended family was Juliette Gordon Low, founder of the Girl Scouts of America. "Daisy," as she was affectionately known, was family in the sense that both Caroline and she were nieces to Aunt Eliza Stiles. Daisy and her Gordon siblings spent their summers at Etowah Cliffs and the dozens of children created a unique world among fields, pastures, orchards, gardens, rock cliffs, and the river. Daisy's connection with Caroline was later reinforced when Daisy married Caroline's first cousin, the Englishman William Mackay Low. The two friends kept in touch throughout the years, and, after Daisy died in 1927, Anne Hyde Choate and Helen Farris of the Girl Scouts organization asked Caroline to contribute a short memoir of Daisy's childhood summers at Etowah to a memorial volume they were editing. Caroline's endearing chapter, titled after Louisa May Alcott's *Eight Cousins*, was "Twenty Cousins In The Summer-Time And Daisy Low One Of The Cousins."

Although she was sixty years removed from the experience, Caroline captured the joys and trials of childhood with the perception of one who was just there. When *Juliette Low and the Girl Scouts* was released in 1928, it was read widely by family and friends who encouraged Caroline to expand her efforts; she took their advice and the final outcome was *The Light of Other Days*, which was completed in late 1933. Caroline's brother John Couper Stiles of Brunswick, Georgia, took a lively interest in the memoir, and Caroline eventually left her manuscripts to him. He annotated the originals with his own commentaries and also removed one page in some copies to purge an account he felt too sensitive to release. Permission to publish *The Light of Other Days* has been granted by the kindness of Mr. Stiles's two surviving children, Mrs. Henry Cate and John Couper Stiles, Jr., both of Brunswick, Georgia.

Caroline's energies produced one final manuscript that was finished in 1935. "The Bend of the River" was a continuance of *The Light of Other Days* and detailed her early married years on Palmyra Island and in Natchez. The rich narrative details the agricultural enterprises as well as the lives of the freeman tenants, and the chapters on Natchez give the reader personal tours of the stately homes of that old river town as they were in the 1880s.

Caroline's declining years were spent in close companionship with her beloved Tod. From her 16 September 1924 journal entry, the day of their fortieth wedding anniversary, comes this vignette:

> Tod said this morning, "When we were first married I thought, 'If we live together for twenty-five years, I will feel that I have had my share of happiness.' "
>
> And we have had our share, for, as our married life is concerned, we have been perfectly happy. Tod says he wishes he could go back to the beginning and live it all over again!

The dedication to "The Bend of the River" shows the same relationship ten years later:

> To my husband, William Storrow Lovell, who said on our golden wedding day, in answer to a toast, "No place need be reserved for me in Heaven. I've had my heaven here. "

Tod's heaven would last through a sixtieth anniversary, but in 1945 he preceded her in death. Their house on Ridge Park Avenue was closed, and Caroline moved to Savannah to be with her two surviving sisters, Miss Margaret C. Stiles (Margie) and Mrs. Snowden Marshall (Belle). Tannie lived but two years in the city of her childhood before her wish to rejoin Tod was granted. She is buried beside her adoring husband in Birmingham, the other love of her life.

THE COMPLEXITIES OF SOUTHERN SOCIETY following the Civil War are frequently ignored in modern histories, which tend to divide the populace along black and white lines, but that period of flux was inhabited by numerous distinct groups, many discussed in this memoir. Because of

Caroline's background, most prominent consideration is given to her caste, the planter society and their Anglophile traditions. The reader is not schooled directly in the perspective of this class, but an education is acquired through the intimate introduction to older relations and prominent historical figures and through exposure to family teachings. The concept of *noblesse oblige* emerges more as an intuitive duty than a definition. Another class of white Southerners found in the memoir is tenant farmers, referred to as Crackers. Here we catch glimpses of their closed society and the strange values that sustained them. Caroline's perspective on African-Americans offers rich information for racial history. Coming from slaveholding families, she deplored the institution of slavery, but yet did not feel the African to be her evolutionary equal. Her paternalism was based on lifelong intimacy with and appreciation for blacks that was defined by barriers of propriety, not hatred. Years later, she would note with much pride that her brother Hamilton had kept the Klan out of Bartow County, Georgia. In her memoir, Caroline used the term Negro most often, black often, darkie (capitalized and uncapitalized) and colored on occasion. In keeping with now-forgotten social realities, she also used the term mulatto (capitalized) to refer to the mixed-blood community that held itself—and was held by the law—as a group apart from other freedmen and freedwomen. Many of Savannah's mulattos formed St. Stephen's Episcopal Church and maintained separate institutions from whites and blacks until Georgia's segregation laws of the 1880s placed all people of color under the same oppressive yoke.

As in any Victorian-style narrative, the famous and the prominent are showcased as a major feature of *The Light of Other Days*. With an abrupt and peculiar beginning, the book presents an overpowering figure of importance, General Robert E. Lee, as Caroline opens with a short letter from the general to her father that acknowledges her birth in a humorous aside. In addition to Lee, a friend of the Stiles and Mackay families from his West Point days of the 1820s, other prominent soldiers and citizens pass through the memoir: General Joseph E. Johnson and General P. M. B. Young of the Confederacy; the refuge-seeking family of Jefferson Davis and later General William T. Sherman in a defeated Savannah; Juliette "Daisy" Low of the Girl Scouts and the poet Sidney Lanier; Stephen Elliott, first Episcopal bishop of Georgia and a founder of the University of the South; a young Willie Gorgas, before his fame in Panama; and the actor Edwin Booth, fleeing a mob of juvenile admirers.

The Light of Other Days also presents the city of Savannah as a dusty town quite different from its appearance today. Caroline tours her readers through the elegant rooms of the Bulloch-Habersham house, the soaring nave of Independent Presbyterian Church, the democratic classrooms of Massie School, and the scarlet azaleas of Bonaventure Cemetery. But yet we also see another side of the port city—one of old cultivers in parterre gardens, of the servants' world in cramped alleys, of firebells and hucksters. Her descriptions of Bartow County are a contrast to Savannah: the reality of rural life balances with the beauty of the terrain. Within the upcountry world, however, Caroline reveals that coastal manners and customs were well preserved among the gentry at Etowah Cliffs, Malbone, Valley View, Spring Bank, and Barnsley's Gardens. In leaving this pastoral world, she found another such world in the University of the South at Sewanee, Tennessee, where she introduces us to the faculty, students, and villagers in their wooded cluster of clapboard buildings and residences.

IN *THE LIGHT OF OTHER DAYS*, Caroline draws her audience close, revealing her secrets and sometimes her doubts; but yet, as one who realizes a confidence has gone too far, she will suddenly move on to another thought, leaving the reader a bit perplexed. It is her intimacy though that keeps the reader in the process. Although we may want to linger a moment longer or may wish for more details, we are pulled away by our guide who wishes to cover more ground. Caroline reveals the dark side of childhood guilt, feelings of inadequacy and doubts about her faith and character. The confessions she gives are profound yet trivial: a case of stealing candy, a belief that she was a repulsive child, a fear of hideous old relatives, even an accusation that her grandmother had culpability in the death of an ill brother. Such thoughts are normally omitted from nostalgic memoirs, but for Caroline there seems to be a need to expel these old demons through the process of writing. The gothic tone of this good-versus-evil theme stands as an outgrowth of the puritanical form of Anglicanism taught to Caroline first by her Mackay aunts and then by her aunt Eliza. This act of writing serves as the confessional that Caroline otherwise would have been uncomfortable in using; hearing her confession becomes an endearing honor for the reader, a fascinating journey to another time and place.

Tannie, may I present you with a new audience.

Introduction
by LeeAnn Whites

aroline Couper Lovell was born at a pivotal moment in the history of her class, her race, her gender, and her region. In 1862, the year of her birth, the Confederacy was locked in mortal combat with the Union. Even members of the white Southern planter and merchant elite, to which her family belonged, were beginning to experience the hardships and shortages brought on by the war effort. In the first year of the war her mother's family, who were wealthy slave-owning rice planters on the coastal islands off Georgia, had been forced to flee by the invasion of Union naval forces. When the family returned at the end of the war, it would be to a transformed region where much of their property had been ransacked or burned, while their fortune in slave property had been abolished with the emancipation of their former slaves. This economic loss was matched by a loss of male family members. Several of Caroline Couper Lovell's uncles and cousins never returned from the war, and others returned seriously wounded in spirit, if not in body. In the hard first year after the war, both her grandfathers died, unable to overcome their multiple losses in wealth, in family, and in social position. The death of these family men left Lovell's female relations behind to face the difficult postwar years alone.

Over sixty years later, in the closing passage of her recollections of her childhood and her youth, which are published here for the first time, Lovell acknowledged her debt to the older generation of her family, especially to the women, who somehow managed to carry on despite their losses. According to Lovell, the men and women of her parents generation "never repined," but instead set about to raise their children and to mend their fortunes as best they might. In so doing they enabled their children to experience the joys of childhood and the promise of youth.

This was a gift that Lovell claimed was more valuable than all the wealth and land which they had lost during the war.

Historians have considered the ways in which the antebellum elite persisted in the South despite the social and economic losses they experienced in the context of the Civil War and its aftermath. Generally these discussions have focused on the ways in which the planter class was able to retain land ownership. According to this line of discussion, it was their continued land ownership that allowed antebellum elites to reconstruct their domination over the newly freed people in the form of the sharecropping system. This, in turn, enabled them to eventually reclaim regional political power through "redeemer" movements throughout the South. What historians have generally failed to consider, however, is the role that the family and the persistence of cultural values played in this ability of antebellum elites to maintain their social position despite their economic losses. In Caroline Couper Lovell's recollection, appropriately entitled *The Light of Other Days*, the reader is offered an intimate view of the inner workings of one such Southern family in the postwar era, as well as a larger window onto the social experiences of their class more generally. Thus, this work is important because it reveals with such clarity the ways in which antebellum race, class, and gender relations persisted through the structure of the postbellum elite white houeholds while simultaneously being transformed in the context of an emergent "New South."

This then is a story of how family and larger kin connections facilitated the cultural persistence of antebellum elites in the altered conditions of the postwar Southern world. In this account, the greatest accomplishment of the antebellum elite did not reside in the restoration of either their economic or their political position, which many were unable to achieve in the postwar period; their greatest accomplishment was the replication of their class through the successful rearing of their children. Caroline Lovell was herself precisely such a child, and she carried on the cultural values of the antebellum Southern elite, even in the face of the decline of their economic and social privilege that had given those cultural values birth in the first place.

Lovell wrote these recollections of her childhood and youth in the postbellum South over a six-year period, completing it in 1933 when she was seventy-one years old. At the same time, she also wrote a history of the Georgia coastal islands, *The Golden Isles of Georgia*. The virtually simultaneous production of this antebellum history of her region together

with her own postwar childhood recollections is particularly fitting because for Caroline Couper Lovell the larger history of her class and her
region merged almost seamlessly with the particular history of her own
family. Thus while the total white population of the Georgia coastal
islands in 1850 numbered only 700 and the black slave population numbered 4,232, Lovell's history of these islands is told almost entirely as the
history of the white slaveowning class. Based in large part upon the
recollection of her uncle Charles Spaulding Wylly, *The Golden Isles of
Georgia* not only tells the story of the region as the story of the slaveowning planter class, it goes one step further and tells the story of the
region's planter class through the story of her maternal family, the Coupers, who were amongst the earliest white settlers of the islands, and, at
the outbreak of the Civil War, were leading slaveowning rice and cotton
planters of St. Simons Island.

For the Couper family and their fellow coastal planters, the Civil War
constituted a virtually unmitigated saga of loss and destruction. In both
her history of the islands and in the opening of her own childhood recollections, Caroline Couper Lovell describes the impact the Civil War had
on this white elite. Yet Lovell's account evinces no understanding that
the same course of events that represented loss to the white slaveowning
class, could have represented gain for the region's slaves. The fact that
the Civil War created the moment of liberation for the slaves, even as it
made for the destruction of the economic and social position of the white
slaveholding elite, is beyond the scope of her vision. It is, however,
precisely this myopic focus on the experience of the slaveholding white
elite as the *only* experience, even sixty years after the fact, that enabled
Lovell to avoid a more comprehensive understanding of the war and
emancipation. It was her underlying assumption that the ligaments of the
white household constituted the ligaments of the social order more
generally that allowed for the continued cultural cohesion of her race and
her class, even in the face of its economic and social transformation.

The primacy of the white household is reflected in the very structural
organization of Lovell's recollections. Each chapter in the first half of
The Light of Other Days is named for one of the households in Lovell's
extended family. She tells the story of her childhood and youth through
the description of these households. No description is ever complete without a discussion of the damage that Sherman and his troops wreaked
upon these households. In the case of the Mackay household in Savannah, where she spent many winters of her early childhood, Lovell notes

that only the wine cellar was damaged. At Etowah, her paternal grandfather's antebellum summer home in the Georgia upcountry, where her immediate family and her father's brother's family were forced to set up collective housekeeping for lack of any other alternative after the war, she records more extensive damage by Sherman's men. The Union soldiers stabled horses in the house, broke the windows and mantles, and took up the flooring. It was her mother's family on the coastal islands, however, which suffered the greatest loss. The damage was so extensive that her grandmother, Caroline Wylly Couper, was forced to give up her home on St. Simons Island altogether and move to a small wooden house on the nearby mainland at Brunswick.

For Caroline Couper Lovell, Sherman and his troops represent a sort of shorthand for all that was lost by her family and her class with the war and emancipation. Indeed, her memoir opens with an account of the occupation of Savannah by Sherman's troops in the spring of 1865. According to Lovell, the invasion of Savannah by Union forces when she was barely three years old constituted her earliest childhood memory. If, however, descriptions of the depredations of Sherman and his men represent wartime losses of her family for Lovell, the image of Robert E. Lee represents a critical antidote to this loss. As much as the Yankee Sherman had despoiled her family and the white Southern antebellum elite more generally, the ever loyal Confederate, Lee, served to reclaim and sanctify it. "Our family," Lovell wrote, "had a more exalted opinion of Lee than anyone on earth."

Although Lovell's earliest memory was of Sherman's invasion, she prefaced her memoir with an excerpt from a letter from Robert E. Lee congratulating her family upon the occasion of her birth in the midst of the war. She later recounted a visit of Lee to her aunt Kate Mackay's house in Savannah, where she was living at the time, and noted her good fortune in having actually been kissed by him. In a later section of the journal, she explained the basis for the depth of her family's relation to Lee; he had been a "dear family friend" since 1829, when he and John Mackay, her great-uncle, had attended West Point together. Indeed the family still had twenty-one letters from Lee.

Precisely because her own family had suffered such intense economic decline, their continued connection with notable personages like Lee, as well as with the wealthier members of their own extended kin networks, took on added significance after the war. For example, Lovell describes the impact that a visit from her wealthy British relatives had on her. The excitement of hearing about their houseparties and hunts and balls, the theatres and operas that they attended, and their travels on the continent is palpable in her account. To their impoverished American relations, these British relatives appeared to be "rolling in wealth."

Lovell's own experience was much more like her upcountry neighbors, the Hugers, who were descended from the "blood royal" of South Carolina, but were impoverished by the war. True to their elite upbringing, however, the Hugers could "live without necessities, but they cannot live without luxuries." Similarly, Lovell herself lived surrounded by the artifacts of her family's antebellum wealth, the furniture her grandfather Stiles brought back from Vienna, the family portraits on the walls, the extensive book collections, while at the same time wearing hand-me-downs and never owning more than one pair of shoes at a time.

If one basis for the cultural reconstruction of the antebellum elite was formed by the persistence of antebellum class connections, the other side was to be found in the rigid exclusion of those who were not socially acceptable. As the case of the Hugers would indicate, social acceptability was dictated as much, if not more, by one's genealogical descent and one's presumed cultural accomplishments as a consequence of these connections, as it was by a family's actual postwar economic status. Thus Caroline Couper Lovell carefully records the considerably "more common" social structure of the Georgia upcountry, where her family was forced to move after the war, as compared to the low country from whence they came. When the Lovell family first moved there after the war, they found few families with whom they could associate. The one exception was the George Warings, who themselves being originally from the coastal region and old friends of her family in Savannah, were of the "same caste."

While Caroline Couper Lovell was preoccupied with the experience of wartime economic loss on the one hand and the persistence of social connections amongst the antebellum elite on the other, she was not insensitive to class difference. Indeed, she was acutely aware of the common white and black folk in her environment. She claims that it was the very loss of her family's economic position that made her sensitive to the experience of poverty. This understanding on her part seems to have allowed her to perceive poverty in a way that she might not have if her own position in the economic order had not been disrupted. At the same time, it also caused her to cling to her class difference with a kind of desperation that had been unnecessary in antebellum days.

Economic loss and the persistence of class privilege and position are therefore uneasily intertwined in these recollections. Lovell's family made their living in the upcountry by planting and renting out some of their land to tenants. She describes social occasions with these tenants that are both redolent with noblesse oblige, while at the same time shot through with class ambiguity. She describes, for instance, the Sunday services held at Etowah that the white tenants attended and the ceremonial distribution of sugar cookies on the piazza afterwards. She records as particularly memorable the gathering of the tenants to admire the Christmas tree. As the assembled company paraded around the piazza, an orange on the tree caught Lovell's eye. She remembered desperately wanting that orange, an orange that she never received because it "probably went to some Cracker girl."

If the uneasy combination of economic loss and persistence of class privilege provided the filter for much of Lovell's discussion of white tenants, the ambiguity of her position as a member of a fallen white elite is even more apparent in her discussion of postwar race relations. These observations are particularly telling in the opening chapter of her memoir, which focusses on her early childhood when she still spent every winter in Savannah with her father's aunts, Sarah and Kate Mackay. While her immediate family had lost much of their wealth in the war, her aunts retained their Savannah home, as well as a large retinue of black domestic servants. Once again, Caroline Couper Lovell's larger kin connections allowed her to experience a kind of persistence, this time in race hierarchies. For Lovell, pleasant memories of Savannah were always intimately associated with black singing and with squares filled in the afternoons with white children tended by their "old black maumas." Lovell recounts her own experiences of learning to be a properly raised young white woman, as well as a gracious hostess, from her aunts' domestic servants.

For Lovell, the fact that she could claim to have learned her manners from loyal black servants indicated that whatever her family may have lost, she was still culturally a true member of the white elite. But as with the story of the white tenant girl and the orange, here too the story of a seamless, benevolent white elite world suffers from breaks in the text. Thus while her account of race relations after the war generally presents a picture of loyal black domestic servants and benevolent white mistresses, she includes one discussion of "colored girls" who forced her off the sidewalks. While she attributes this behavior to "northern carpetbaggers" who were "poisoning the minds of otherwise peaceful folk," she nonetheless concludes that even though this kind of behavior was in the end "subdued," it was not without lasting consequences in the "alienation of the races."

Lovell also records a sort of lasting alienation of the sexes, as a result of the war and its aftermath. This alienation was in the first instance a purely structural consequence of the death of so many men. She recollects that as a child growing up in the shadow of the war, she hardly ever saw a grown person wearing anything besides black. Old ladies seemed much older because they all lived so much in the past, like her maternal grandmother, whose greatest interest resided in "ceaselessly speaking of the dead." For the younger generation of women, with children to support or their own living to earn, such a total retreat into the past and the memorializing of the dead was not possible. Lovell recounts the lengths to which her female relations and acquaintances went to make ends meet, from the war widow who took in boarders to support her children, to her own mother who was forced to make and remake all of their clothes and hand-me-downs, to the impoverished governesses from the first families of the South, who earned their own support by taking positions in more fortunate elite households.

While the men of Lovell's class clearly suffered in the postwar era, and Lovell is sensitive to this, her recollections reflect the ways in which the women of her race and class constituted the bottom line of elite cultural defense. For while Caroline Couper Lovell was more fortunate than many of her female relations in that her own father survived the war, nonetheless, he also died young as a result of an accident when she was only twelve years old. This premature death of her father intensified her family's economic burdens and the weight of responsibility that fell upon her mother. Male recklessness, which Lovell witnessed both in the war and in peacetime, combined with the ultimate accountability of the women such men left behind, perhaps explains Lovell's most caustic comment concerning postwar gender relations. Noting that many men behaved as "tyrants" toward their families, she suggests that the best solution would be for men to establish their households and their wealth and then conveniently die young, leaving their wives and children to a happier existence.

Male privilege rankles her from the outset in her memoirs. As proud as she is of Lee's letter congratulation her family upon the occasion of her birth, she also notes that Lee indicated that what the Confederacy needed was not more girls, but boys. Growing up in the aftermath of the war, her brothers and male cousins replayed the conflict endlessly, always excluding the girls. On one occasion, however, Caroline Lovell and her cousin Daisy Low insisted upon being allowed to play as well. Apparently determined to teach them their place, with much hilarity the boys assigned to Lovell the role of Sherman, while Daisy was given the part of a Union spy. Excluded from direct participation in the most pivotal moment in the history of their class, the war itself, even the younger generation of girls were excluded from the reenactment of it. From Lovell's vantage point of over a half a century later, too many women were left, like her grandmother, with "lined face and hopeless eyes" to recount the losses. No wonder Lovell suggested that in an ideal world men would establish their households on an economically sound basis and then conveniently exit this world early.

Of course this account is not a journal written actually at the time the events occurred, but rather a recollection written many years later. This makes the actual authenticity of the account at times suspect. Would Lovell have depicted her antebellum experiences with black domestic servants so warmly at the time? Would she have recognized the gender asymmetry in her early upbringing? The main interest in the memoir as a historical document is not, however, in how literally accurate Lovell's description of her childhood was, but rather in the way that she chose to remember it. Indeed the memoir tells us more about the adult she became than the child she was. While her family was largely stripped of their wealth with the destruction of the war and the emancipation of the slaves, they nonetheless retained much of their cultural heritage by clinging to the social relations that remained to them, their own family circles and their wider kin and class connections. Lovell grew up then in a divided world, part cultural persistence, part economic decline. Toward the end of her life, she returned to the beginning through the writing of these recollections, much as her own parents had clung to the past while moving inexorably into an uncertain future.

From this vantage point, it is understandable that the memoir at times seems to war against itself. On the one hand it is a testimony to a happy childhood as reflected in her dedication of the memoir to her siblings, "when we were seven." On the other hand, the barely concealed evidence of the difficulties of doing without reflects her family's efforts to persist if only on a cultural level, surrounded by the artifacts, the books, the furnishings handed down from earlier, more prosperous days. The closing passage of the memoir brings these two themes together forcefully. In this final passage Lovell juxtaposes the death of her aunt Kate as well as that of Grannie Gordon—which left her mother and her aunt Eliza to scrape by as best they might—with an account of her own marriage to Tod Lovell, by all accounts a long and happy one.

A Note on the Editing
by Hugh Stiles Golson

wo manuscript versions of *The Light of Other Days* exist today. Manuscript A, the template for this published edition, was passed directly from Caroline Couper Lovell to John Couper Stiles to his two surviving children, Mrs. Henry Cate and John Couper Stiles, Jr. Caroline provided the original typed version to her descendants; either no complete handwritten copy existed, or it was lost or destroyed. The manuscript was later retyped in the 1940s by Elise Stiles Walker of Texas for redistribution to her branch of the Stiles family. This second manuscript, Manuscript B, shows slight alteration of some sentences and, invariably, some typographical errors of names. Also, Caroline's overuse of exclamation points was toned down. Manuscript B has been important because it provides several words blurred or incorrect in Manuscript A; thus referenced, this published edition of *The Light of Other Days* reflects the "corrected" text of Manuscript A.

We have attempted to edit *The Light of Other Days* in such a way as to insure that the authenticity and uniqueness of Caroline Couper Lovell's voice remains, while at the same time barriers for the general reader are kept to a minimum. No sentences have been added or taken away from Manuscript A; we have even kept her "The End." On occasion, we the editors have felt it necessary to provide full names in the text where Caroline provided only first or last names. We have removed dozens and dozens of commas from the manuscript because they impeded the flow of the narrative or clouded the meaning of the subject in question, yet the reader may still find an overabundance of commas by modern standards. We have also added punctuation marks, often correcting what was clearly a mistake from an age where correcting a page meant retyping a page. Caroline's hyphenation in particular has been altered because it is not internally consistent in the memoir—*sidewalk, side-walk,* and *side walk*

all appear, for example. We have adopted modern hyphenation rules to benefit the reader; *Webster's* notes very few changes in this area since the 1930s. We have corrected misspellings such as *it's* for *its,* but, in cases where the spelling of certain proper names has changed since her day, we have left the words spelled as she had them. Thus, *St. Simon's Island* remains instead of *St. Simons Island*; this system provides the greatest continuity between *The Light of Other Days* and her 1932 history, *The Golden Isles of Georgia.* Like many women and men of her day from the coastal area, Caroline used the British spellings of many words, and we have left them in that form. The words *centre* and *center* are both used throughout the memoir without any apparent system, so we settled on the more prevalent British *centre.* Regarding capitalization, we have lowercased words such as *presidency* but have left unaltered incorrectly capitalized words of a historical significance, such as *Mulatto* and *Quadroon*, and have left unaltered capitalized common nouns such as *The Shoals* and *River Path*, where the reference site takes on special importance. With certain words, such as *Poor Whites* and *Mauma* (child nurse), we have left them capitalized where she capitalized, lowercased where she lowercased them; thus the reader can better know Lovell's own emphasis. We have not altered her style of grammar; thus prepositional phrases often exist as *with Daisy and myself* instead of *with Daisy and me.*

The Light of Other Days catalogs numerous family members and neighbors, as well as authors and painters now obscure. We have added an appendix with very brief sketches of the individuals and landmarks most prominent in the text. In addition, a genealogy and a photograph section has been provided by Hugh Stiles Golson and THE NATIONAL SOCIETY OF THE COLONIAL DAMES OF AMERICA IN THE STATE OF GEORGIA to help the reader keep the most frequently mentioned faces and places straight. After much thought, we decided against adding explanatory footnotes because we feel that their presence might disrupt a story that flows quite well on its own. Hopefully the extratextual material of Mr. Golson and Dr. Whites will satisfy the reader searching for more information about Caroline Lovell; as for the story itself, it needs little outside explanation of its characters, no outside explanation of its virtues and achievement.

The Light
of Other Days

Caroline Couper Lovell

To My Dear Brothers and Sisters
In Memory of the Days
When We Were Seven

1.

I Remember

Richmond 18 May 62

My dear Mr. Robert:

I have recd your letter of the 10th. Capt. Echol's letter has not yet reached me, but I applied on the strength of yours. Your Commission as Lt. is made out and waits the Secty's signature, which I will probably receive to-night. I will then send it to you. In the mean time I send this as several days have elapsed. Please present my kind regards to your good Grandmother, Aunts and all the family. Do not forget Mrs. Low and Miss Carrie. Tell Mrs. Maggie we want boys not girls now. Soldiers are the need in time of war. Remember me to your father and mother. Give my love to all my sweethearts.

Very truly yours.
R. E. Lee.

 his letter was written by General Lee to my father, Robert Mackay Stiles, just after my birth at Etowah Cliffs in Cass County, Georgia. Father was a civil engineer, and had written about his commission to General Lee, who had been for many years a friend of the family.

Only two months before this, General Lee had been called to Richmond and assigned, under the direction of President Davis, to the conduct of the military operations of all the armies of the Confederate States. That at such a time he should have been so considerate of a young man's request shows the genuine kindness of heart of Robert Edward Lee, one of the greatest of men.

My mother had been Margaret Wylly Couper of Hopeton plantation on the Altamaha, and I was the second child of my parents, my brother Robert Mackay being nearly two years old at the time of my birth.

The first winter of my life must have been spent in Savannah in the old Mackay home at 75 Broughton Street. The Confederate troops were in the city at this time, and our mauma used to take Mackay and myself to the encampment to see Father and his comrades. Mackay was mother's one beautiful child, and Uncle Charlie Wylly has since told me that the officers made a great pet of the handsome little boy, while even *he* turned away from the plain baby girl in the hideous mob cap. Fortunately at that age she did not care.

My very earliest recollection must have been of Christmas Day, 1863. I remember being on the floor of the front piazza at Etowah Cliffs, and seeing a little red table. My first cousin, Gulie Stiles, who was two years older than myself, was standing beside me, and when she finally made me understand that that marvelous table was my very own, I fell upon it, and, clutching it fiercely, felt the first passionate joy of possession.

My next distinct recollection is of the entrance of Sherman's army into Savannah, which took place on December 21st, 1864. From a preceding blank, I find myself in Mother's bedroom with the two low windows looking out on Broughton Street. The room is darkened and I am conscious of subdued excitement. There are only servants in the room with me, and I presume that Mother, with Mackay and my younger brother Hamilton, have taken refuge with my great-aunts Kate and Sarah Mackay, in another part of the house. The servants have evidently been told not to open the shutters, but they turn the slats of one, and I look down on the street which seems to me to be paved with loaves of bread. From the east there comes pouring a sea of blue-coated soldiers, shouting, leaping, and brandishing their muskets. Mother told me afterwards how the loose women of the town rushed out in the streets to welcome the Yankees, kissing and embracing them, and dancing in an abandon of joy.

Father had left Savannah with the Confederate army when it evacuated the city and, being on the engineer corps, was one of the last to cut the pontoon bridges, after it crossed to Hutchinson's Island, while the Yankees swarmed in from the south over abandoned fortifications.

In his diary he wrote:—

Savannah, Georgia, Dec. 20th, 1864. Tuesday.
Evacuation of the city began at dark. Was with my company on pontoon bridge all night on guard. Everything passed successfully.

Dec. 21st., 1864. Wednesday.
Cut away pontoon bridge from Savannah shore at 20 minutes before 6 A.M. Yankees at that time coming down West Broad Street yelling. Cut away the 2nd and 3rd pontoon brides over Back River and marched to Hardeville. Rained off and on during the day.

Charleston, S.C. Jan. 6th, 1865.
Entered on duties as Assistant to Chief. (Colonel Clarke.)

Jan. 12th, Thursday.
Heard from home of my fourth child being born. (John Couper Stiles.)

Father's rank in the Confederate army was captain, Company E, 2nd Regiment of Engineers.

I remember the white tents pitched in Oglethorpe Square, in front of Aunt Elliott's house, and I recall passing with my nurse a long-legged Yankee soldier who stalked by with two loaves of bread impaled on his bayonet. I suppose he was out of earshot when Mauma said something scathing, and I realized that he was an object of scorn.

The following March, wishing to join Father, who was outside the lines, Mother had to request permission from General Sherman to leave Savannah, and she never forgot the mortification of that interview. Sherman, surrounded by his officers, was standing at the street corner, and it was some time before he would notice Mother or allow her to speak.

When her request was granted, Mother took the three little boys, Mackay, Hamilton, and John the baby, joined Father out in the country, and they trekked to southwest Georgia, where her parents Mr. and Mrs. James Hamilton Couper were refugeeing near Tibeauville. They drove in a wagon, and at night camped in the pine woods, and I have heard Mother say this was the happiest time of her whole life.

I, having chicken pox, was left behind in Savannah with Aunt Kate and Aunt Sarah Mackay. When I became convalescent, Aunt Sarah wrote a letter for me to my brother Mackay, which began, "I tired all the time." And continued, "Some of the time I am happy, but if anybody comes in to see Aunt Kate and Aunt Sarah, and they do not give me their entire attention, I get very cross and bad." I cannot think that this confession was voluntary, and it makes me realize that Aunt Sarah had a poor opinion of me from the first. However, as I added, "Aunt Sarah had made me a sponge cake all for myself," she must have been good to me in spite of it.

In a postscript to my mother, Aunt Sarah adds, "Mrs. Jefferson Davis is here at The Pulaski with all her children. Crowds of people have called on her, and Mrs. Owens brought her children here this morning to let us see the poor little things. Master Jeff was remarkably polite and well behaved, and the little girls looked gentle and quiet, and excited our sympathy much. Their clothes were actually taken from them, and people sent in for the children what could be gathered. I hear that Mrs. Davis is much gratified at the kindness she has received."

The Yankees established themselves in Savannah, their soldiers being stationed in the barracks on Bull Street in the heart of the city. The Union Flag hung across the pavement in front of the archway, and, when in passing Aunt Sarah stepped out into the street to avoid it, she was seized by two soldiers, pulled back to the pavement, and forced to walk beneath it.

This archway was the identical scene of the story, which has since been told of almost every city in the South. A Savannah beauty, with cheeks like a damask rose, was passing by. "Painted by God!" said a Yankee soldier to another. "Yes. And by God alone," retorted the beauty.

The military occupation of Savannah lasted until 1870, and I always turned cold when I passed the barracks and glanced through the archway into the great open court in the centre where the soldiers drilled, for I felt that we were at the mercy of some sinister power. And I suppose those blue-coated soldiers, marching back and forth with their guns on their shoulders, were as harmless as possible, and, so far from home and their own children, would have been more than glad to be friendly to a little child.

As a child, the words "The Yankees" suggested to my mind vast hordes of men marching on the horizon, a mysterious and murderous host, the very thought of which was terrifying.

And the word "Rebel" was the most beautiful word in the English language to me, for its connotation was, "A Southern soldier." And that soldier was typified by my father, one of the handsomest men I have ever seen. He was six feet, two inches tall, with a superb figure and a fine carriage. Brunette, with the beautiful Mackay skin, a clear olive, with the slightest coral tinge of color. His eyes were dark and his hair as black and glossy as a raven's wing. His features were fine, the nose straight, the lips clear-cut, and the chin square and strong. Uncle Charlie has told me of his wonderful smile, when his usually grave face would be illumined as though a lamp had been lighted within.

I have left my own plain little self recovering from chicken pox in Mother's front bedroom in Savannah. Some kind friend of the family sent me at this time a wonderful little table. It was strong and well made and the top was covered with colored pictures, the alphabet running around the edge, and the whole finished with shining varnish. I do not remember being half impressed by this work of art as by the sight of a joined wooden doll which I saw in an opened bureau drawer. I had a fleeting glance, for, some senseless confusion ensuing, I never saw the doll again, and for years I had a sense of aching loss when I thought of it.

It was probably during my convalescence that my first fool performance took place. All that I recall of it is persisting stubbornly until I worked my head through the bannisters in the upstairs hall. Afterwards I learned that they had tried in vain to pull me out, and then, as they could not pull off my ears, a carpenter had to be fetched, and the bannisters sawed in two to release me. For years afterwards an unpainted post marked this historic spot, and I always felt a sense of personal importance when I glanced at it.

My life at this time seems to have consisted of long blank periods, varied by occasional moments of vivid consciousness.

The next picture of the past that I recall is in a strange bedroom at night, and I am aware that I am on the ground floor of a cottage deep in the woods. It is a small room, for the great bed on which I have been placed takes up the whole of one end of it. Candles are lighted, and two old ladies are near me and leering horribly. One is so hideous that I cling to my aunt Rebecca Couper who has brought me here. We have stopped overnight on a journey to Altama on the Altamaha. Aunt Rebecca, who is my mother's youngest sister, tells me that I must love my great-aunt Fannie, that she has given me a silver cup. I always loathed that cup, but out of respect to Great-Aunt Fannie's memory, I had to keep my loathing to myself. It always made me a little sick to use it and I have never liked to drink out of silver since. Nothing ever gave me greater satisfaction than passing on that cup in later years to a godchild of my own.

Another secret aversion of mine was for my name. As long as Grandmother Couper lived, after whom I was named, I could not acknowledge it, but now I can say openly that I detest the name of Caroline. No parents should inflict an ugly name on a child. I believe I would have been a different character had I been named Margaret or Catherine, my favorite names. There could have been but one worse fate for me. I could not have survived being named Sarah, although it is the name of one of my dearest friends.

When I grew older, Mother overheard me once rebelling, and she said, "Well, suppose I had not named you, and had let you choose for yourself. What would you have chosen?—Julia?" Imagine my scorn! At that age I would undoubtedly have named myself Maude.

The Altama house, which was nine miles from Brunswick, had been built just before the war by Grandfather Couper. He died in 1866, and both of his plantations, Hopeton and Altama, had passed into the hands of the Corbin family of Paris. Mother's brother James Couper had charge of these two places at this time and was living at Altama. He had married Miss Dora Harper of Vicksburg, Mississippi, and they had now two children, Mary who was a year younger than myself, and Hamilton, her little brother.

It was at Altama that I saw Mary Harper for the first time. She was a plump little girl, and was leaning against the wall, sucking a stick of candy, and she laughed and said there was a surprise in store for me. The next morning we were taken into a large empty room upstairs, where a wonderful dolls' house stood. There were two lower and two upper rooms and, in my eyes, it was beautifully furnished, everything having been made by Aunt Rebecca. She must have been just out of her teens at this time, though she seemed to me then as old as when she died at sixty-five.

It must have been during this visit at Altama that we were driven one day to a small house out in the woods where Mr. Brown, the Episcopal minister, lived. He had three lovely daughters, and these children had arranged a dolls' wedding for our benefit. As we entered the front door, I was dazzled by a vision of fairyland, for, on a table at the end of the room was a little altar glittering with lighted candles, in front of which was a procession of dolls dressed in shining white, one of them wearing a gauzy veil and orange blossoms. I suppose there was a bridegroom, but I noticed him no more than he is generally noticed at a wedding, where he is merely a painful necessity.

Mr. Brown was a Northern man, and later on he returned to the North, where his daughters grew to be great beauties, and I hope made wonderful matches and were very happy ever after.

I remember distinctly when I was four. We were up the country, and Mackay and I were on the River Path, which lead from Etowah Cliffs to Summerland, the Elliott's place. It was dark under overarching trees, and suddenly I became panic-stricken. What if a lion should spring out of the bushes? Then I looked up at Mackay and all fear left me. My brother would protect me. *He was five.* Never has any age seemed to me as old and trustworthy as that.

This beautiful boy lived to be six. He died of meningitis at Etowah Cliffs the year after the war. His death must have been torture to Mother, for Grandma Stiles, who was a very strong character, would not allow her to feed him, and she felt that he was starved to death. She never got over it, and could never even speak of him. He was buried in a remote part of the garden, under a magnolia tree, but I knew nothing of this at the time.

I remember sitting on the floor in Mother's room, cutting pictures out of a paper, when I was aware Mother was crying. Father put his arms around her, and they told me that Mackay had gone to heaven. It embarrassed me to see Mother cry and what they said made no impression on me, nor do I ever remember thinking of Mackay again.

In spite of her powerful character, Grandma Stiles was not much more than a shade to me. Her bedroom at The Cliffs was the delightful large southeastern room downstairs, the windows of which looked out on the grass and flower garden. It was furnished in Circassian walnut, a set brought over from Vienna by Grandfather Stiles, when his term as Austrian minister expired. There were twin beds placed near enough, Gulie said, for Grandfather and Grandmother to hold hands. Grandfather died in Savannah the last year of the war, and Grandmama, who was an invalid in her last years, I always remember lying on the bed nearest the door. We children were taken into her room on Sunday afternoons, and she gave us chinquapins out of a little bag. Then all of us were sent out of the room except Henry, our eldest cousin, and Johnnie, who were her favorites. They stayed as long as they liked and ate all the chinquapins that they wanted.

There was an amusing episode connected with Grandmama's room. One piece of the Austrian furniture was a standing mirror in a carved frame. A pet donkey once made its way into the house, reached Grandmama's room, and saw itself in the looking glass. Its immediate reaction was to kick the mirror to pieces. I suppose nothing likes to find itself a donkey.

Grandmama Stiles died at Etowah Cliffs in 1867 and was buried near Mackay under the magnolia tree, the first two graves in our family graveyard, where there are now so many that it has had to be enlarged twice.

Judging from my own experience, death makes no particular impression on a child. All ideas of fear and horror are suggested, and, in the South, usually by the Negro servants. A friend of mine has recently found that her little child has a mortal terror of *The Cold Man*, of whom she must have heard in this way.

The first corpse that I ever saw was that of Grandmama. The servants were wildly excited, and I heard them say that I ought to see her. Unknown to my elders I suppose, I was taken into her room, where I saw her lying on the couch beside the window. Her head was lifted, her high nose profile clearly out against the light, and her face as white as the handkerchief bound under her chin. The servants who had taken me in hurried out, but I was not in the least affected, nor particularly interested. I knew nothing of her burial, and it was wise never allowing us to go to a funeral, for the lowering of the body into a hole in the ground and covering it up with dirt would have made a frightful impression on us I am sure.

It must have been at about this age that I was taught the alphabet. I remember perfectly my first attempt at learning. Aunt Sarah was seated on the little back piazza upstairs, and I stood at her knee. I was gazing blankly at a page covered with hieroglyphs, when I heard her say, "This child is so stupid, she will never learn her ABC's." I have no idea how old I was, but they managed in some way to penetrate my skull, for at five I could read. I know this because I heard Grannie Gordon say—she had just arrived from Savannah and was unpacking her trunks—"I suppose there is no use giving Caroline this book as she is only five and cannot read." I was deeply mortified, and murmured that I *could* and, though not believed, was good naturedly given the book. It was called *Susie and Her Pet Horse*, my first essay in literature after *Reading Without Tears*, and I remember how dull I thought it.

I do not know how old I was when I first became conscious of dress, but I remember being in a little chair in Aunt Sarah's room, pleasantly aware of my beauty, for I had on, for the first time, a little sack of pink sprigged calico, which some kind aunt had made for me.

It is as great a mistake I think to tell a child that she is plain as to tell her that she is pretty. The question of looks had never entered my mind, when, once in the park in Savannah, a nurse joined our party, leading by the hand a very beautiful little girl. Her long curls were as yellow as jasmine, and she wore a black velvet bonnet, lined with lace rushing. I supposed I gazed at her entranced, having been born with a love of beauty, when I heard my mauma say, "This child would give her head for that one's." She did me an injustice. No such thought had entered my mind, and she sowed the seeds of a mistrust as to my personal appearance which has never left me.

I am sure that I remember the first wrong that I deliberately did. In some way I found out that Mother had some candy on a shelf in her wardrobe. I had to tiptoe and lift my hand above my head to get it, and

I took one of the little squares. It was yellow and opaque, and I remember the delectable taste to this day.

Now as far as I know, no one had ever told me not to take what was not my own, but as I did it, I knew that I was stealing, and I stole.

I believe that consciences have gone out of fashion, but we had them then, and mine made me very uncomfortable at the time, not, however, to the point of confession.

2.

The Mackay House

here is an age in childhood which differs from all others. An age when we first become aware of the world around us, and find it mysteriously beautiful.

I passed this Age of Enchantment in the home of my great-aunts, Catherine and Sarah Mackay, in Savannah. I was a fortunate child, for I had two homes. A winter home in Savannah and a summer home in the upcountry.

The Mackay house faced north and was built directly on Broughton Street, its small front porch and high flight of side steps extending half-way over the pavement. It was an unpretentious wooden house, two stories high, with a basement and garret. The garden was on the eastern side, the yard and servants' houses on the west, both concealed from the street by high brick walls, topped with broken glass.

At the back of the house the yard extended to the lane, and on one side of the large gate was a two-storied brick stable; on the other a brick storehouse, beneath which was a deep wine cellar. When the Yankees took Savannah, the only damage they did to the Mackay house was to break into the wine cellar. It was full of old Madeira, and what they could not drink, they destroyed.

The backyard opened into the lane, and it was a shortcut along this to the back gate of Aunt Elliott's house, which stood on the corner of Abercorn and State Streets, facing Oglethorpe Square. Though our elders disapproved of it, we children always left the house by the lane. When

I was very little it was rather terrifying, for on the way there was a dark cavernous opening, in which a very old black man sat, making splint baskets, and I was sure that he was a Booger.

On each floor of the Mackay house was a hall and three rooms, and along the eastern side, upstairs and downstairs, were broad piazzas. As you entered the front door you faced the flight of stairs on the right, and a door on the left opened into the drawing room. A number of English sporting prints hung in the hall, and I recall the scarlet coats of the men, who were dashing along on their hunters, following the pack of spotted hounds.

The drawing room was square, with two north windows opening on Broughton Street, and two east windows on the piazza. It was separated from the dining room back of it by a narrow transverse entry, which led to the piazza.

As I remember it, it was a rather stiff and formal room and kept always in semi-darkness. There is usually a good reason for the customs of a country, and this was done to keep the room cool and to keep out flies and mosquitos. Between the piazza windows was a high black mantlepiece, with divans on either side, at the ends of which were hard rubber bolsters. There was a square rosewood piano, and a rosewood étagiēre, on the shelves of which were many fascinating forbidden *objets d'art*. I remembered particularly a tiny Chinese bowl, as fragile as an eggshell, in which there was a little turtle whose feet quivered if the bowl was touched.

On the mantlepiece were five miniatures by Malbone, including the first one he ever painted, at seventeen. *Shakespeare on the Lap of the Muse*, a sepia after Angelica Kaufman. I also remember a picture in an oval frame that hung on the wall. The head of the Reynold's child in *The Age of Innocence*, which had been exquisitely copied in India ink by my uncle Robert Couper. I remember it because I had an idea that it was a picture of myself!

The dining room was one of the most delightful rooms I have ever seen. Two windows opened on the piazza, and across the whole south end was a bay window which flooded the room with sunshine. Outside of this was an arbor of cloth-of-gold roses shading the side yard. The loveliest thing about the dining room was its coloring. Aunt Kate had it painted one summer, and I will never forget the rapture I felt when I first saw the white woodwork against the buff-colored walls. I had never seen anything but dark woodwork and hard white walls before.

On the eastern side of the dining room, between the two piazza windows, was an alcove, in which stood the old English sideboard. Above it hung a large oil painting of one of Great-Grandfather Mackay's ships. He had been a merchant, dealing directly with Liverpool, and this picture may have represented the ship which the French government seized and never paid for, a disaster which contributed to his failure.

There was another high black mantlepiece in the dining room, and in front of the small coal grate, there always stood a Japanned tin warmer, in which the breakfast plates and toast were kept hot. On each end of the mantlepiece was a missionary box, one blue and one pink. One for Foreign, the other for Domestic Missions. These belonged to Aunt Sarah, and as I recall it, almost every cent we received had to go into one or the other. We children favored the Domestic box for the Indians. There was some romance connected with that, and we were mildly excited when the boxes were opened, and the money counted. Never a large amount, I imagine.

The finest piece of furniture in the dining room was the large mahogany desk bookcase, with its doors of diamond-paned glass. Great-Grandfather had it made at the North after an English model. It belonged to Aunt Sarah and is now owned by my sister Bessie, Mrs. Frank Screven of Savannah. In one of its locked compartments Aunt Sarah always kept a black bottle, and after dinner she would pour some spirits from this into a glass of water and drink it. She had always been infirm, and this probably strengthened her, and I am glad to think she allowed herself this one indulgence. As a child I use to say, "Aunt Sarah likes everything beginning with B. Bible, Bessie, brown bread (she ate no other kind), and bottle."

In the dining room were two mahogany sofas, one of which I particularly disliked. It was rectangular, with thin straight legs and a flat seat. I remember to this day how the horsehair stuck to my legs as I sat with them straight out on the wide seat. One day when Great-Uncle Joseph Stiles, the noted Presbyterian divine, came to call, Aunt Sarah asked him to have prayers in the dining room, and in broad daylight we children had to kneel an interminable length of time beside this sofa, while the old gentleman with the long silvery hair prayed loud and fervently.

This sofa was eventually sent up to the country, and as we could never afford to have old furniture repaired, it became so dilapidated that it was finally put up in the garret. I think the possum family which lived up there—going up by the way of the muscadine vine on the piazza—

must have made it their home, for when after many years it was eventually brought down, the rusted springs had busted their bonds, and the horsehair seemed to have exploded into a hurrah's nest. It was as forlorn a looking object as I have ever seen, and this was the one piece of furniture that my sister Belle, Mrs. Snowden Marshall, coveted. She made each of us look at it and say we were willing she should have it, and she had it crated and sent to New York. I am told that it is now a thing of beauty, upholstered in blue damask, and that it is greatly admired by connoisseurs, as an example of a chaste and refined period.

Mother's bedroom in the Mackay house was over the drawing room, with a dressing room adjoining it over the front hall. In this room I remember two colored French prints in oval frames, of old fashioned beaux and belles, which hung above the mantlepiece, on each end of which were hexagonal Chinese vases of lovely blues and greens, with monkey handles.

My personal recollections of this room are few, as I only slept in it when I was a very little girl. I remember one episode vividly however, and that was when I was slapped for the one and only time by my father. God know what I had done, but I was suddenly slapped, and then thrust into the dressing room and shut in. Perhaps Mother was sick, and Father worried, and I had made myself unbearable. I remember to this day my sense of burning shame. After I had cried myself out on the floor, I found not only consolation but pleasure in picturing my death, and the finding of my body behind the door by my agonized and remorseful parents. Then I crawled out on the sloping tin roof of the front porch and forgot all about my wrongs in my interest in the street below and the passersby.

An interesting feature of the Mackay house was the different levels of the rooms. When you left Mother's bedroom, you had to mount three little steps to the transverse hall behind it, on which the two back bedrooms opened. This hall was not over five feet wide, and on one side it was lined with tall bookcases, filled with fine old books.

The company room came first, cold and cheerless, without a fireplace. Not that fires were much needed in Savannah. We seldom had one, except a hard coal fire in the dining-room grate. We children used the company room once to have a play in. But the plays were such an important part of my life, I feel that subject deserves a separate chapter.

Aunt Kate's bedroom was over the dining room, and looked down on the cloth-of-gold arbor. A little dressing room opened from this, made by the enclosed south end of the upstairs piazza. There was a large white curtained bed, in which I slept with Aunt Kate, and on the walls hung many pictures, one of which I especially loved. It was a colored English print called *The Birth of the Thames*. A group of beautiful nymphs emerging from reeds and water plants were holding up in their arms a darling little naked dripping boy. I am sure I would think it a lovely picture even now, and I would give much to possess it.

Every night Nancy May put me to bed, and sat in the chair beside it, telling me about her beaux until I grew sleepy. Then she drew the fringed curtains together, and I fell asleep in an airy white tent.

Nancy was the only child of Aunt Kate's housekeeper, Lizzie May. Nancy was a Quadroon and was very refined and could be trusted not to tell me a thing I ought not to know, which was more than could be said about some of my aristocratic little white friends.

Sometimes in the dead of night I would be awakened by the sound of the fire bell. A tremendous dismal boom that struck terror to my heart. This bell hung originally in the belfry of the Customshouse on the Bay, and could be heard all over the city.

I had a perfect horror of fire as a child, but I have overcome this by going through two fires since I have been grown. Once we barely escaped with our lives in the middle of the night, and our house and everything in it, including the old Mackay sideboard, was burned to the ground. The excitement was so intense that my brain was paralyzed, but I felt no physical fear. The fire was a formidable foe, from whose clutches we must escape, but that was all. And realizing that we might have lost our lives, the loss of even our most treasured possessions seemed as nothing by comparison. There is usually time however to snatch something, so it is a good plan to decide beforehand just what you want to save. I did this before our second fire, and when the fire came, my brain worked automatically, and I saved every one of the things I decided on, and then it ceased working at all, and, try as hard as I might, I could think of nothing more, though I still had time to spare.

We never had a fire in the Mackay house, which must have been very well built, for after a century, when it was sold, it had to be pulled down in the end. So I need not have quaked in my white tent bed, when I was waked by the sound of the fire bell.

In the early morning we used to hear the calls of the crab and shrimp sellers, passing along the street under the windows, crying in their high-pitched flat but musical voices, "Cra-ab Buyer here!" "Swimp Buyer here!" On their heads they carried—without the support of even a hand—round flat baskets, called fanners, filled with fresh crabs and shrimp.

In April they came in from the country, with wonderful coronals on their heads, fanners filled with delicate white swamp lilies, which they called "Naked Ladies," and sold for five cents a bunch. The sound of Negroes' voices, sweet but melancholy, still means to me Savannah and my early days.

There was a divan in the southern bay in Aunt Kate's room, and here in the mornings the ladies of the family often sat and sewed together. The sewing machine stood nearby, and once when Aunt Kate was using it, her hand slipped, and the long needle went entirely through her finger. The others rushed to help her, and I remember how perfectly self-controlled she was, not uttering a sound, while the needle was lifted and her hand drawn out.

It was on a table in this same bay that I experienced the rapture of first trying to write. Aunt Kate's dearest friend was Mrs. Joseph Huger, who lived across the river on their rice plantation, Murray Hill, and it was she who brought me a little book, and suggested my keeping a diary. I "kept a journal" until I was seventeen, but every volume of it has since been burned, voluntarily or otherwise.

There was a third half-story in the Mackay house, for a steep staircase led up to the garret, where the large front room belonged to Aunt Sarah. In this room there were two dormer windows on the north and east, and on the sill of the latter, cages of canary birds were always kept. I still remember the smell of hard-boiled eggs cooking in the sun, with which the dreadful young birds were fed. I should add Birds and Black to Aunt Sarah's B's, for she always kept birds and she always dressed in black.

My little sister Bessie, who came next to Johnnie, slept in this room with Aunt Sarah. In fact she was Aunt Sarah's child. Whether Bessie was born good, or owed her goodness to Aunt Sarah's training, I do not know. After putting her to bed, Aunt Sarah always left her alone in the dark garret room. On one occasion I officiously went up to tell her goodnight, and before leaving her said sanctimoniously, "There is nothing to be afraid of, Bessie. You are not alone. *The Angels are with you.*" Before I was halfway down the stairs, I heard the poor little thing crying in the dark.

There was a stairwell from the garret, and once, when Bessie was very little, she fell through this and landed on her head on the second floor. The angels were with her on that occasion, so that she might live to be a blessing to her entire family.

Aunt Sarah had a trunk full of Confederate money, and at one time she thought of papering her room with it. Had she done this I am sure it would have been a much prettier room than the one I remember, with its hard white walls. I still have a ten-dollar bill that Uncle Charlie gave me, printed in faint rose and blue, across the face of which is written, "Representing nothing on God's earth now. A pledge of a nation that is dead and gone."

Aunt Sarah had her own books, and these she kept on shelves in her room. There were complete editions of Maria Edgeworth and Mrs. Sherwood, and I think it was in the latter set that I read an exciting story, in which several beautiful nuns were rescued by a number of handsome young men. It inspired me to write my first story, the heroine of which was a lovely nun, and every chapter described a hideous torture to which she was subjected. Aunt Sarah also subscribed to *The Spirit of Missions*. I have only to be told that a person subscribed to this publication to know that they were aristocratic.

In the long low garret room back of Aunt Sarah's, "Mr. Pink" had his abode. Pinckney was one of the many sons of Mrs. Huger, and, just grown at this time, he had come to Savannah to work for a cotton firm, and Aunt Kate had given him a room in her house. We children were very fond of him, and one of our excitements was to see him dressed up in his uniform, on the nights that the Guards drilled. In his immaculate gray and scarlet outfit, he was literally the "Pink of perfection," as he entered the drawing room to be inspected by the family.

There was a lumber room next to Mr. Pink's, which was filled with treasure. Boxes of valuable family letters which included 21 from General Lee to his West Point classmate "Jack Mackay," their headings showing the deep affection he held for him. "Dearest Jack," "Delectable Jack," "My beautiful Jack," "My glorious Jack," "Darling Jack," and "Mackay, my Child." But of especial interest to the boys were the old firearms, the bell-mouthed blunderbusses, the boxes of duelling pistols, and the glossy beaver cocked hats in their perfectly fitted cases.

The piazzas in Savannah were usually built on the eastern sides of the houses to catch the sea breezes, and the end on the street being for privacy. The street end of our downstairs piazza had a wooden wall and window, and I remember once hanging out of this to look at a grand carriage which was standing in front of the house. Some of the Lows, our wealthy connections, had come to call on the family, and their colored coachman in livery was seated on the box. He turned his head and surveyed the house from top to bottom. Then seeing me out of the tail of his eye, he said disdainfully, "Dis house sho' need paint!" It was the first time I had ever thought of it having a flaw, and, deeply mortified, I slid down from the window.

I have only to mention the pantry and Maum Lizzie's room in the basement to finish describing the important part of the Mackay house. The pantry, open from the dining room, was a large, pleasant room, where Maum Lizzie reigned supreme. She was not only Aunt Kate's factotum, but was her trusted and devoted friend. A Mulatto, she was short, square, and yellow, with a stubby nose and long upper lip. She was very neat and always wore a colored bandanna handkerchief wound around her head like a turban.

I remember seeing often in the pantry a little old humpbacked lady, dressed in black bombazine, with a black coal-scuttle bonnet. Her name was Williamson, and she was related to us. Aunt Sarah was especially good to her, but she never went into the drawing or dining room, poor soul. Maum Lizzie treated her with the greatest respect, and prepared little collations for her, which she ate in the pantry, but I was afraid of her, she was so ugly.

The basement of the Mackay house was always mysterious to me. The kitchen was under the dining room, and a dark narrow entry led to Maum Lizzie's room, which was under the drawing room. Along this entry were doors opening into what looked like black cells. The Yankees probably would have thought they were torture chambers. At the Hermitage outside of Savannah, Northern tourists are told by the Negroes there that a basement room, with barred windows, was used for this purpose. Uncle Charlie says they were right. It was the McAlpin's wine cellar, and the slaves were tortured by not being able to not get into it!

When I first remembered Nancy May she must have been about sixteen. She was tall and had a fine figure, a creamy skin, red lips, and dark sparkling eyes. Maum Lizzie worshipped the ground she walked on, and told me once, "She was brought to me by fairies in a chariot." Nancy received a higher education at the colored public schools, where she was taught by Northern teachers to play on the piano and guitar. When she was graduated and became a young lady, her mother and herself moved into the two little rooms over the brick stable in the yard. An outside flight of steps led up to their little porch, and here, at night, Nancy use to entertain her beaux, singing to the accompaniment of her guitar. She had many admirers, and finally married well, and, after Aunt Kate's death, took her mother to live with her, and cared for her devotedly to the end.

There were other servants who lived in the little brick houses in the side yard, and I remember seeing the cooks churning ice cream in a large wooden churn under the cloth-of-gold arbor. I have never tasted any ice cream that could be compared to Aunt Kate's. It was made of richest cream and chocolate, and looked like a round tower when brought to the table, and there was so much of it that we always had two helps. Years later I heard in Baltimore someone say, "They do not know what ice cream is in the South. They have never tasted anything but frozen custard." To this day that remark riles me when I think of it.

At an early age I had an individual nurse, but I do not remember much about her and have forgotten her name. We always called them "Mauma," which was sufficient. She took me once to an old part of the town, where there was a quiet square in the centre. In early days all the squares had pumps in them in case of fire. As we left the square, I looked back and was horrified to see a crowd of large boys dragging a small one to the pump, under which they held him and drenched him with water, while the square rang with his screams. I was so overcome by this act of cruelty that I wept all the way home. I suppose my nurse told Mother about it, for she comforted me by giving me a large stick of striped candy to take back to the little boy. When we reached the square again, he was swinging on a gate. He had a round face and very red cheeks, and he looked quite dry and cheerful and seemed astounded when I handed him the candy, without a word, and hastened away.

The Mackay house was a very simple one compared to the grand houses of Savannah, but it possessed a realm of beauty and mastery in its gardens, and today my heart quickens when I think of it.

The garden extended from Broughton Street to the lane and was surrounded on three sides by high walls, which made it as private as the garden of a convent. It was laid out formally in beds of different shapes and sizes, each one edged with pointed bricks. The soil being sandy, everything grew clean out of the ground and not a blade of grass was to be seen. In the centre was a circular bed, in which there grew a large sago palm, its stiff green spikes curving out and downward like an overflowing fountain. Against the southern wall was an arbor, covered with bouquets of tiny buff colored banksia roses, and under this arbor we used to play in the ecru sand.

I remember an episode connected with this arbor. One night we had sweet rusks for supper, and I smuggled mine upstairs and hid it in a bureau drawer. Then I decided to give a party. I invited three of my little friends, who arrived promptly with their dolls, and were met by Maum Lizzie at the front door. Then she drew me aside, and made inquiries, and I was obliged to confess that I had invited them. She asked me what I had for refreshments, and I gave her the rusk, which I had cut up into little cubes, which were by this time as hard as a rock. The little girls and myself went out to play in the arbor, and after a while Maum Lizzie brought out the rusks on little plates. I have never forgotten her perfect manners. In a tone of gentle reproach, she said, "If Missie had only told me in time, we would have had nice refreshments for you. You must excuse us, young ladies."

Many a time since then when I have invited guests to a party, I have been seized with panic at the last moment, for fear that my refreshments might be comparatively as inadequate as those that I served in the banksia arbor so long ago.

A wisteria vine covered the eastern wall of the garden, and I still recall the wonder of its downpour of lilac clusters in the spring. There was a tall magnolia tree, a pomegranate, ablaze with scarley blossoms, and lemon trees against the piazza rail. The fragrant leaves of these lemon trees used to be put in our finger bowls at the table, and I remember to this day the sharp aromatic odor when one was crushed. Little green lizards darted up these trees and sunned themselves on the warm brick walls, blowing out the scarlet balloons beneath their throats. Aunt Kate never allowed them to be harmed, anymore than the tiny land turtles that lived in the remote corner of the garden and appeared at long intervals out of the earth.

It was near this corner that I caught sight of the first snowdrop I had ever seen. It had pushed its way through the winter leaves and was so exquisite I could hardly believe that it was true. I knelt down to see it nearer and held my breath. A snow-white bell, with pure drops of green on every petal. I had never seen anything lovelier in my life.

But then everything in nature is lovely, if we have eyes that see.

We used to play with the pomegranate blossoms on the high piazza steps. Inverted they made perfect ladies with their red kid basques and fluffy ruffled skirts. The fruit itself was nothing much. Beautiful to look at when broken open, disclosing rows of transparent seeds in their snowy setting. If you only ate the seeds, they were acidly sweet and refreshing, but if you bit into the white, your mouth was instantly puckered, and your teeth set on edge.

There was one fascinating bush in the Mackay garden which I have never seen since my childhood. We called it The Rooster Bush. At the time of flowering it was leafless, and its bare thorny branches were hung with adorable little pink and scarley rooster. I have since been told that its proper name is erythme, but I think our name much more interesting.

There were roses in the garden of course—I remember the safrano—but there is not enough clay in the Savannah soil for roses to be fine. It takes the marsh mud for that, and they only reach perfection on a rice island like Mr. Manigault's.

In the eighties, this old gentleman, who was a bachelor, would invite his special friends to spend an afternoon at Pennyworth Island. We would row up the river, disembark on the island, and walk along an embankment to his little house, where cake and ice cream would be served. Then we were each given a basket and a pair of scissors and turned into the acres of roses, free to cut the most magnificent blooms on the longest possible stems. It was simply intoxicating, and by the time the afternoon was over, the boats would be piled from prow to stern, and we would row back to the city, literally on a bed of roses. The most regal form of entertainment I have ever known.

Of course the glory of the Mackay garden, as all of Savannah gardens, were the camellia japonicas, which grew to a great height and bore every kind of blossoms. The simplest were the single reds, with the yellow tasseled centres, which we did not think much of. The red and white striped ones were handsomer, but the most gorgeous of all were the double whites and shell pinks, so perfect that they looked as though they were made of wax. The most beautiful decoration I ever saw was done entirely in japonicas. Aunt Elliott had an entertainment and I was allowed to see the drawing room. A great mirror stood between two windows, resting on a low white marble pier table, and this was banked with double pink camellias, laid on soft gray moss.

A clever woman said to me once, "I do not like camellias, they are so perfect, they make me feel a sinner."

Mrs. King of St. Simon's Island, who had a wonderful garden at her home Retreat, would never have a camellia in it because they are without fragrance. "Flowers without souls," she called them.

They are perfect. So perfect that you can hardly touch one without leaving a stain, and they are as scentless as if they were made of wax. In spite of which I love them, for they mean the South to me. There is only one flower more typical, and that is the yellow jessamine, which I adore.

Once, many years later than the time of which I am writing, I went to see Cousin William and Cousin Sidney Elliott on their Golden Wedding Day. Under no circumstances would there have been a celebration, for they were modest, retiring people, but Cousin William had been very ill and was still in bed. Cousin Sidney took me to the window and said, "I want you to see our Golden Wedding decoration." And there, from the ground up to the second-story window, over the entire side of the house, was a yellow jessamine vine, which was simply a golden glory.

I cannot imagine anything more intoxicating than the woods on the Georgia coast in spring, when the great live oaks, swathed in filmy gray moss, are garlanded with fragrant yellow jessamine, and vocal with the music of mockingbirds.

In the Mackay garden there was a magnolia tree, so tall that we could never pick a bloom, but it was thrilling to find one on the ground, even if it was shattered, and its creamy petals were turning saffron, for many were filled with tiny lucifer matches, which had spilled from the cone in its centre.

The Japanese magnolia was much less beautiful, though the lilac pink chalices upheld on its bare silver twigs, had a sort of Oriental charm. This tree grew near the garden gate, where there was a hydrant for watering the flowers, and I remember seeing Aunt Rebecca Couper there giving old Herks Habersham a drink. She was then, as always, very delightful and amusing, and she had named a bulbous cactus in a pot after the old red-faced gentleman, whose vocation was imbibing.

It was at this same hydrant that I concocted a tumbler of chocolate ice cream out of mud and water. I put the tumbler on a plate, covered it with a napkin, and sent it in to Harry Elliott, our cousin, who lived next door. He was at dinner when the ice cream arrived, and seizing the tumbler and inviting no one to share it, he took a large spoonful, forgetting that it was April Fool's Day.

But I think after all Harry had the last laugh.

The largest mispilla plum tree I ever saw grew against the Mackay house. Its branches reaching to the upstairs piazza. I tiptoed across this once to purloin some of the delicious golden fruit, leaned over the rail, and looked straight down into the grinning face of Harry Elliott. Unseen, he had climbed up the tree, and, hidden smugly in the thick foliage, was stuffing plums. Although a fellow criminal, I had not the courage to acknowledge it, and fled, followed by his chuckling laugh.

I was willing to do evil, if it could be done without detection.

3.
In Savannah

he city of Savannah, built on a high bluff above the river, is laid out as symmetrically as a chessboard, the streets running east and west, crossing at right angles those running north and south. Every alternate street is a broader one, and the longitudinal streets widen out every two blocks into a square, around which the street circles. These open spaces were said to have been planned as places of refuge for the country people, when threatened by Indian raids. The broader streets that run east and west have wide grass plats down their centres, shaded by live oaks.

Bull street is the central street of the city, and when I was a child, it ran from Bay Street on the north to Forsyth Park on the south, and in every one of its five squares there was an interesting monument, erected in honor of someone who had been notable in Savannah history.

I cannot imagine a more beautiful business street of the city than The Bay. Extending east and west along the top of the bluff, it is wide and airy, with a broad parkway of grass and shady trees down its centre. The countinghouses, built on the lower level of the riverbank, rise two and three stories above Bay Street and are entered by little bridges thrown across from the bluff.

Savannah was not as beautiful when I was a child as it is today, for no avenues of crepe myrtle flowered into pink foam in the summer, down the centres of its broad streets, and no miles of palmettos and fragrant oleanders extended to the sea. Above all, no Bonaventure, idyllic City of the Dead, blazed scarlet with azaleas beneath its gray cathedral aisles of moss-draped oaks.

It was not so comfortable a city either, for while there were brick sidewalks, the streets themselves were deep in sand, and only outside of the city limits did the white-shell roads extend in every direction, a delight for the drivers of fast horses.

Most of the dwelling houses were built directly on the street, whole blocks of them side by side, and if they had space for a garden, it was always hidden by a high brick wall. It made the gardens as private as Spanish patios, but it did not add to the beauty of the town. Only where the handsomer houses were built on their isolated lots, two on each side of a square was there a small garden in front surrounded by an iron fence, in addition to the walled garden at the back. Wrought iron was the fashion of the day, and there are still many beautiful grills and balconies on the old crumbling houses.

At that time Savannah had a rather deadly climate, with its malaria and not infrequent scourges of yellow fever, and at best the heat of its long summers was exhausting. General Joseph E. Johnston, who came to live there after the war, was once asked what he thought of the climate. "Sir," he answered, "I consider it the most *corroding* climate that I know." In winter there was a penetrating chill from its nearness to the sea, in spite of which few Savannah people had fires in all of their rooms.

Aunt Kate and Aunt Sarah Mackay had lived in Savannah all their lives, and as young people had been educated at the North, often spending their summers at Newport, where their cousins, the Malbones, lived. They were the only unmarried daughters of a large family and were comfortably off—not rich of course like Grannie Gordon, who lived in a fine house on Bull Street, drove out in her own carriage, and had bananas, powdered sugar, and cream *every* day for dinner, in addition to another dessert—but well enough off to take care of the great-nieces and -nephews, who came at pretty regular intervals of eighteen months, until there were eight of them in all.

Aunt Kate and Aunt Sarah had been particularly devoted to our father and had wanted to adopt him and have him change his name to Mackay, as there were no men of the name left. He was unwilling to do this, but they helped him all the same, and after his early death, took virtual charge of us. They were the good angels of our family, and I do not see how we could have survived without them. They were devoted to all of us, but each one had her favorite. Aunt Sarah's was Bessie, and Aunt Kate's Margie, the next little sister. She was also devoted to me, and how unworthy of her love I must have been!

Aunt Kate was the elder, and as her judgement was excellent and she had a great executive ability, she had entire charge of the household and of their finances. She was small and slender and had large brown eyes, a straight nose, and thin firm lips. I always thought Jane Eyre must have looked like her. Beautifully neat, everything about her was kept in perfect order, and after all these years, I could almost say where every article was kept in her top bureau drawer. I do not think Aunt Kate had any sense of humor, and I never remember hearing her laugh. She was very reserved but impressed everyone by her quiet force and great dignity. And *never* have I known a more perfect lady.

Every day after breakfast Aunt Kate washed the glass and delicate china at the breakfast table, and I sat beside her and wiped it. It bored me almost as much as learning to hem, for at that age I had not the slightest taste for any domestic duties. After superintending the cleaning and filling of the tall bronze lamps in the pantry, and giving out the daily supplies in the basement storeroom, Aunt kate went up to her dressing room and spent an hour in prayer and Bible reading. Every Sunday afternoon she lay on her couch—she was not very strong—and, when I grew older, I sat beside her, and she read aloud the collect, gospel, and epistle of the day, with expositions. I can recall the torture of trying to keep awake.

Aunt Sarah was tall and gaunt, and, to me, she was very plain. Both sisters dressed alike in black, their dresses made with full plain skirts which touched the floor, and basques, the white ruches in their high necks, fastened with mourning brooches. Both wore their hair parted in the middle and brushed down smoothly over their ears, and both wore immaculate white caps.

Aunt Sarah was undoubtedly a Puritan. Deeply religious, she was intolerant of everything that she considered worldly. I once asked her if she had always been good, and she said, "No. I was a very wicked girl. When I was twenty-one I had a terrible illness, and when I recovered, I became a Christian."

And she was a real Christian, for hers was a religion not only of words, but of deeds. She spent her entire time visiting the poor and sick, going regularly to see the awful old women in the Old Ladies Home on

Broughton Street. Up the country she visited the tenants, black and white, taking them food and medicine, and reading the Bible to them.

She did her duty by me, taught me to read and saw that I learned the catechism, but she did not care for me, and I know now that she saw through me and knew that I was not religious. I used to try hard to please her, and everything that I did or said was wrong. I remember saying once what I thought would meet with her approval, "I know when I die I am going to hell." But I slipped up there, for she rebuked me sternly.

Aunt Sarah was very plain spoken, as I remember on one occasion when a gentleman came to call at night. He was a perfect Don Quixote in appearance, long, lean, and yellow, with the most frigid manners. We were in the drawing room, and when my bedtime came, I started around as usual, to kiss everyone goodnight. Out of sheer politeness, the visitor leaned over to kiss me too, when Aunt Sarah said severely, "We do not allow Caroline to kiss gentlemen." I escaped in some confusion, and the fury of Don Quixote can be imagined. I do not remember his ever calling again.

There is one memory however for which I am truly grateful to Aunt Sarah. I remember once coming in the front door, and seeing an old gentleman, with snow-white hair and beard, seated in the drawing room. He took me on his knee, and kissed me, and Aunt Sarah, who was standing by, said, "Child, never forget this moment."

The white-haired gentleman was General Lee!

Our family had a more exalted opinion of General Lee than of any man on earth. He had been a dear and intimate friend of the Mackay family since 1829, when he had been stationed on Cockspur Island at the mouth of the Savannah River. He was then a young and exceedingly handsome man, with dark wavy hair, perhaps wearing the "side burns" he sported in the Mexican War. He was at this time very much taken with Grandmama, and we had several of his letters, from the days when he addressed her as "Eliza, my Sweetheart," to those written later on, when he offered her beautiful little daughter Mary the devotion of his little son Custis.

Next to General Lee, Bishop Elliott came first with the Mackay family. "Stephen the Magnificent," he was called. To hear him preach in Christ Church was the greatest pleasure that Aunt Sarah had, and she must have taken me once, when I was four, for I still remember his beautiful face and silvery hair above me.

I once heard a new acquaintance say to Aunt Sarah, "I have been told that if ever there was a saint on earth, it was Sarah Mackay." Aunt Sarah shrank as if she had been struck. "Oh, no, no!" she protested, horrified. But I do not think this person had been misinformed, if to be a saint is to be "one eminent for piety and virtue." Aunt Sarah's entire life was spent ministering to others. She always took what was least desirable for herself and denied herself everything but the barest necessities.

Bessie's feelings can be imagined then when the following indignity was offered to such a saint. Wearing a clean little stiffly starched dress, she was walking one day on Bull Street with Aunt Sarah, when, at the corner of the Gordon house, they passed a little boy who was playing with a stick in a mud puddle. As the tall, black, severe figure of Aunt Sarah approached, he shouted, "You old dink!", struck the puddle with his stick, and covered Bessie and Aunt Sarah with dirty water. But then this little boy was the worst little boy I have ever known. His favorite occupation was leaning out of the windows of Grannie Gordon's house, to spit on the heads of the passersby.

As Aunt Kate and Aunt Sarah had entire control of us, our religious training was thorough. We said our prayers night and morning and read one chapter of the Bible once a day. I remember how virtuous I felt, when I read a chapter of seventy-two verses once before breakfast. The Bible I always felt was a sacred book. No other book was ever put on top of it. If the house should ever burn down, I knew that I must save the Bible, *if nothing else.* Needless to say the Bible was not saved in either of my fires.

We had family prayers before breakfast and grace at every meal, the children taking turns saying this. In Lent we denied ourselves something that we really liked, and for the entire time. No indulgence on Sunday for *us.* And never could we tell anyone but Mother or our aunts what we had given up. Let not your right hand know what your left hand doeth. It was severe discipline, but I suppose it helped to teach us self-control. And I have lived long enough to appreciate the good training I received as a child. However you disregard it at the time, it stays with you, and in the end you find it of inestimable value.

On Sundays we went to church in the morning and to Sunday School in the afternoon. Christ Church, which we attended, had been founded by John Wesley, who had come over from England with Oglethorpe. The church building was not erected until after he left, and, having been burned down later on, our grandfather James Hamilton Couper was requested to design a new one, which is still in existence. With the classical taste of the day, he designed a Greek temple with a portico and Ionic columns in front. His concern can be imagined when the Greek temple was erected upon a high basement with a wide flight of steps leading up to the portico!

The Mackay pew was the third from the front on the right-hand side of the central aisle, and the walk up that aisle used to seem to me a mile long. I do not remember the services but they wearied me, as the very sound of a church bell makes my heart sink to this day. I do remember Sunday School in the basement, and the tiresome hours we spent there. It was nothing to me that the first Sunday School in the world had been originated in Christ Church.

Aunt Sarah took me once to the Presbyterian Church, and I thought the arched tops of the great windows, with their green shutters, were fan palmettos. The Presbyterian Church is more beautiful than Christ Church. It is perfectly proportioned inside with an oval ceiling and oval galleries: the whole church surrounded by immense arched top windows, reaching from the floor to the ceiling. Everything is white, and the effect of the whole is snow barred with silver, where the sunlight gleams through the slats of the shutters. This church, which has the highest steeple in Savannah, was a copy of St. Martin-in-the-Fields, London, and was described at the time of its erection as "A poem in architecture, a dream in stone, and a sculptured religion." The president of the United States, James Monroe, with his suite, attended its dedication on May 9th, 1819, having come down to see the *Savannah*—the first steamboat to cross the Atlantic—start on its perilous journey. In April 1889, there was a great conflagration in Savannah, and the Presbyterian church was burned to the ground, only its foundation being left. In time it was rebuilt exactly as it was before, and the baptismal font, which was saved, is still in use.

Our Sunday afternoons were rather dreary, as on our return from Sunday School, we spent them sitting on the piazza steps leading down to the garden. We could only read religious books on Sunday—and I have yet to read an interesting one—we could not study our lessons—not that was any deprivation—nor could we play. We could not even go to walk.

The fashionable Sunday-afternoon walk was out Bull Street to the park. Only one side of the street was *comme-il-faut*, but I have forgotten which side it was. Gulie and her cousins Nellie and Daisy Gordon walked out to the park every Sunday, but Aunt Sarah considered this worldly and we stayed at home.

Forsyth Park is a lovely park. A grove of tall pines, palmettos, and oak trees traversed the broad paths, in the centre of which is a graceful fountain, modeled after those in the Place-de-la-Concord. The circular enclosure is surrounded by an iron railing, within which a wreath of brilliant azaleas is reflected in the water, where tritons blow their conch shells and swans send graceful sprays from uplifted beaks when the fountain plays. The main promenade is the broad walk to the fountain, its entrance formerly guarded by a sphinx on either side. A bronze copy of John of Bologna's *Mercury* soared from its pedestal, halfway up the walk, along which were iron benches on which the young men sat to view the Sunday procession of girls.

A bazaar was held once in the park for Christ Church, and I was allowed to help with other little girls. We carried grab bags around, and, from being painfully shy at first, I became hardened and bold before the evening was over, and I have no doubt we made ourselves perfect little pests.

I remember seeing General Joseph E. Johnston there, small, trim, and dry, with a gray mustache and imperial, walking around with his large, dark, showily dressed wife. Major Mims of Mississippi was also there with his second wife, and his refined looking little daughter Emma, who was to become such a noted beauty and belle. Mrs. Mims, who was as pretty as a French Marquise, wore a black lace dress and a broad turquoise silk sash. I am sure this was considered scandalous, but it gave me the keenest pleasure, for I have always loved color above everything. I had hardly ever seen a grown person in anything but black, and many of the Savannah ladies wore long crepe veils down to their heels. After the war the entire South was in mourning, and many women wore black for the rest of their lives.

I remember my excitement when once in the shopping district of Broughton Street, two handsome young women passed me, dressed in the gaudiest colors I have ever seen. One was in purple and the other in emerald green silk, with kid gloves to match. They had come from the North and evidently enjoyed flaunting their gorgeous plumage in the midst of so many black crows, for they attended a service in Christ Church on the following Sunday, and I had the bliss of seeing them again.

Our Stiles cousins, who stayed every winter with their Grandmother Gordon, lead a much more luxurious life than we did. They were handsomely dressed and were each given twenty-five cents for pin money on Saturdays. We were given five, with a cent deducted for every bad mark we got at school. I remember once being reduced to two cents, and it took all of my courage to enter a pastry shop and ask whether I could buy anything for that sum. Much to my surprise I was given a delicious macaroon. The pastry shop nearest to us was Derst's, on Broughton Street, and the ambition of my life was to buy one of the snowballs displayed in its window, an ambition I never achieved, as a snowball cost ten cents.

We were also given five cents to put in the plate at Sunday School, and once Hammie, tempted by an older colored boy, spent his for licorice! This remained a dark secret, which was never divulged to our elders. But Hammie's crime was as nothing compared to my own.

The first school I ever went to was kept by Miss Lucie Blois, whose family had been refugees from the French Revolution. Miss Lucie was a dried-up but very sprightly old maid, and she taught us in the garret room of their house on Chippewa Square. Meta Habersham, my second cousin, and myself went to school together, but one morning I happened to be alone, and on South Broad Street I met Satan in the form of a little Mulatto girl. She asked me where I was going, and I told her. "Why don't you play hooky?" she suggested. I had no idea what she meant, and she explained. "You go and sit on somebody's steps for a long time. Then you go home and tell your mumma teacher was sick." I did exactly as she told me, and I remember the very flight of steps on which I sat, at the corner of York and Drayton. It was dreadfully tiresome, and I soon returned home and told the lie. But I had not counted on Meta Habersham. That afternoon I went over to Aunt Elliott's and into Cousin Leila Habersham's room. She was kneeling on the floor, cutting out a dress for Meta, and she looked at me closely. "Why did you say that your teacher was sick, Caroline?" she asked. "Meta went to school, and she was not sick at all." I was covered with confusion and could not answer her, for I did not know myself, and for the first time I realized that what I had done was wrong.

The next day Mother herself took me to the school and went in first to explain. Then I was taken up to the garret room and seated on a little stool near Miss Lucie, who was kindness itself, and you may be sure I never played truant again.

One of our schoolmates was the most beautiful little girl in Savannah. She was named Maude Elliott, and, was the cousin of a little boy at the North, who was named Theodore Roosevelt. Her complexion was like peaches and cream, and her hair, which was as yellow as gold, was always crimped and let out. She was always beautifully dressed and wore a black velvety toque, which was most becoming. It was suspected by our elders that her mother blondined her hair and painted her face, and this was probably true, as, later on, when I met her as a young lady, both her health and complexion were ruined and she had lost her looks entirely.

The prettiest girl of our neighborhood was Jessie McIntosh, who lived on the square below us nearest the Bay. She came some times to play with us in Oglethorpe Square, and when she started home in the evenings, she was always chased by Alfred Mills and the other boys and invariably was caught and *kissed*. I witnessed this myself on one occasion and was scandalized. No boys had ever chased *me* to kiss me. Perhaps I might have been more lenient if they had.

The Savannah squares are green oases, shaded by live oaks draped with gray moss and picturesque palmettos. In the center of each one along Bull Street there is a monument, the two most imposing being those of Pulaski and General Greene. Pulaski, the young Polish patriot who came over to fight for American Independence, was mortally wounded near Savannah in 1779. After the Revolution, General Nathanael Greene came South to live and was given a plantation on the Savannah River, where he died in 1786. His body now lies under his monument.

In the afternoons all of the Savannah squares are filled with little children tended by their old black maumas. In my day the maumas all wore brilliant bandanna handkerchiefs, wrapped, turban-like about their heads, the ends tied in a bow like rabbits' ears on one side.

A friend of mine was once passing through one of the squares on Bull Street, when her attention was arrested by the behaviour of a little boy who was simply raising Cain. "Why, Mauma," she said "What a temper that child has!" The old body snorted, " 'E bleege to hab a temper," she said, " 'E Ma got a temper. 'E Pa got a temper. 'E get it frum 'e *off-spring*."

Young Roosevelt had other relatives in Savannah. Miss Louisa Bulloch and her sister Mrs. Locke. Miss Louisa was one of Aunt Kate's best friends, and came often to dine with us. She must have been quite old, for she shook the entire time with palsy, with a constant tinkling of earrings and bracelets, but she was a gay little soul, enjoying everything and always trilling with laughter. I owe Miss Louisa a dept of gratitude, which I will acknowledge later.

Mr. and Mrs. Locke had lived for many years in Italy, where their only child was born, and named in honor of her birthplace, Florence. Miss Florence Locke had the most wonderful hair I have ever seen. It reached below her knees, and the favorite sport of the young men of the Elliott family was to pull out the pins that held it up and let it cascade down her back. In spite of her hair Miss Florence Locke was never married, and she spent her last days living alone with her cats in an apartment in Washington, at the time that her famous cousin was president.

A pleasant experience of mine at this time was going to dancing school in the old Habersham house on Orleans Square. We were taught in the long drawing room, which seemed to me of vast dimensions, and the rainbow lights from the prismed chandeliers were strange and fascinating. Robert and Annie Coleman stayed here when they came down from the North, their mother having been the beautiful Ellen Habersham. But while they were very kind to us, they were so fabulously rich, they were entirely outside of our world.

The Habersham house had been built by Jay, the English architect, who had designed the Telfair and Owens homes. In the latter home, Lafayette had stayed when he visited Savannah in 1824. In the middle of the Habersham house was an octagonal hall, surrounded by columns from which rose a circular stairway of wrought iron. One of my elders once said to me, in a low tone, "They could never get a corpse down those stairs. The dead had to be *let down*." When you think of it I suppose that is a drawback in the home, as all of us will be the dead some day. The Habersham house is no more. Being one of the handsomest and most unique houses in the city, the Savannahians never rested until it was torn down and a modern auditorium erected in its place.

Every winter we children were sent up once to pay Uncle Low a visit, a hateful experience for him as well as for ourselves. Mr. Andrew Low, a Scotchman, had made a fortune in the cotton business in Savannah before the war and had married for the second time, our Aunt Mary, the beauty of the Stiles family. She had died during the war, leaving four children who were at this time in England with their older half-sisters, Amy and Hattie. Mr. Low had been very kind and generous to our family, and Aunt Kate and he were good friends. The old gentleman came back every winter to Savannah to attend to his affairs, and must have had a rather dreary time all alone in his big house.

No house in the world will ever seem to me as grand as the Low's house, and I always approached it with trepidation. It stood on the west side of Lafayette Square, with a small garden in front, enclosed by an iron railing and a walled garden filled with camellias at the back. It was a square brick house stuccoed coffee color, two stories above an English basement. The long windows had heavy dark green shutters, and in front of them were little iron balconies. On each side were double iron balconies, and at the back were broad shuttered piazzas. The high flight of stone steps in front, with a recumbent red-stone lion on either side, was positively awe-inspiring; while the massive white door at the top, decorated with round knobs, seemed the very symbol of riches. By the time that this was opened by old Tom, the Negro butler, I was absolutely petrified.

With my little brothers and sisters pressing to me, we would be herded into the dining room at the back of the hall, where Uncle Low, like an old bear in his den, would be seated in semi-darkness, reading his paper beside the fire. He was a stout old gentleman, with light eyes, and a full reddish beard, and his voice was like a growl. To save my life I could not understand a word he said, and, as the other children were always speechless and I hadn't an idea left in my head, the interview was mutually awful. Why we were sent to poison a perfectly good after-dinner hour for the old gentleman, I cannot imagine. Children should *never* be sent to see *anybody*.

Old Tom, Mr. Low's butler, who was as black as a coal, was once taken to England by his master, and there he had a trying experience. He all but died of the cold, but what he minded much more was the constant quarrelling of the white maids for the honor of "walking out" on his arm!

Before the war, Mr. Low had entertained Thackery in his home, when he came to America on a lecture tour. It has been stated that Thackery wrote *The Virginians* while staying with Mr. Low, a visit of probably a few days! While there he dined with the Mackays, and Aunt Kate afterwards sent two pretty little colored boys, Jim and Sady, up the Low's house to see him. They went up to Thackery's bedroom, where he had an amusing conversation with them, which he jotted down. One was older but the other was fatter, they said. When they left he gave them a quarter, which excited them so that fat little Jim fell down the stairs, to Thackery's perfect delight.

General Lee also stayed with Mr. Low when he came to Savannah after the war, and he was received with such honors, so after all the house was historical, and worthy of respect and awe of small countrified visitors.

Although we spent every winter in Savannah, we remained country children and loved the things that country children do. Climbing, for instance, especially if it was dangerous, for like all children, we had a passion for doing dangerous things.

One of the favorite stunts in Savannah was sliding down the lightning rod from the upstairs piazza to the ground. To this day I remember the scrape of rusty twisted iron burning the palms of my hands, as, with my skirts over my head, and my panties exposed, I shot down into the garden below. Another was hanging out of an upstairs window, holding on to the ledge with our hands. I have climbed from an upstairs window to the ground hanging on to the ivy that grew on the stuccoed walls at Etowah Cliffs, and I never rested until I had climbed down one of the columns on the front piazza there, which was really difficult because of the protruding capital.

As far as I can judge I did not have a ray of sense when I was little —and not so little either. On one occasion Hammie and I had been taken to call on Grannie Gordon, and I suppose to get rid of us we were sent out in to the garden. A very high brick house, belonging to the McAlpins, bounded the east end of the garden, and suddenly we were attracted by the antics of a little boy up in the third story. He called out that he was locked into the bathroom, and couldn't get out, and then he let himself out of the window, and hung on by his hands. I glanced at Hammie, who looked at me with perfect trust, and I realized that he was expecting me, his big sister, to save the little boy. I thought in a wild way, and then I lifted my skirt with both hands. "Drop!" I cried, "*And we will catch you*." Before the little boy could follow this sage advice, his big sister, with a scarlet face and wild white eyes, rushed into the garden and ordered him back into the bathroom. He obeyed with the agility of a monkey, and she then told him to throw the key out of the window. This he did, and the excitement ended as far as we were concerned. I have no doubt that there was further excitement for the little boy.

When I was older I went to the Massie School in Savannah, and after all these years it is just the same today that it was at that time. Three square squat buildings, stuccoed a mild rust color, and connected by corridors. When I stood for the first time outside of the great door of the central schoolroom, I almost died of fright. How I ever got inside I do not know, but it did not take me long to feel at home, in the overcrowded, ill ventilated rooms, and I thoroughly enjoyed being with so many other little girls, Jews as well as Gentiles. I remember that the two prettiest girls in my class were Mary Footman and Sallie Champion.

At recess we played out in the sand square, where, if we had the means, we bought sticks of molasses candy from the young little Negro boys, who carried them around on trays and sold them for five cents apiece.

The first time that I had to say a "piece," standing on the teacher's platform, I all but lost consciousness. But I soon became used to it, and revelled in it, and finally had the honor of reciting "The Rebel Sock" before a large audience of enthusiastic parents on Examination Day.

At this time I had a genuine coast pronunciation, saying gyrls, cyars, gyardens, and so on, a pronunciation that I unconsciously lost later on, though I can still be spotted by my speech as coming from the coast. I myself think the coast pronunciation very flat and ugly, but in hearing coast people talk, I realize that this is compensated for by the usually lovely quality of the Southern speaking voice.

We were trained to say "Sir" and "Ma'am" to our elders as properly behaved children of English descent should do, and to this day when a child says "No" and "Yes" to a grown person it gives me a turn. Of course I know that they are suppose to add the name of the person addressed very prettily, but it is almost impossible for the poor little things to remember the new names they hear. We said "You all" of course, as it was biblical English, but we never used it in the singular. In spite of Northern assertions, when addressed to a single person the family is always implied, even by a Negro with his "Y'all," and a Cracker with his "You uns." We must never say that we "loved" anything to eat for that was "common." And, speaking of eating, I do not think I had to be told, I think I knew by instinct, that I must never eat anything in the presence of others, *especially of an inferior*, without offering them some of it. The consequence was that on one wonderful occasion when Maum Lizzie gave me the saucepan, in which chocolate blancmange had been made, to scrape, I flew to the most secluded spot I could find, the entrance of a cellar window, where seated with my feet on the ground and safely concealed from every little brother and sister, I could eat every spoonful of that delicious concoction by myself. I remember to this day that the performance gave me no pleasure at all, and that, for some strange reason, the blancmange was absolutely tasteless.

When we wrote a letter we were taught to fold the front page *in* and not *out*, and even now if I receive a letter folded in the wrong way, I feel that its writer has not been properly brought up. It is almost as bad as leaving your coffee spoon in your cup. We girls were trained rigidly not to stoop, and we would never have thought of holding our arms akimbo, or of crossing our legs when seated. It takes a childhood of training I suppose to civilize us, as we come into the world such little barbarians.

It was a long walk up to the Massie School, past the old cemetery, and through three squares, but I never remember being "tardy" but once, and I can still recall the deadly feeling when the great green gate closed in my very face. When I came home at two o'clock, Maum Lizzie always had a thick slice of bread spread with soft yellow butter sprinkled with brown sugar ready for me, as we dined at the uncomfortable hour of three.

Sometimes in the afternoon we played in the old cemetery, where General Nathanael Greene and Malbone the painter were buried, and I remember the gravestone of one of my great-great-grandfathers, Joseph Smith, who Aunt Sarah said "was common only in name." She also told us that any good there might be in us came from the saintly man. Many of the doors of the old vaults had fallen in, and I always glanced a little fearfully at the cavernous dark inside, but the spookiness did not prevent us from cracking coconuts on the tombstones and eating them with relish.

These were the days of Reconstruction, when the Northern carpet-baggers were poisoning the minds of the Negroes against the Southern whites. Once Meta Habersham, another little girl, and myself were coming home from the Massie School, when a crowd of half-grown Negro girls darted in front of us, and, holding hands, tried to force us off the pavement into the street. I was alarmed, and said nothing, and they let me pass, but Meta gave them a piece of her mind, and I have no idea how long she was detained and scoffed at.

Of course it was not long before the poor creatures, who are not naturally belligerent, were subdued, but the lasting harm that was done came in the alienation of the races.

4

Brunswick

y Grandmother Couper, Mother's mother, lived in Brunswick, Georgia, and when we went down to visit her, we went usually by boat. The island passage between the coast and sea islands is a beautiful one, and Mother loved it especially, as it recalled her happy childhood. Though banished to the mountains of North Georgia, it was the coast she always long for, and I must have inherited her love for it, for, to this day, the first sight of a palmetto tree on the edge of a marsh thrills me as nothing else has ever done.

I never saw the ocean until later life, and when I first stood on Pawley's Island and saw the rush of white breakers along the beach as far as eye could see and heard their thundering roar, I was simply overwhelmed.

The first trip to Brunswick by water that I remember was on board the *Lizzie Baker*, which plied between Savannah and Palatka, Florida. Above the cabin there stood a short, sturdy, painted wooden figure of Lizzie Baker—whoever she was—which I thought frightful. There was a gay crowd of young ladies aboard, who abashed me by asking me which one I thought the prettiest. I could not say as I thought them all as ugly as the figurehead. I must have been very little at this time, as these young ladies seemed to me gigantic. But then we live in a world of giants in our extreme youth.

After leaving Savannah, the steamer makes its way at first through an expanse of quiet, level marsh, its color and values changing imperceptibly. At times a pale pure green, with a feeling of purple in the shadow along the water's edge; at times so dark, that the creeks winding through it shine like quicksilver.

At the edge of the marsh is the blue bloom of the mainland, and there the boat glides into a wide and shining channel, and along its shores are deep woods of oaks, magnolia, and bay. And now comes the tang of the salt air, and the soaring of white gulls, and only a misty sea island lies between you and the great Atlantic, which booms on its outer beach.

The largest of these islands are Ossabaw, St. Catherine's, Sapelo, St. Simon's, Jekyl, and Cumberland, and the Spaniards called them the Golden Isles.

From the earliest times, when the Creek Indians used them as hunting islands, through the century of Spanish occupation, when missions were founded and chapels were built upon them, to their settlement by the Scotch and English under Oglethorpe and their highest development, when owned by the planters of prewar days, their history has been romantic and interesting.

Not that I knew anything about it as a child, or was the least interested in the subject.

A friend of mine once said, "It is a sign of old age when you stop making New Year's resolutions."

But I think the first sign of old age is when you begin to be interested in your ancestors. A pity, for then it is generally too late to secure the valuable information you long for later on.

Mother had lived as a girl at Hopeton, her father's rice plantation on the Altamaha, which was about eight miles above Darien. One of a large family, she had led a happy life, going down every summer to St. Simon's Island where they stayed at Cannon's Point, the home of their old Scotch grandfather, John Couper. There were many families living on the island at this time, and others came from the mainland for the summer, and their intercourse was friendly and delightful.

But the war had come, and desolation followed. Most of the people on the coast lost everything they possessed, but though their lives had been utterly changed, I never heard one of them repine. Grandmother's sorrow however was stamped in deep lines on her face, and I have never seen more hopeless eyes. She had lost two sons in the war, and her husband just after it. She had to give up Altama, which has been built for her dower house, her share of Hopeton, and all that she had owned on St. Simon's Island, and, now reduced to a slender income, she was living in a small wooden house in Brunswick.

As I remember Brunswick at that time, it consisted mostly of small wooden houses, many of them unpainted and grayed with age. The wide streets were deep in sand, with only boarded sidewalks, but the great live oaks bordering them were magnificent, and the air was full of fragrance from the pink and white oleanders blooming in the gardens.

However dreary life must have been to our elders, it was entrancing to us who were just entering it, and my visits to the old house in Brunswick were filled with interest and excitement.

In addition to Aunt Rebecca, Grandmother's maiden sister, Aunt Harriet Wylly, lived with her. She was a merry little soul, with a round, shriveled, downy face, and was devoted to young people. She was especially devoted to my cousin Mary Harper, though she had a funny way of showing it. Mary used to come in from Altama to spend the night with me, and in the morning Aunt Harriet would come into our room and slap Mary soundly to wake her up. How Mary took it I do not remember, but anything more infuriating than being waked by a stinging slap, I cannot imagine.

When Aunt Harriet lived at The Village on St. Simon's, they had a little black boy, who sat on the back piazza, and pulled a cord, which waved the fan suspended over the dining room table. Gradually the fan would begin to slow down, and at last it would come to a standstill. Then—Uncle Jimmie told us—Aunt Harriet would slip out on the piazza, find the little boy sound asleep, take off her slipper, and whack him. So slapping was evidently a habit of hers. In spite of which she was the kindest little old person in the world, and the best natured.

Aunt Harriet enjoyed above everything else Mary's and my foolishness and would laugh at our pranks until the tears rolled down her withered cheeks. Grandmother enjoyed us too, in spite of herself, and would laugh almost as heartily as Aunt Harriet when Mary and I would jump up from the table in the middle of dinner, sing and dance around the room, and make ourselves perfectly ridiculous. It was the sheer joy of living, for we were overflowing with life and had to express our feelings in some way. I did not stand in awe of Grandmother and Aunt Harriet as I did of Aunt Sarah and Aunt Kate, and I suppose that was one reason that I had such a delightful time whenever I visited Brunswick.

They were all fond of flowers, and at each end of the narrow downstairs piazza were tiers of potted plants. In one pot there was a fat double cactus that belonged to Aunt Harriet, and once when Mary and I were playing ball, my ball struck it and knocked its block off. I was horrified, and wept, in spite of the fact that Aunt Harriet laughed merrily when she heard of it. She immediately stuck the top on, and it grew back perfectly, with only a pinched waistline, in the fashion of the day, to show for its mishap. And it lived for years and years, and, for all I know, it may be living yet.

Old ladies seemed to be much older in those days than they do now. Perhaps because they all wore black and brushed their hair down over their ears. Perhaps because so many of them were deaf or nearly blind. Perhaps because they lived so much in the past. Grandmother's greatest interest in life was talking, and she always talked of other days. When Uncle Charlie Wylly married Aunt Rebecca, he wrote me once, "Your Aunt Rebecca is reading, and I am writing, and your grandmother sits by the fire, ceaselessly speaking of the dead."

Poor Grandmother! As the years went on, she became almost stone deaf and could hardly see to read or sew, and the only pleasure she had was talking. I might at least have listened to her, and I did try at times. I think of her now as a lonely shade against the light of a window, her face brightening if she heard a footstep, then changing to despair when it died away.

Mother was a devoted daughter to her, but she died before Grandmother, who lived to a great age. At the time of which I write, Grandmother was in her fifties, which seemed to me then aged, and seems to me now the prime of life.

When in Brunswick, we used to drive out sometimes to Altama to visit Uncle Jimmie Couper's family. It was a very monotonous drive as I remember it, as the road ran perfectly straight for about nine miles through pine barren. Where the road was low, there were stretches of corduroy, and anything more sickening than driving over corduroy road, I cannot imagine. There was a tradition that the Altama road had been cut originally for a railroad. Possibly for that Southern Pacific, which the Honorable Thomas Butler King of St. Simon's, had suggested. A road which was to extend from Brunswick to San Diego, California. The first transcontinental line ever advocated.

The house at Altama is a square, substantial tabby building, and, painted yellow at that time, it was very attractive, surrounded by dark orange trees. It stood on the sight of an old Indian field, which sloped down in front to the lower level of the rice fields and river and, on the lawn surrounding it, were magnificent live oaks, swathed in gray moss.

Mr. Richard Corbin and his son, who now owned Hopeton and Altama, came from Paris occasionally to spend a winter here. Whether the old gentleman thought the gray moss would kill the splendid trees, or whether he found it melancholy, as many outlanders do, I do not know, but he spent his entire time trying to rake it down.

When Mr. Corbin and his son first came to the South after the war, they called at the Mackay house in Savannah, and one of my aunts congratulated the father on having a son to love him in his old age. Mr. Corbin shook his head, and there was sadness in his tone. "*Love descends*," he said. I think perhaps he was right.

I do not remember much that we did at Altama, but I always enjoyed it, and it seemed wonderful to have all the pecan nuts you wanted to eat. As the oranges were sour, they were used only for making marmalade, though Mary ate them as they were, with salt.

Mary's two brothers, Hamilton and Jimmie, were little boys at this time and could not have been much attached to the place, but to the end of her life Mary Harper loved Altama more than any spot on earth.

At this time Uncle Aleck Couper was living in the woods of Altama, but I do not remember seeing him at the house. He was Grandmother's second son, and had always been peculiar. After the war he tried planting but was unsuccessful, and he then determined to lead the life of a hermit. Selecting a small house with a clearing around it, in a remote part of the Altama woods, he took possession of it, was never molested by the owners, and spent the rest of his life alone. He had bee hives and sold honey enough to supply the few wants he had outside of his vegetable garden. He was a great hunter, so probably had all the game he needed, and his dog was his devoted companion. Once when he went after wild ducks in the swamp, he saw what he thought was a duck on the surface of the water, shot, and killed his dog!

Grandmother worried a great deal about the lonely life that Uncle Aleck led, and the privations he endured, and once she sent him some money by mail. He used to walk to the railroad station several miles away for his mail, and when he received her letter, he walked on to Brunswick, entered Grandmother's house, and, without a word, laid the money on a table at which she was sitting, and then walked back to Altama.

I do not think that Grandmother need have worried about Uncle Aleck, for I am sure that he was perfectly happy, leading the life that he preferred. He had his bees and garden to occupy him, and a little Negro boy to wait on him. He was fond of reading and subscribed to a number of papers and magazines, a French one among them. Uncle Aleck was rather a small man with a rather large head. His features were aquiline, and he wore a fierce mustache and imperial. At one time he became interested in phrenology, and, studying his own head carefully, he discovered that he was irresistible to women. He afterwards remarked that phrenology was a most accurate science!

At this time Uncle Jimmie had charge of Hopeton, Altama, and Butler's Island and planted rice on all three places. There was necessarily a great deal of ditching to be done, and bands of Irishmen used to come through the South at certain seasons for this purpose. They were admirable ditchdiggers, being far superior in this capacity to the Negroes. It is interesting to know that Sir Thomas Lipton was one of this set, though his digging was done in South Carolina and not in Georgia. Uncle Jimmie used the old abandoned house at Hopeton for his Irishmen to stay in, with the result that one winter it was burned to the ground.

Finding rice planting under such changed conditions unprofitable, the Corbins gave it up and sold Hopeton and Altama for ten thousand dollars to a set of Quakers from Ohio. The first thing that the Quakers did was to smash up the fine old English machinery in the sugar mill and sell it for junk. Unsuccessful themselves in whatever it was that they undertook to plant, and hating the climate, the Quakers abandoned Altama in disgust, and it was eventually bought by Mr. William DuPont, for a winter home, and is now one of the finest game preserves in the South.

When Uncle Jimmie gave up planting, he moved with his family into Brunswick to live and built a comfortable house on Union Street. Being a horticulturist like his father and grandfather, he beautified the lot surrounding it with shrubs and flowers.

Uncle Jimmie was a delightful man, having a keen sense of humor and being one of the best storytellers I have ever known. Aunt Dora was quite talented, a fine musician, and fond of poetry and recitations, and as both of them liked people, their house became a social centre for the little town.

As a girl, Mother had been intimate on St. Simon's Island with Sarah Butler, the daughter of Fannie Kemble, who afterwards married Dr. Wister of Philadelphia and became the mother of Owen Wister. On one occasion when I was a girl, she came down to Brunswick, probably to visit her sister Mrs. Leigh who had taken charge of Butler's Island.

Mrs. Wister must have been a woman of great intelligence and force, and was, I imagine, interested in all social betterment. Once when Mother and herself were walking along on of the sandy streets, under the great overhanging live oaks, they happened on a little darky boy who was driving a dilapidated cart and belaboring the donkey that drew it.

Mrs. Wister stopped at once. "Little boy," she said sternly, "You should not ill treat your donkey. You should pet him."

The little boy rolled his glistened white eyeballs.

"I pet um wif me wip," he said. And wham!, it came down on the donkey's hide.

Mrs. Wister evidently understood the darkies no more than her illustrious mother.

To Mrs. Wister and Mrs. Leigh the change on St. Simon's Island must have been appalling. As girls they had stayed with their father in the comfortable old tabby house on Hampton's Point, and the homes of their many hospitable friends on the island were attractive and pleasant. Many of these homes had been burned and many abandoned, while the friends they remembered had died or been scattered abroad. Those who had taken refuge in Brunswick now lived for the most part in small and insignificant houses, and, in their reduced circumstances, were unable to keep up any but the simplest form of sociability.

The society of Brunswick was decidedly limited at this time, and the only other young ladies in Aunt Rebecca's set were the Nightengale sisters, Miss Anna Drury, and the beauty Mrs. Westmorland.

The Nightengales, who were the grandchildren of General Nathanael Greene, had formerly lived at Dungeness on Cumberland Island. This handsome old house had been burned by the Yankees during the war, a former tutor having lead the soldiers to it, and the family had come to Brunswick to live.

Old Mrs. Nightengale, now a widow, had been Miss King of New York, the daughter of Mr. Rufus King, and the family, though very kind and friendly, was a rather exclusive one. The two sons and four daughters were all very tall, well made, and handsome.

There was a strong bond of friendship between the Nightengales and Coupers, as our Grandfather Couper had saved the lives of Mrs. Nightengale and her infant daughter Louisa when the steamer *Pulaski* was wrecked in 1838, off the coast of North Carolina.

Miss Louisa Nightengale was a godmother, and, while she was kindness itself to me, I never felt perfectly at ease with her, perhaps because she was so religious. She was an unusually large woman, and I think one reason she refused my Uncle Hamilton Couper was because she was taller than he was.

There was a tradition that the Couper men always fell in love with the Nightengale women. Uncle Robert Couper, Grandmother's youngest son, was in love with Miss Ellen, who was very lovely. He proposed to her by letter, and as she wrote an undecipherable hand, he never knew whether she had accepted or rejected him, and the affair went no further. Later on she married Mr. Fuller of Beaufort, South Carolina.

The beauty of the Nightengale family was Mrs. Troupe, who had the face of a Bellini Madonna. All of the Nightengales had perfect teeth and perfect complexions, the latter so unusual in the South. I think they took great care of their complexions, for even the little granddaughters had to wear veils when they went out in the scorching sun.

Of Aunt Rebecca's friends, Mrs. Westmorland had the most dramatic life. She had been Miss Fannie Slaughter, and when, at seventeen, she returned from boarding school in Athens, the whole town went down to greet her at the steamboat wharf. During her absence, a young Englishman named Westmorland had come to Brunswick to live, and, much amused over the excitement, he decided to go down and take a look himself. When Fannie Slaughter, dazzlingly beautiful and entrancing, walked down the gangplank, he instantly lost his heart.

Another man fell as desperately in love with her, and for a year the two were rivals. The morning that Fannie Slaughter married young Westmorland, he was shot and killed by his rival, and she was left a young and beautiful widow.

The last one of Aunt Rebecca's particular friends was Miss Anna Drury, the daughter of Le Baron Drury, the British consul. As I remember her, she held herself very stiffly erect, was quite fine looking, and always well dressed.

At this time ladies dressed most elaborately. In the first place they wore underclothes, and many of them, corsets, which were like plate armor. Their skirts touched the floor all around and ended in short trains, and overskirts were looped up on both sides and bunched out behind. The waist was a basque, pointed in front and at the back, and fitting like a glove. In the daytime the necks were high and the sleeves were long, but at night they wore square necks and elbow sleeves. And around necks and sleeves, and over and under skirts there were always ruffles. It was no wonder that Rosalie Quitman used to exclaim at night, as she started to undress, "Off with these trappings!"

I remember a beautiful old Empire gown of bronze satin, which Aunt Rebecca cut up to make herself a dress, and the train was so long that she had ample material even for one of those voluminous costumes.

The ladies of this day also dressed their hair elaborately and wore chignons, which were becoming. The hair was waved in front, and the chignon, a plastron of three lengthwise plaits, was pinned on at the back, with a curl or two falling behind the ear.

There were even fewer beaux than belles in Brunswick at this time, for mostly women and children were left in the South after the war. The only beau of Aunt Rebecca's that I remember was named Day, and for once she was caught napping, when someone asked her if she ever dreamed at night, and she replied, "No. My dreams are all Day dreams."

The excitement in the society set can be imagined then, when once while I was there, it was announced that a large party of society men were coming down by boat from Savannah to attend a ball that the Brunswick people were giving in a warehouse on the wharf. Mr. James Postell came over from St. Simon's and requested Aunt Rebecca to teach him the latest round dance steps, and I remember seeing him practicing in the dining room.

The night of the ball Mrs. Westmorland came around for Aunt Rebecca, and Mary Harper and I were allowed to see her. She came upstairs to our bedroom, and I was mortified to have her see me in night drawers. I never dreamed that as pajamas they were destined to become ultra fashionable. Mrs. Westmorland wore a gauzy white dress, low-necked and short-sleeved, with a touch of heavenly blue about it. She stood and smiled at us, and never have I forgotten that vision of loveliness. She was so dazzlingly beautiful that I could hardly look at her. It was like trying to look at the sun. Though her features were irregular, being on the order of Ellen Terry's, I have never seen a lovelier face, nor a more enchanting expression.

Aunt Rebecca said next day that she saw all the old Savannah beaux cutting their eyes at the widow Westmorland, and I have no doubt that she reigned the undisputed queen of the ball.

Later on Mrs. Westmorland married again—the handsome John DuBignon—and they went to live on Jekyl, where for years she was a virtual exile but perfectly happy, as she loved nature and poetry as well as her husband. That their only child, Josephine, should have been a beauty, goes without saying, but it was beauty of a different type, the beauty of pure perfection. When the DuBignons sold Jekyl Island to the one hundred wealthy Northerners who bought it for a winter club, they returned to Brunswick, and in later life I remember Mrs. DuBignon as a most interesting looking, though no longer beautiful woman. Alas, that spring should vanish with the roses!

I mentioned that Mr. James Postell came over to Brunswick from St. Simon's. That island is separated from the mainland by Fredericka River and a broad stretch of marsh. An occasional steamer leaving Brunswick made its way across the sound and landed at a pier on the southern end of the island near the lighthouse. The row through the marshes could only be made at high tide, and was so intricate, that only one knowing the channels should have attempted to thread them.

Mrs. Gould of St. Simon's and her youngest daughter once had a terrible experience here. They had been to Brunswick and were returning to the island with a young Englishman who had offered to row them over. When they failed to reach home that night, the Gould family supposed they remained in Brunswick. There was little communication at that time, and it was not until three days had passed that it was discovered they were not on the island, or in town. The winding channels of the marsh were searched, and they were found at last, all but dead of fright and exhaustion. The tide had receded and left their boat stranded on a mud bank. They were unable to make themselves seen or heard, and there they had stayed for three days and nights and, but for a timely rain, might have perished of thirst. There were those who said the Englishman could have made his way through the marsh grass at any time!

These were the days when the younger sons of English families were shunted off to the wilds and almost invariably came to grief in America, on sheep farms in Virginia, on plantations in the South, and on ranches in the far West. They were a helpless lot, and almost all of them lost their money, but one thing that they never lost was their gallantry.

As I remember St. Simon's at this time, it seemed a lonely and desolate place, cut off almost entirely from the world. Most of the plantations had been abandoned, most of the houses had been burned or were in ruins, and gardens and fields were reverted to jungle. Only one or two of the old families were left on the island, and these were in sadly reduced circumstances.

The James Postells had a large family of children and at this time were living in the great tabby house of Kelvyn Grove, on the edge of

Bloody Marsh, where the murder of Thomas Cater had taken place early in the century.

Mr. Postell had scientific tastes, was a conchologist, and had made a valuable collection of shells. He told me once of an experience Bishop Elliott and himself had when searching for shells. Coming to a little stream that ran into the sound, and seeing a shell that he wanted in the water, the Bishop knelt down, reached out his hand, and all but touched a huge rattlesnake, which was coiled on the other bank. Keeping his eye on the reptile, he drew his hand back quietly and rose. Mr. Postell started at once to kill the snake, when the bishop said, "The nobel fellow has spared my life. Let us spare his."

Mr. Postell himself had no fear of rattlesnakes and said they were never dangerous unless molested. Once he saw one lying across the road asleep and decided to try an experiment. He stepped over it, dragging his cane behind him. The snake did not stir. He stepped back, and again the cane touched the rattlesnake, and it shivered. A third time he stepped across, letting his cane drag as before, and the snake coiled instantly with a warning rattle, and Mr. Postell walked on.

A cousin of ours, who lived at this time on St. Simon's Island, had, I think, the saddest fate of any of our contemporaries. Margaret was a little older than Mary and myself, and when she was a young lady, she came over to Brunswick occasionally to stay a few days, and I think this was the only glimpse of the world she ever had. She was fine, intelligent and high spirited, and naturally longed for the pleasures that every girl should have. Her family, who at one time had been wealthy people, had been badly off ever since the war, and, living in such isolation, she had no advantages of any kind. Unfortunately she had an unhappy love affair with a handsome, fascinating, and quite worthless young man, who lived near Brunswick and who was eventually drowned on the beach at St. Simon's.

It was not long after this that Margaret, sitting at an open window in her home, was struck by lightning and found unconscious in a pool of water. The rain that poured in had saved her—alas!, for a sadder fate. In the lonely old house in the woods, within sound of the surf on the sands, she slowly went mad and died in her twentieth year.

How unfair life is! How unfair!

I feel the same when I think of Sidney Lanier. Being threatened with tuberculosis, he probably came to Brunswick on account of his health. And he must have come just after a serious spell of illness, for he writes of, "The wood smell that swiftly but now brought breath/From the heaven side bank of the river of death."

It was a tragedy, not only that Sidney Lanier should have had to work to the bitter end in his desperate condition to support his family, but that his work should have prevented what was to him the greatest joy on earth, communion with nature.

Only before daylight, could he go out in the woods, for he writes:

I have come o'er the dawn, O, beloved, my live-oaks, to hide
   In your gospelling glooms,—to be.
As a lover in heaven, the marsh my marsh and the sea my sea.
And then, when the rapturous hour had sped,

I must pass from thy face, I must pass from the face of the Sun:
Old Want is awake. . . .
The worker must pass to his work in the terrible town.

An old oak still stands outside of Brunswick on the edge of the marsh, which lies between the mainland and St. Simon's, and beneath it Sidney Lanier is said to have written his marvelous "Marshes of Glynn."

And in the home of Uncle James Couper, he read this poem aloud for the first time from the original manuscript.

No one has ever written, or can ever write more beautifully of the Georgia coast than Sidney Lanier, and in his Marsh Hymns he has immortalized it. What could be more perfect?

Of the dim sweet woods, of the dear dark woods,
   Of the heavenly woods and glades,
That run to the radiant marginal sand-beach within
The wide sea marshes of Glynn;—
            •
O braided dusks of the oak and woven shades of the vine,
While the riotous noon-day sun of the June-day long did shine,
Ye held me fast in your heart and I held you fast in mine;
            •
To the edge of the world I am drawn, I am drawn,
Where the gray beach glimmering runs, as a belt of the dawn . . .
With a step I stand on the firm packed sand,
            Free
By a world of marsh that borders a world of sea.
            •

How the still the plains of the water be!
The tide is in his ecstasy.
The tide is at his highest height:
            And it is night.

     •

And I would I could know what swimmeth below when the tide comes in
On the length and the breadth of the marvellous marshes of Glynn.

5

Etowah Cliffs

towah Cliffs is in Bartow County, north Georgia, on the Etowah River, seven miles from the town of Cartersville. In 1540 De Soto and his cavalcade of Spanish cavaliers may have passed through Etowah Cliffs on their hopeless quest for gold, for they stopped at an Indian village on the banks of a river and then followed that river up to the present sight of Rome. Near Cartersville there are five Indian mounds in a field, surrounded by a deep ditch, both ends of which touch the river. The top of the largest mound is half an acre in extent, and is reached by a broad inclined roadway.

"The governor was quartered in the house of the cacique," writes the Portuguese, "which stood on a mound, and was surrounded by a terrace wide enough for six men to go abreast."

It was in Georgia that De Soto found such quantities of pearls. Pearls which were procured by the Indians from the mussel shells in the rivers. As children we used to find these empty shells on a sandpit, where the river curved above our shoals. It may have been on our very place that Juan Terron, the foot soldier, tired of carrying his heavy wallet of pearls, "untied the bag, and whirling around, scattered the pearls in all directions among the thickets and herbage." How pleasant it would be to find some of these large lustrous pearls at this late day, perhaps a cache of them in the hallow of an old tree, where an enterprising squirrel has stored them for winter use, four centuries ago!

North Georgia was originally owned by the Cherokee Indians, and its fertile lands were coveted by white settlers from early times. It is a picturesque, mountainous country with a fine and bracing climate. The peaches for which it is famous, as well as the Cherokee rose, were said to have been introduced by the Spaniards. The Indians loved and valued their land, and were loath to give it up, but were finally forced to do so, and to go out to the Indian Territory to live.

Grandfather Stiles rode up on horseback from Savannah, with gold to pay them in his belt, and stopped at the cabin of a trader, which was built above cliffs that rose directly from the Etowah River. He was so pleased with the situation that he bought the cabin and surrounding land, and afterwards built his house on the same spot.

Etowah Cliffs contained about a thousand acres of land, two hundred and fifty being on the other side of the river, while its wooded lots were on the mountain nearby.

The first part of the house, which was built of wood, was finished in 1845. Under President Polk, Grandfather was sent as minister to Austria, and not until the return of the family in 1850, was the remaining part, of brick and stucco, added.

One wing of Sherman's army marched through the place during the war, but fortunately all of the furniture had been taken from the house and carried down to our plantation in Terrell County. The Yankees stabled their horses in the house, shattered some stained glass windows, and broke two marble mantlepieces. When the family returned, there was no flooring in the downstairs rooms, but at least the house had not been burned, and we had a roof over our heads.

The only trace of Sherman's army on the place to this day is the two long trenches dug down to the river, where his soldiers made their pontoon bridge to cross to Raccoon Creek on the other side. The tradition of the Yankees still lingered however, for at the foot of one of the cliffs on the riverbank there is a small opening into a black cave, and we children had an idea that a Yankee soldier was hidden there, and gave it a wide berth.

Grandfather Stiles died in Savannah in 1865. He had been colonel of the Sixtieth Georgia Regiment, which he organized, and both of his sons were captains in the army. After his death, Grandmother, her two sons, and their families came back to Etowah Cliffs. It was all that they had left, and they decided to make it their home.

The house was amply large. Standing high on the cliffs above the river, it faces west, with upstairs and downstairs piazzas, about a hundred feet long. Uncle Henry and Aunt Eliza took the northern end, the old part of the house, which was built of wood, and we, the southern, which was built of brick. And we shared the drawing room at the southern end of the piazza, between us. I think we had the best of the bargain, for our rooms were flooded with sunshine, and overlooked the garden. But Uncle Henry, I imagine, had chosen his side to keep an eye on the yard and barn beyond. From the piazza, through a vista out in the trees, we could see the Etowah, then a clear and sparkling stream, as far south as the shoals, where it came around the bend.

There were eight children in our family and nine in Aunt Eliza's, though one of ours and three of hers died in childhood. Each of us had a cousin about our age, and I do not think there could have been a happier set of children. We did not mind being poor. We had known nothing else, and I have lived to realize that we were *blessed*. None of us are dependent on money for happiness; poverty has no terror for us; and we can feel for the poor as no one can who has not known what it is to do without.

I am not one who thinks that childhood is the happiest time of life, perhaps because my idea of happiness is independence, but I do think we were as happy as children could be.

In our family there were three boys and five girls. After Mackay's death, I was the eldest, and then came Hamilton and John, and the four little girls, Bessie, Margie, Katie, and Belle.

My first recollection of my brother Hamilton is this. One Sunday morning he did not appear downstairs. What had become of him no one knew. The dining room door was accidently pulled forward, and he was found standing behind it, in an agony of self-consciousness. He was wearing his first pair of pants!, which were made of homespun and came to his knees. He could not have been much older when he fell into the sugar barrel in our storeroom, as I remember seeing the same little pair of pants waving in the air.

Everything was bought in barrels in those days, and every winter Mr. Willie Gordon, Aunt Eliza's brother, sent her up from Savannah barrels of rice, sugar, and flour as a Christmas present.

I could not have been much larger than Hammie myself, for I remember about this time going to the little community church which the neighbors had built on the road to Cartersville, and sitting on a high bench, unable to touch the floor with my feet. It was winter, and my legs became blue with cold. Aunt Kate discovered this, and put her huge ermine muff upright on the floor, and made me put my legs in it up to my knees, which warmed me deliciously.

I do not remember suffering much from cold up the country however, though the rooms were large and high ceiled, and warmed only by wood fires, but poor little Johnnie once had an awful experience. He had been taken into Cartersville and left by accident to come home in the wagon. It was bitterly cold, and the slow drive of seven miles must have taken at least an hour and a half. When the wagon reached The Cliffs at last, the poor little boy, perched up on the high seat, with his bare legs exposed, was almost frozen, and Mother, I am sure, suffered as much as he did.

When Hammie and Johnnie were little, they slept on a trundle bed in Mother's room. Hammie had been a delicate baby, and, as a little boy, he used to have nightmare spells when he felt that Mother was leaving him, and he would cry out in terror. He told me once that, because of these spells, he was haunted by the fear that he might be a coward. If he had such a tendency, he overcame it, for I have never known a braver man. Hammie had a strong will, and a high temper, and punishment had a bad—instead of good—effect on him. I remember one of the only times when he was whipped, he hardly spoke to anyone for three days. He was the only one who had blue eyes in our family, and he hated it, and nothing made him madder than being called "Blue-eyed Beauty."

Johnnie had a very sweet disposition, being amiable and fun-loving, and the wit of our family. With him it was peace at any price, for, like myself, he hated quarrelling. Mother did not have to tell us on her deathbed never to quarrel with one another. We would never have done it anyhow.

Bessie, in spite of being so good, had the keenest sense of humor and was vividly interested in life, and Margie was from the first the most entertaining member of the family. From the time she could talk, she was a little mimic and would imitate the drawl of the Crackers on the place, to the great amusement of our elders. Hamilton and herself were the two most interesting people I have ever known.

Katie was our only delicate child. Perhaps that is why I have always had an especially tender love for her. I am sure she never felt perfectly well when she was little. A contrast to the rest of us, to me especially, who has always enjoyed positively "rude health." Katie's talent was for housekeeping, and if Mother had only let her help in the housework, she would have been perfectly happy. Bright little Belle had many interests and was busy from morning till night, cutting out, sewing, painting, and always singing at her work.

It was Katie who originated the name of "Tannie," which Belle and herself, and my little nieces and nephews have always called me, and it is a name that I love. My brothers and sisters looked up to me and admired me, and how intensely selfish, and utterly unworthy of it all I was!

We were almost all brunettes in our family, like our father, and most of our Stiles cousins were blondes like theirs.

The four oldest of these were Henry, Gulie, Gordon, and Mary. Alfred, the next, died as a tiny baby, and the four youngest were Ellen Beirne, Ethel, Robbie, and George. Henry was older than any of us, George was the younger.

Henry did not have much to do with the younger children, except to lord it over us and invent games to tease us. We played church in the cottage out in the grove, and Henry was always the minister. Standing in front of us, he would say, "Bretherin and Sisterin, this is my text. The Lord made a blue tree and a green tree. One of them goes to heaven. One to hell. Which one will you climb?" I sometimes hit it right, but no matter whether Gulie said "blue" or "green," Henry always answered, "Then you go to hell!" Finally he would get tired of playing, and would say, "The minister will now go into the vestry room to change his robes. The congregation will sing 'I Want to Be an Angel,' until he comes back." And then he would run away and leave us.

"I Want to Be an Angel," and "There is a Happy Land, Far, Far, Away," were the first two hymns we ever learned to sing as children. Aunt Eliza used to sing her children to sleep, and I believe it would break my heart to hear "Saviour When in Dust, to Thee," as she sang it at twilight to those little children so soon to leave this world.

Gulie was a strong and spirited character from the first. She was named after her aunt, Mrs. George Harrison of Brandon-on-the-James, who had been given her father's name, William, in its Italian form, Gulielma. Gulie was tall—she grew to be six feet—and had one real beauty in the wonderful Stiles hair, pure gold, and curling like grape tendrils.

A year's difference in age makes a world of difference to children. They prefer to play with those of their own age, and, as a rule, look down on anyone younger than themselves. Gulie was two years older than myself, so it was very good of her to allow me to play with her, which she did.

Gordon and I were the same age, and both of us had been born at Etowah Cliffs: I in the beautiful southeast bedroom, over Grandmama's. Whatever Gordon did he did thoroughly, for though slow, he was painstaking and determined. We used to play stick horses in the grove when we were very little, and none of us had a stable that could be compared to Gordon's. His horses were fine, strong peach switches, all of the same length, with their tops neatly rounded. His stable was in the corner of a worn fence, and each horse was tied by a string halter in its stall, and I remember how fussed he was if any of us ever disturbed them. It was a natural development that Gordon should, in the end, be the owner of a large cattle ranch in the Panhandle of Texas.

Mary was Hammie's age, but they never cared for one another, while Gordon and I were very friendly. Being all of two years younger than myself, Mary was barely tolerated, though sometimes allowed to play with Gulie and myself.

Ellen Beirne, who was Margie's age, was a little saint. Ethel who was Katie's, was lovely, even as a child. Robbie, Belle's contemporary, was a dear little boy, and George, who came last of all, was a fine, sturdy, handsome child, and the pet of both families.

Aunt Eliza, who had been Eliza Clifford Gordon of Savannah, had a very strong and decided character, and Mother herself had very different ideas about bringing up children. Aunt Eliza believed in strict discipline and was an advocate of spanking. Mother was not.

On one occasion several of us went down to the riverbank. Who suggested it I have no idea, but we all pulled up our clothes and waded into the river, holding on to an overhanging branch. Our wrong doing was revealed, and Aunt Eliza, in great excitement, insisted that we should all be spanked. I have never forgotten that mortifying ordeal. Mother took Hammie, Johnnie, and myself into the drawing room and shut the door. Then she laid me across her knee and struck me with a cotton switch, which broke in her hand. I made the mistake of laughing, and she went out and brought back a peach switch, with a vicious sting to it. That made me cry, and Hammie and Johnnie laughed. Then Hammie's turn came. I doubt if he cried, but Johnnie and I laughed. Then poor little Johnnie was switched and he wept. None of us knew at the time what we were punished for, and I know Mother was sick over the whole horrible affair. She never spanked one of us again, and at least none of us have turned out to be criminals.

When we were little we all went barefooted in the country in summer, and I have no doubt that accounts partly for the splendid health that most of us have had. I remember how strange it felt when you pulled off your shoes and stockings for the first time and your bare feet touched the earth with a delicious intimate contact that made you feel a part of it.

In the middle of our park there was a low place that after a rain would be filled with red muddy water. Mary and I walked down there once and found Hammie and Johnnie, with their shoes off, wading about. They offered to carry us on their backs out to the stumps in the middle of the pond. We accepted the offer and sat for some time on the stumps, enjoying the novel situation. When it was time to go home, Johnnie started back for land, carrying Mary, and halfway across his legs gave way. "I can't carry you any farther," he announced. "You've got to!" shrieked Mary. Without further discussion, Johnnie dropped her knees, but she hung to his throat desperately, and, with her shoes dragging in the water, he finally staggered to land. I laughed so that I nearly fell of the stump I was sitting on, and I laugh to this day when I think of it.

Every Sunday at 12 o'clock, we had church in the drawing room with Mother, Aunt Eliza, and Uncle Henry reading different parts of the service. All the white tenants on the place used to come, and after church thick "sugar biscuits" were handed around the piazza. There were two long green benches out there, and on Sunday nights the two families assembled and sang hymns without an accompaniment. Everybody chose one, beginning with the youngest child, and we always knew what everyone would choose. Johnnie always chose "From Greenland's Icy Mountains."

At Sunday dinner the children of our family were allowed to eat pickles, and we took turns choosing the dessert. Sillabub was the favorite, made of sponge cake, blackberry jam, and whipped cream. Chocolate blancmange came next, and we all felt a little desperate when Johnnie's turn came, knowing that he would choose boiled custard.

Our birthdays were great events. Everything was mysterious for a day or two before, and on the momentous morning we entered the dining room, frightfully self-conscious, with the eyes of every child fastened on us eagerly, for each one had given a present, however small, and these were piled up on our plates. My birthday came on the seventh of May, a lovely and propitious month, while Johnnie was the unlucky one, as his came the week after Christmas. One present that Margie invariably received on September the second was a pile of the first delicious brown scuppernongs, on a green pottery vine-leaf plate.

We thought our Christmas wonderful. We never believed in Santa Claus, which I think was a pity, but Mother never told us anything but the truth. We hung up our stockings at the foot of our parent's bed, and at the first screech of dawn, tiptoed into the room in our night clothes and bare feet, and secured them. I do not think that we ever got over two or three presents a piece, and these were of the simplest and most inexpensive kind. When I see children of the present day receiving as many as fifty handsome presents, I, being my Aunt's niece, think it *wicked*.

We only had one Christmas tree, that I remember. A very large one in the "harness room" at the north end of the long piazza. All of the tenants came, and we marched the length of the piazza and entered the room, where we were fairly dazzled by the splendor of the lighted tree hung with gifts. I caught sight of a painted candy peach, and I hoped and hoped it would be presented to me. It was not, being probably presented to a little Cracker.

I do not remember in what year it was that we saw such wonderful displays of the Aurora Borealis, whether immediately after the war or later. They would illumine the whole northeastern sky after dark, with fanning lights of rose and gold, and we used to look at them from the window of our dining room, which had been Grandmama's bedroom. Johnnie was terrified of them, and though he was once offered ten cents to go to the window and look, he would not do it. Nor would he ever sleep with his face in the moonlight, for fear of being moonstruck. I suppose some servant had filled him with fear.

I was more fortunate, for when I was very little my nurse took me to the window during a storm to look at "the pretty lightning," and I have loved storms ever since. When we saw the rain coming across the river, we would run out into the fields, then turning back, would lift our skirts like sails and be blown before the coming storm, wild with joy and excitement, and to this day the reverberation of thunder fills me with exultation.

I mentioned that the drawing room at Etowah Cliffs was used in common by the two families. It was at the south end of the piazza, and was a most attractive room, large and square, with two French windows opening on the piazza, and a wide bay overlooking the grass. The furniture, which had been brought from Vienna, was of Circassian walnut upholstered in blue and yellow brocade, the curtains lambrequins to match. There were some real treasures in this room. Goethe's autograph, beautifully illuminated and framed, which had been given to Grandmama by his daughter-in-law, Ottilie von Goethe, and a bowl, cup, and saucer of Washington's Cincinnati china, which had been a gift from General and Mrs. Lee.

On the wall hung four exquisite watercolors. Portraits of Grandmama Stiles and her three children, Aunt Mary Low, Uncle Henry, and my father, which had been painted from life in Vienna. Aunt Mary is perfectly beautiful. A fine, tall, upstanding girl, with wonderful amber-colored eyes, a piquant nose, and a most entrancing mouth. Her hair is amber-colored too, and waves down on either side of her face, ending in graceful curls which fall to her shoulders. She wears an evening gown of sky-blue silk, trimmed with fringe, which is out very low off the shoulders. It seems strange that beauty was a genuine outdoor girl, who was said to ride and shoot even better than her brothers! The pictures of Father and Uncle Henry show them as handsome schoolboys, wearing white trousers and short dark blue jackets.

On the tables and étagières in the drawing room were many interesting ornaments which our grandparents had brought from Europe. I remember a marble Hadrian's column, a Venetian gondola inkstand, and a bronze Pompeiian lamp. There were also several boxes with trays filled with delicate little cameo reproductions of the famous statues of antiquity.

The object that interested me most was a little china statuette, one side of which represents an Austrian officer, the other a Hungarian. I had an idea that the blonde Austrian, with the fair hair, mustache, and imperial, wearing the white uniform, was Uncle Henry, while the dark Hungarian, with the black hair and mustache, in the Zouave costume, was my father.

Uncle Henry was as handsome as Father, and an inch taller, being six feet three. Both had fine figures, with broad shoulders and flat backs, and I remember how good looking they were in their well-fitting suits of dark blue broad cloth.

They were as different in character as they were in looks. Father was gay and good natured, and I remember how he whistled and sang about the house. Uncle Henry was a sterner and more masterful man. He was very powerful, and, placing a heavy stick on the rims of two goblets filled with water, he could break it with one blow of a sword, without spilling a drop. Henry told me that he had seen his father and mine each lift a rock weighing eight hundred pounds a few inches from the ground. And a Mulatto barber of Savannah declared that Captain Henry Stiles had almost frightened the life out of him, when, once, on a wager, he had held him by the coat collar with one hand, out of his second-story window.

Both Father and Uncle Henry were devoted to horses, and both were fine riders and drivers, though, trusting to their strength, they were both utterly reckless. As far as I know neither of them was afraid of anything on earth, and this undoubtedly caused their tragic deaths.

Courage is, I think, the finest attribute of the Stiles family, and, selecting what I would rather have inherited from each line of my immediate ancestors, I wrote,

From the Coupers—the intellect
Stiles—the grit
Mackay—the morale
Wyllys—the wit.

Father and Uncle Henry never talked of the War. That was over and done with. Nor did I ever hear either of them, or any other Southern gentleman, abuse the Yankees. The nearest to it was when I heard a nitwit ask Uncle Charlie what he thought of Sherman. "What do I think of Sherman?" he growled, "I think of him what he thought of war!" Like all brave soldiers, the Southerners respected their enemies. They had fought through four bitter years, but it never occurred to them to complain of "shattered ideals." They had to work too hard to repair their shattered fortunes.

Father and Uncle Henry made no legal division of the farm, Father planting the south end of it, and Uncle Henry the north, in addition to the acreage across the river. At that time wheat and other cereals were planted in the upcountry, as well as corn and cotton. Our cotton was ginned in an old-fashioned gin on the lane, where horses were harnessed to long beams attached to the press in the center. Occasionally we children were allowed to sit on the beams and ride around the circle in the shade of the wide-spreading roof.

Part of the place was rented to tenants and part they planted themselves, and every day Father and Uncle Henry rode over it. When they came in, they always had a toddy at the sideboard. Like all the men of that day, they drank freely, but I never saw either of them intoxicated. I remember that Father used to make a drink called cherry bounce, whatever that may be. It sounds quite refreshing in these arid days. Needless to say no young person ever touched a thing to drink at that time, nor did the ladies, unless it was wine at a party.

During the war, the name of our county had been changed from Cass to Bartow, Cass having been a Northern man. As the spirits of the county people revived, it was decided to have an annual fair in Cartersville, and to make it more attractive, tournaments were held, where the men could tilt for prizes. My cousin Ida, Mrs. Page Couper, tells me that as a young girl she attended one of these tournaments, and that when Uncle Henry in blue and silver and Father in scarlet and gold road on to the lists, she felt that the knights of old had come to life again. In spite of their superb horsemanship neither of them ever won a prize, as both were rather nearsighted. At one of these fairs, Henry, following in the footsteps of his father, drove his goat cart around the entire track, in spite of the maddening obstinacy of his team.

Grandfather Stiles had imported some cashmere goats from Europe, and Henry and Gordon trained several pairs of their descendents which were always named Tom and Jerry. They had a little three-seated wagon painted green, in which they used to drive us about, and I remember once falling off the front seat, and feeling the back wheel rolling over my jaw. I opened my mouth to scream when Henry said, "We know Caroline isn't going to cry. She's a brave girl." And I shut it.

The cashmere goats lived and multiplied and became a perfect plague, finally stripping the bark from the fruit trees. This was too much, and they were exiled to an island on the river, and what became of them I never knew.

It was on the path leading from the orchard where the goat wagon had run over my face that I once had a terrible experience.

I was tripping back from the orchard and still at some distance from the house, when, crossing a side path, I hear a piteous crying. I looked down the path, and to my terror, saw a snake coiled at its edge, its neck and head lifted, and in its wide open jaws a little frog, from whose body blood was dripping.

The frog was crying for help, and with one tiny hind leg trying feebly to push away from the hideous jaw. It was not a long snake or large one. One good whack on its neck would have released its victim. *And I ran away!*

I do not blame myself for running. Snakes have always filled me with loathing, and I was terrified. But—I never told a soul! I ran and ran and tried to forget what I had seen. And my punishment has been that I have never forgotten it. That I can wake up at night now, after all these years, and hear the pitiful crying of that little frog, and still see the bright red drops of blood dripping from its body. I only tell it now in the hopes that by this confession I may expiate my sin and be allowed to forget.

Our family had a two-wheeled cart and a donkey, named Caroline, the most obstinate creature that ever lived. I was riding it bareback once, when, in spite of all I could do, it bolted through an osage orange hedge and scraped me off under a low-limbed cedar. My first attempt at writing for a magazine was on the subject of this donkey. It was called "Caroline's Letter" and was published in *St. Nicholas*, with a picture of the donkey and cart by Uncle Robert. I am sure that it was accepted because of the perfectly drawn illustration.

My fall from the donkey was nothing unusual, for we were continually having falls, and they never seemed to hurt us. I was out driving once, seated on the backseat with the nurse and baby, Father and Mother being in front. We were going up the steep hill in the lane near the gin, when the backseat turned over, and the nurse, the baby, and I were left at the bottom of the hill. As I lay on the ground, I looked up and saw Mother turn around when they reached the top. Otherwise I suppose they would have driven home without us.

Aunt Kate and Aunt Sarah spent every summer at Etowah Cliffs, Aunt Kate's bedroom being the pleasant one over the drawing room, which opened on the upstairs piazza. I slept on a hard couch beside her bed, and I always went to bed alone. Sometimes when I knelt beside the couch to say my prayers, I would be petrified with fear. What if a lion should spring on me from the dark piazza at my back? I think my fear of lions must have come from a little book Aunt Sarah had called, *The Lion in the Path*. In it there was a picture of a lion springing on a bad little boy. The fact that the story was an allegory did not mend matters, and I have disliked allegories ever since. Aunt Sarah's favorite book next to the Bible was *Pilgrim's Progress*. Perhaps if I had read it as a child it might have thrilled me, but I did not happen to read it until I was middle aged, when it bored me almost to tears.

I remember having an attack of fever on my little couch beside Aunt Kate's bed, and experiencing the utmost terror as I felt myself receding farther and farther away from her, my brain swinging in great circles. I had seen a hideous caricature of a man in a paper, and I saw the dreadful creature grinning as he came after me, swinging in the same slow circles, and getting nearer and nearer. I could have screamed with terror but for the fact that it was Aunt Kate who lay in the high white bed, and I knew I must control myself.

Aunt Sarah's bedroom was back of Aunt Kate's. She had taken for herself of course the most disagreeable of our bedrooms, a small dark one, which opening with glass doors on the front and back piazzas, was a mere passageway to the other side of the house. Here Bessie stayed with her and neither of them seemed to mind it.

Mother's room was the nicest of all. Very large with an eastern window and a bay to the south, and overlooking the garden and grass. I like to think I came into the world in such a beautiful bright room as that.

Grannie Gordon came up from Savannah every summer also, and had the immense room upstairs in the center of the house, which had been built for Grandfather's library. She was small but so fat that she moved with the greatest difficulty, and I remember seeing her always seated at one of the front windows which opened on the piazza. Because of her looks and her wealth I always thought of her as a sort of Queen Victoria. In reality she was a timid, gentle old lady, very kind to all of us, and greatly beloved by her grandchildren.

Etowah Cliffs was seven miles from Cartersville. Uncle Robert Couper once asked, "How many young ladies would it take to reach from here to Cartersville?" "Seven. For a miss is as good as a mile." They were the longest seven miles in the world I know, for the roads were something terrible. We would drive around our garden hedge, through the grove and park, and out of the pink gate into the public road, which ran through our place. Then we skirted our mountain and the Sproull's, drove along the river, and, about halfway to town reached the Red Hill, a long steep climb, which we always struck in the hottest part of the day. At the top of the hill was Ladd's Lime Kiln, where they were cutting into the side of the Three Sisters' Mountain. Beyond this a narrow road skirted a precipice, which Uncle Henry always took at a tearing pace, perhaps because it was so narrow that two vehicles could not pass on it, and then we plunged into Pettis Creek, which seemed to be forever rising and coming perilously near the bed of the buggy. After this you could breathe again, for the rest of the road, though full of deep ruts and large stones, was not dangerous. It took us always over an hour to make the seven miles.

What we saw of Cartersville was not attractive. Four blocks of Main Street, unpaved and unshaded, and lined with commonplace stores, some of them with false fronts above to make them more imposing. The railroad ran straight through the town, and in its centre was the depot. The great excitement of the day in Cartersville was the coming of the passenger train in the afternoon, when most of the inhabitants gathered at the depot to see it arrive.

Every fall Robinson's Circus came to Cartersville, and going to see it was the greatest event of our lives. The whole countryside was excited. The Negroes could not go inside the circus because it was a sin, but they could go to town to see the parade, and many of them walked miles to do it.

It was expensive taking such a host as the children of the two Stiles families, and of course we never went into a sideshow, sat on reserved seats, or stayed to the concert. We could not even buy pink lemonade— Dr. Tanner's favorite beverage—or stale peanuts. But the performance itself was enough, for what we saw was glamorously beautiful, especially the circus girls in their tarlaton skirts and pink tights, standing on the broad backs of the satiny white horses, and jumping through the paper hoops held up by the painted clowns. I longed to be a circus girl for years, and, by a coincidence, my husband, then a little boy in New Orleans, longed to marry one!

Every January, Aunt Kate and Aunt Sarah took us down to Savannah, on the Central of Georgia Railroad Script. In this way the road paid its dividends, and the cars were always crowded with upcountry people going to the coast for a two-week jaunt. As we always went in a day coach, we carried our pillows, but I never remember the luxury of having a seat to myself, and being able to stretch out at full length to sleep. We also carried our own provisions in a large market basket, with a calico cover drawn over it. Hammie confessed when he grew older that he hated traveling with this mob, and always felt mortified. But, apart from feeling rather sick all the way owing to the sulphur smell, smoke, and cinders, I did not mind it, and I was always thrilled the next morning when I looked out of the window at dawn and saw the flat stretch of white sand and the great black oaks hung with long black streamers.

It was always bitterly cold when we started for Savannah, and we always left at night. During all of my youth, trains seemed invariably to leave everywhere between two and three in the morning.

I remember Uncle Henry driving us into Cartersville once at night in a heavy snowstorm. We were all perched high up on a sort of three-seated, uncovered carryall, and had finally reached the outskirts of town. The snow was blinding, and in addition Uncle Henry was shortsighted, and suddenly we ran up on an embankment, and the whole blamed thing turned over. I remember sailing out in an arc, and landing as softly on the snow as on a featherbed. And at this juncture we heard the train blow up the track for Cartersville!

There was nothing to do but drive back to Etowah Cliffs, and the next night try it again!

6.
Summerland

bout a half mile north of Etowah Cliffs, the Ralph Elliotts of Savannah had built, in the fifties, a summer home, which they called Summerland. The large brick house, with bright and airy rooms, and double southern piazzas, was, in their day, a comfortable and delightful home.

A shaded walk, along the river, which we called the River Path, connected one house with the other, and on this the older people used to walk back and forth every afternoon. An avenue of elms led from the river to the flower garden at Summerland, and you walked through the garden to the house. All that I remember of the garden was a smoke tree in its centre, which seemed to me strange and fascinating.

Aunt Elliott, who had been Margaret Mackay and older sister of grandmama, Aunt Kate, and Aunt Sarah, was a pretty old lady, very small and dainty, with a pink skin, clear blue eyes, and snow white hair. Of course she always dressed in black, and wore a cap. General Lee used to call her "The Little Madam." Like all the Mackays she had a decided character, and her word was law, even in her family of grownup sons and daughters. Every year she came up from Savannah with her daughters and their children to spend the summer at Summerland.

Two of her daughters were war widows, Cousin Leila Habersham and Cousin Mary Elliott. Cousin Leila had been left with two sons and a daughter, and nothing to live on. Being a strong and capable woman, she did everything that she could to support them, but in those days, with the exception of teaching, there was no work outside of the house for a lady. She made delicious preserves for sale, and I remember her carved oranges, which were preserved whole, and looked like spheres of carved amber. At a later date she could have been a successful cateress, for she was a wonderful housekeeper, and many of her dishes were famous in Savannah, notably her white terrapin stew, made with quantities of cream and eggs and wine. She kept house for her mother and kept things stirring, as she was full of life and keenly interested in everybody, and in everything that was going on. Cousin Leila loved young people, understood them, and sympathized with them, and her nieces and nephews, who called her "Munna," were devoted to her.

Fred and Charlie, her sons, used to fight fiercely at times, and as they tussled on the floor, Cousin Leila would light into them indiscriminately, until she separated them.

Charlie must have borne a charmed life to have lived as long as he did, for he was always having narrow escapes. He climbed to a high hickory nut tree once in front of the Summerland steps, and was doing some monkey tricks to show off in the top limbs, when he fell to the ground, and split his nose right in two on the dividing line. Once a crowd of boys from the two houses found a huge snake on the River Path. Armed with rocks they surrounded it, and Charlie directed that, at his count of three, every boy was to throw and stone the snake. Arthur Elliott, a much smaller boy, who was afraid to get up in the circle, stood back behind Charlie, unnoticed by the others. At the count of three, not to be left out of the sport, Arthur cut loose, hitting Charlie in the back of the head, knocking him down. A big gash was cut, and he bled like a beef, and for a month after had a lump on his head as big as a hen egg. Once when Fred was chopping wood with a hatchet, Charlie laid his thumb on the log. "Chop that off, if you dare," he said. And Fred chopped it off.

I do not suppose that Fred and Charlie Habersham fought more than any other boys. Fighting seems to be one of a boy's most powerful instincts. When Hammie and Johnnie met anywhere in our house, there was always a clinch and a thud as they fell to the floor, though I do not remember that they ever quarrelled. Once at Sewanee, seated at a window, I watched the grammar school boys pour out of their barracks into the street. Their first impulse seemed to be to haul off and hit each other as hard as they could drive. I suppose it is one way in which boys get their necessary exercise.

The idol of Cousin Leila's heart was Meta, her youngest child. She was Gulie's age and was a handsome girl with a fine figure and wonderful hair. This reached below her waist, and was nut brown, glossy and as soft as silk. Every night of the world, Fanny Lloyd, her little colored maid, brushed it with a hundred strokes, and woe to Fanny, if she ever cracked a hair.

Meta was brought up by her mother to think only of clothes and society. They were as one in their interests, and every thought was for Meta's personal adornment and social advantage. Their goal was her "coming out" in Savannah, and being a belle.

Cousin Leila made all of Meta's clothes, and they were all made in the latest style. I remember one night in Savannah when Meta was brought around to the Mackay house by her mother and Uncle George Elliott. She was going to a soiree given by her dancing master, and they came to show us her costume, which was made with bouffant panniers, which had just "come in." As they went out to get in the hack that was waiting for them, Cousin Leila, afraid that Meta's dress might be crushed, gave a little scream, and Cousin George shouted gleefully, for our benefit, "For goodness sake, don't hurt them panniers."

I would have adored going to dancing school, but I only went once or twice to look on. Gulie and Meta both took lessons, but only in round dancing. The pupils who did the "fancy dances" were the stats, and we all worshipped them. These ballerinas were Marie Cobart, Sissy Taylor, and Phelie Henderson. They danced "The Highland Fling," "The Cracovienne," "The Cachucha," and other ravishing solos, while we looked on in hopeless envy. I would have given anything on earth to have been Phelie Henderson, even if her father did keep the barroom underneath the theatre.

We had Meta once in one of our plays, giving her the part of a fairy. She had a single quatrain to learn beginning with the word "Hither I come from the Silver Moon." Cousin Leila made her costume which was lovely, being layer on layer of crisp white tarlaton, but it took her four weeks to learn the four lines, and we were afraid she never would.

Meta was not a highbrow, but she had what was far more important, good judgement and tact. And when she entered society her *savoir faire* was perfect, and beside her, we country cousins were simply gawks.

Cousin Caroline Elliott had married her cousin, Robert Barnwell Elliott, son of the beloved Bishop of Georgia. He himself was a minister, and later on became the Bishop of Western Texas. Cousin Carrie had been the beauty of the Elliott family, and I was told by Dr. Orme of Atlanta, that he considered her more beautiful than our Aunt Mary Low.

Cousin Mary, the youngest, was a very pretty and attractive widow at this time. She also had married an Elliott cousin and was left with a very dear little boy, Arthur Beverly, the little one who had felled Charlie Habersham.

The Three Sisters' Mountain, on the way to Cartersville, was called after the three Elliott sisters.

Aunt Elliott's oldest son, William, was a doctor. He had married Father's double first cousin, Sidney Stiles, and they lived next door to us in Savannah. Cousin William was one of the best and kindest men I have known. He was literally "The beloved physician" with his patients, and Cousin Sidney and himself were always as good as possible to us. Of their five children Harry was the oldest, and the oldest daughter, Clelia, absolutely straightforward and loyal, was and is my sister Margie's dearest friend.

I never remember seeing any of Aunt Elliott's sons at Summerland. They were all at work in Savannah, and the household consisted entirely of women and children, and was for that reason was a very happy one.

Samuel Butler says, "The reason that all ministers' families are unhappy, is because the father stays at home all day." I could not imagine anything more hateful myself. In fact, I think the ideal thing for a father to do is to die after the birth of the last child, leaving the family in comfortable circumstances. Then the mother could bring the children up, and they would all be happy ever after. The very finest men I have ever known were brought up by their mothers. And how about George Washington and General Lee?

I must however acknowledge the improvement in fathers in recent years, but in my day there was many an unbearable old tyrant among the fathers of my relatives and friends.

At Summerland at the front there was a pretty grove, through which the carriage road wound to the highway, or public road, as we called it. In a secluded spot Fred and Charlie Habersham had built a perfect little wigwam of saplings. They were very clever at this sort of thing, and constructed the neatest little bridges across the gullies on the River Path, as well as their boat and bathhouse. They were both good swimmers, and when they went to Sewanee, Charlie was the finest swimmer at the university.

All Southern boys of that day went to Sewanee, and, as it was a church school, many scholarships were given. It was also inexpensive compared to other universities, and had for its professor the very finest class of men. Fred and Charlie were sent to Sewanee by their generous aunt, Mrs. Coleman, and Henry by his Grandmother. The three went up to the university together and so passed out of our childhood.

Summerland was always filled with company, and I remember perfectly the visit of Miss Hessie and Miss Sada Elliott, the old Bishop's daughters, when they were of their way to Sewanee to make it their home after the war. Miss Hessie was graceful and refined looking, and Miss Sada was very pretty, very coquettish, and very attractive.

I remember one afternoon that Gulie and I were walking alongside of the grown people who were on their way to Summerland. Miss Hessie and Miss Sada had called, and, as they invariably did, some of the family, including Uncle and Father, were walking back with them. We had reached the Red Hill going down to the ferry, beyond which was the River Path.

The group of people were talking and laughing, and I happened to turn and see Miss Sada's face, and I thought how pretty she was. For once I was quick witted. "I claim Miss Sada for Papa," I said.

There was no one left but Miss Hessie, but Gulie, being game, appropriated her for Uncle Henry. I felt the deepest satisfaction. For once I had triumphed over an older girl.

I suppose it was several years after this that Miss Sada's literary career began. Her first book, *The Felmeres,*—every word of which I read—was a serious, and, as I remember it, rather a dreary one, written in the style of George Elliott [sic]. Its subject was atheism, the burning question of the day. Miss Sada's technique was admirable, and her stories and books always began in a promising way, but, as I recall them, the interest was never sustained.

There was another Southern authoress at this time, a Mrs. Westmorland of Atlanta, who wrote a thriller called *Heart Hungry*. I could never get through that, and all that I remember of it is that she used five and ten exclamation points where other writers used only one.

I happened to hear of something that Mrs. Westmorland said once. She was a very handsome woman and evidently a very advanced one, for she remarked on one occasion, "All that I want in the world is Robert Stiles." I did not know whether to consider it a compliment or not.

Another attractive visitor to Summerland was Mrs. Blackford, who had been the charming Mrs. Potter of Savannah. She came to Summerland on her second honeymoon, and brought her little son, James Potter along. He was my first sweetheart, and I have never forgotten him. "I have something to ask you," he said to me once. We were seated, Gulie, Jimmie, and I, in an abandoned pigpen. "My father told me to say it. Darling will you give me your heart?" Gulie laughed immoderately, and, horribly embarrassed, I said "No," when I would liked to have said "Yes." Jimmie was visibly downcast, and it consoled me to know that when he left Summerland for the North, he cried on the train, and said, "I will never have another sweetheart like her." I have never seen James Potter since.

The river which flowed past Etowah Cliffs and Summerland meant much in the live of both families, for all summer long we used it for boating and bathing. When I was a child it looked to me as wide as the Mississippi, and now, every time I see it again, it has become smaller, and I think of it as a little yellow stream, shimmering below the high gray cliffs, its voice the ceaseless murmur of the Shoals.

When Father and Uncle Henry came back to live at Etowah after the war, they floated two of Sherman's abandoned pontoons down the river and anchored them opposite our spring. On these they built a platform and a bathhouse, and we would row across to this to go in swimming. One of my earliest recollections of Father is when he took me in his arms and dove into the river from the platform; I can still recall the frightful strangulation I experienced before we came up again. This bathhouse was probably carried away in one of our winter freshets, for it disappeared, and the next one was built farther up on the riverbank below the Shoals.

I had a terror of the water before I learned to swim, and especially dreaded crossing the river on the flat in the double buggy with Uncle Henry driving. On our side of the ferry there was a gradual slope to the water's edge, but even here there was a muddy space, in which the horses always bogged, their hoofs pawing, slipping, and resounding as they finally struck the flat. Then the buggy would be jerked upon this, and we would rush clattering along the loose planks. How terrifying that dark water was to me, as I looked down from my high seat. There a narrow cut ascended a steep bank, with deep ditches on either hand. It was always wet and slippery, and as the flat struck the land, the horses were furiously slashed, and rushed, panting, up to the top.

There never was a tragedy connected with the river for us, though there might have been. Mother and Aunt Eliza were in bathing once at the Shoals. Neither of them could swim, and Aunt Eliza lost her footing and was swept down by the current. Lifting despairing eyes, she saw, as she thought for the last time, the white columns of her home above the cliffs. Unable to help her, Mother turned her back and covered her face with her hands, so as not to see her drown. Another instant and Aunt Eliza's feet touched bottom, and she was saved.

We children were taught to swim at an early age, the boys being thrown from the flat in mid-river, while the girls learned by the hardest, with empty gourds tied under their arms. Uncle Henry would row us across the river from the foot of Termination Rock to the fine sandy bottom on the other side. Then he would plunge in, and three or four of us would cling to this broad shoulders, while he swam about. The boys all became fine swimmers, and we girls at least learned how to swim, and swimming is to this day our favorite form of exercise.

We never went in swimming together, for the boys were nudists. They had their part of the river, and we ours, and they stayed in theirs almost all day long. They would swim up the river to someone's watermelon patch, float some melons down, and eat them warm on the riverbank. It never seemed to hurt them to eat all that they wanted and go right in to the river again. Once two of them were up in a scaly bark tree on the riverbank, getting muscadines. Suddenly they heard the voices of girls, and, with no time to spare, they came streaking down, being all but scarified before they struck the water and safety.

We girls wore bathing suits of heavy dark blue flannel, all-overs, with skirt buttoned to the waist, and very cumbersome for swimming. Perhaps this handicap accounted for the fact that we were not as good swimmers as the boys. When little Belle could sew, she made a bathing suit for herself out of a flour sack. She had from the first an instinct for style, and hers was a one-piece suit, but not being an expert seamstress, one leg was baggy, and the other skintight, and diagonally across her back, in large blue letters, were the words "Belle of the West." I once saw the Belle of the West floating downstream. She could not swim but could float, and had no idea that she was out of her depth.

Opposite Termination, in the middle of the river, was what we called the Big Rock. It was below the surface but could be located by the ripples above it, and it made a fine seat on which to sit and rest, after the long swim down the river from the Shoals. There was a hole at the base

of this rock, and the boys used to dive down and go through it. Once
Hammie Couper failed to come up and Henry dove down and found him
stuck in the hole. I never saw the Big Rock but once in my life, and that
was when the river was so low that it stood up for a foot above the
water, like a square table, and you could walk almost dry-shod across the
Shoals. Only once as far as I know was the river ever filled with ice. It
was one winter during a spell of intense cold, and Uncle Henry walked
across it on blocks of floating ice.

The Shoals became our final bathing place for the water was shallow
there for some distance out. One disadvantage was its rocky bottom, and
it was hard work making our way up the river in our bare feet against the
swift current, to the fish trap, which Father and Uncle Henry had built in
the middle of the shoals. We would climb upon the big beams, slippery
with moss, lie down and feel the delicious cool water rushing over us.
Then, striking out, we would be whirled down by the current, swept over
jagged rocks, and finally reach the deep water below. Our objective was
the snag in the middle of the river opposite our spring. This was a protruding limb of a drowned tree, and we would sit along it to rest, feeling
it sway under us in the strong current, and then we would sing until it
was time to pull for shore.

Once when Jean Waring came down from Spring Bank to visit us,
we took her in swimming. She did not tell us that she could hardly swim
at all, and she managed to make the snag. When the time came to swim
to the spring across the swift current, she suddenly flagged, and threw her
arms around Mary Stiles.

"All I ask is that you keep away from me!" I hear Mary cry, as she
struggled from Jean's grasp, and I laughed so hard it was all that I could
do to keep my own head above water, and, in some way, get Jean to
shore. Fortunately it was very near.

The tenants on the place never went in "washing," as some of our
neighbors called it, and I doubt if any of them knew how to swim. Perhaps they had no time for this indulgence, for they were very poor, and
had to work from daylight until dark. One father of a large family said,
"Nuthin' sleeps in my house after day." And I am sure he saw that noth-
in' did. He was the patriarch who gave this advice on marriage to my
brother Hamilton when he was grown. "After you git spliced," he said
"the fust thing you better do is knock her down an' tromp her. Then you
won't have no more trouble."

The principal family on Uncle Henry's place was the Bones. On ours the Beans. The Bones lived just above the ferry on the other side of the river. They were big, brawny, rough men, and Crawford the oldest son, was high tempered and insolent, he felt a burning resentment that he had none of the advantages that Henry and the Habersham boys had, and I was always afraid of a clash between Uncle Henry and himself. But the old man and Uncle Henry were good friends, and, after the father's death, the family moved off the place, and I have heard vaguely that Crawford Bone succeeded in life. I hope that he did.

Our principal tenant, Mr. Bean, had good blood in him I am sure. He was refined in looks and manners, and Father was very fond of him. The Beans lived at the far edge of the place, down on the bank of the river, a lonely and isolated spot. Sally Bean, the only child, was a quiet, gentle girl, and what a sad and lonesome life she must have led, without recreation or pleasure of any kind.

All of the women led sad, hardworking lives. I remember once when a crowd of us girls, laughing and talking, crossed a field on our way to the river. A number of women and girls in shapeless, colorless dresses and dark sunbonnets were chopping cotton, and not one of them lifted her head or spoke. How bitterly they must have thought of our lives of idle luxury, compared to their own. No wonder one of them could say when I returned to Malbone two years after I married, in blooming health, "Married two years and ain't broke yet!"

There was one dangerous family on Uncle Henry's place, with one pretty daughter, and a number of strong, high-tempered sons. These men quarrelled dreadfully among themselves, and one afternoon, when neither Father nor Uncle Henry was at home, they had a terrible fight down the lane. Mother ran down to separate them, but by the time she reached them, one of them had stabbed the other. I remember seeing the wounded man lying on a mattress on our piazza looking as white as death. He did not die, but a few years later a fatal tragedy occurred in the family. The pretty daughter had married a short, stocky, surly Scandinavian named Conrad. He was a renter on the Creswell place, which was beyond Summerland. When the time came for the yearly settlement, Conrad met Mr. Creswell at his front gate and demanded his money. There was a dispute as to the amount, and Conrad stabbed him.

It was the first murder I had ever known of, and I remember cowering beside Aunt Sarah's chair, and hearing a horseman tearing past the house in the night, and picturing the murderer fleeing for his life. He was never heard of again.

These poor whites, who were known as Crackers in our day, were like the Indians, proud and independent. They would have died before showing surprise at a thing they had never seen before. We used to go see the tenants on our place, and they always received us with a fine hospitality, but they never came to see us in return, as the more simple and friendly Negroes did.

Several of us went once to see a white woman who lived on our place, and who was noted for the quilts she made. The quilts in a Cracker family are their treasures and heirlooms and are usually the dowries of the girls when they marry. Mrs. Baker had been out in the fields all day, but when we entered her cabin and asked to see her quilts, she obligingly pulled a large trunk out to the middle of the floor and lifted one heavy quilt after another, spreading them out for us to see. They were "Log Cabin," "Texas Star," and "Sunrise," patched or tufted, all beautifully pieced and quilted. I noticed after a while that she was quite pale, and hardly said a word, but none of us realized her condition, and we stayed as long as we liked. No sooner had we left the cabin than she keeled over in one of the "spells" she had habitually, and it took a long time to revive her. I believe she would have had died then and there, rather than have been rude enough as to ask us to leave.

Even when they had illness in the family, the poor whites seldom asked for any help, but I do remember once that Mother was called on for advice when a baby was about to die. Its name was enough to kill it, being Sary Sabiny Emma Elsore Lucindy Angeline. When Mother reached the cabin, the child was in convulsions. She was able to relieve it by hot applications, and she then asked then mother what the baby had been given to eat. "I fed hit sardines and cheese," said Mrs. Bennet.

Bessie had gone with Mother, and, as they left the cabin, she noticed Sary Sabiny's brother hurling rocks at the sky. "What are you throwing at, little boy?" Bessie asked. "I'm a throwin' at that thar moon," answered James Garfield Bennet. "I aims to bust hit plum open."

Margie had many friends among the Crackers, and, calling once on a bride who had been married the day before, she found her seated on the porch with her mother-in-law. When she asked where the groom was, the old lady cheerfully explained that as he hadn't enough to take both of them, he had gone off on the wedding tour alone.

During the Spanish-American War, one of them asked Margie, "Is Cuby sunk?" Having no opportunities to learn, the Crackers were at that time very ignorant, and I doubt if many of the older people knew how to read or write, and there was no school anywhere near for the children. It is pleasant to know that there is now a good public school on the place.

The poorest Cracker family I ever knew lived down in our lane, where the land on that part of the place was rocky and sterile, and only the poorest renter took it. The father of the family drank, and the suffering of his wife and children must have been extreme. There was a girl of my own age who was so poorly clothed that on one occasion when she had a chance to go in to Cartersville, she borrowed a pair of shoes from a Negro girl to wear. It hurts me to think of that even now.

The Negroes of that day had a much better time than the Poor Whites. However indigent and hard worked, they had their pleasures and the excitement of religion. Responsibility rested lightly on them, and they never worried about the future. The truth is that as long as Negroes have enough to eat they are perfectly happy.

The Negro that I remember best was our house servant, Fanny Mann. She was then a young woman, strong, robust and fine looking, with a pleasant smile and a pleasant disposition. She was very good to us and we children were all fond of her, but once, unfortunately, Hammie and I happened to hear and see her beating one of her children in the cotton patch, and were filled with fury. We determined to "pay her back," and that night, when she brought in the supper dishes, we jumped on her from behind a door and beat her as hard as we could on her breasts. She was naturally astonished, as we made no explanation, but she managed to hold on to the dishes. Fanny Mann might have been the heroine of *Scarlet Sister Mary*. She had five children by as many fathers, but this made no difference to Mother. She always said that you could not judge a Negro as you judged a white person, that they were simply following their natural instincts, and to the day of her death Mother remained Fanny's good friend. Fanny Mann is still living, and has now become sanctified, being the only member of the Saints Church in our neighborhood. The last time that I saw her, she said she did not know what the present generation was coming to.

The most respectable Negro family on our place was that of the Kincaids, who had come down from Kentucky after the war, and had probably taken the name of their owners. "Pappy" as the old man was called, was quite handsome, with large dark eyes and a black mustache, and when he was dressed up on Sunday in a black frock coat and beaver hat, he looked the perfect gentleman that he was. He had one daughter, Ellen, and a number of sons, and Ellen's wedding was one of our earliest social events. She married a fine-looking Mulatto from Savannah, named Thompson, and they were married on our long piazza, and afterwards a procession of colored people went down the lane to one of the log cabins, lining it, where they had a wedding feast. Ellen was a gentle, timid soul, and I am sorry to say that Thompson soon deserted her.

Pappy's oldest sons, John and Jim Kincaid, lived on our place until they died in recent years. John married Emma, Grandmama's pretty and indulged little maid. Her mother and grandmother had belonged to the Mackay family, and her children, grandchildren, and great grandchildren still live at our country place in Georgia, so the same family has been with us for seven generations.

We never called the Negroes anything but colored people, so as to not hurt their feelings, though we spoke of them as Darkies. I had never heard the term Nigger used by a Southern lady or gentleman, until I went to live on a Mississippi plantation after I was married, and found they were called Niggers altogether. My Charleston friend, Belle Sumter Roberts, told me that the only time her father had ever punished her as a little girl was when she once used this expression.

Nor did we ever call the Poor Whites "Crackers" to their faces. "Poor White Trash," the Negroes called them, and had a supreme contempt for them simply because they were poor. And the Poor Whites despised and hated the Negroes because they were their competitors. The lower class of Whites still hate them, and it is the middle and lower class of Whites who lynch the Negroes in the South.

The Crackers on our place would never have accepted anything from us, but the Negroes were thankful for what we gave them, and in time Mother gave away so many of her things that she hardly left enough to wear.

In later years when she had no one to help her manage the farm, a white tenant family sometimes pulled up stakes and left, owing her for an entire year's advances.

In the cold light of dawn, they would pile all their belongings on a wagon, tie the hound dog by a rope underneath, and "put out for ole Alibam."

Until I left Mississippi, and came to live in Birmingham, I had a perfect horror of the state.

The Cracker family named Lewis, who lived in our yard, were the ones we knew best. Par Lewis had a hard time of it I think, for in addition to making his little crop, he had to do the work about the place, and, under Mother's direction, he planted all of the trees, which have now grown to such a good size. In the bitterest winter weather I have seen him drive off in the two-horse wagon to cut wood on the mountain and return, almost frozen, at dark. But his hardest task I am sure was taking the honey once a year. We had a row of bee hives under the kitchen window, and I hated the bees myself, I was so often stung. Whether Par Lewis really did not feel their sting, or was too proud to show it, I do not know, for he never uttered a sound, and I have seen him black with bees, while he robbed their hives by the light of a torch, and massacred the wretched insects by the thousands.

Nothing has ever given me greater pleasure than returning to my old Georgia home in recent years and finding the tenants on our place. White and colored, owning secondhand Fords, and driving into town every Saturday, sometimes even going to the movies.

I said, and I meant it, that the most thrilling experience I could have would be to drive to Cartersville in an automobile. When I did, along the beautiful Dixie Highway, which now runs through our place, in less than fifteen minutes, I could hardly believe it was true!

7.
Plays

 have written a good deal about the older people of our family, but, as a matter of fact, they only entered the marginal realms of our lives. Our real, vital, enchanting existence was spent in a world of our very own.

To the south of the old house was a large circular grass plot, almost surrounded by a high osage orange hedge. In its centre was an old mimosa tree covered with ivy, which we called The Ivy Tree, and in this we girls simply lived, each of us having a special "room" of our own. It was a delicious abode, for the mimosa blooms on the ends of the outstretched limbs were like rosy powder-puffs, filling the air with a delicate nectarine fragrance, and the sound of hummingbirds and bees.

Most of our day were spent up in trees, and we loved to hang from the limbs by our knees. The boys could even hang by their feet, and they had the best of us in climbing, being able to "shin" up the very highest-limbed trees. A favorite sport of ours was to have the boys climb to the top of a young and supple tree and bear it to the ground, when one of us would take hold. The boys would then jump off, and the tree would spring erect, carrying us sailing through the air. Then on the riverbank were long, strong muscadine vines, on which we could swing across the deep springs.

Many fine springs gushed out from under the rocks along the river, the largest of these being just below Etowah Cliffs. The limestone water, clear and cold as ice, was always used for drinking water, and in our grandparents' day, was pumped up to the house. The water spigot was just inside the door of the cellar kitchen, and it seemed to me a sinister thing, for an old Negro man who was sitting beside it once, had been struck dead by lightning. In our day the servants brought the water up in buckets, an awful task, as the hill was high, and steep, and often slippery.

I remember once when we were very little, Aunt Sarah took us down to the spring to bathe. Below the overhanging wall of rock the spring formed a circular pool, lined with pebbles which were golden in the sunlight, and the crystal water was deep enough to come up to our waists. Aunt Sarah had a sponge and a quart cup, and she would fill the cup, pour the icy water over us, and scrub it in. I never remember bathing there again. Once was enough.

As children we were all fond of animals, of dogs especially; that is of all dogs except a terrible bulldog, which Uncle Henry kept for a time chained in the cellar. We would peer down through the window and see his green eyes glaring in the gloom.

Our cousins' pet dog was named Tiger. He was also a bulldog, and a real old character, being rather gruff and reserved; but once, when I was in trouble, and was seated on a log in the park with my face in my hands, Tiger came to me, rose, and put both paws on my shoulders. There was no need for words.

Our pet dog was Juno, a little Scotch terrier, who seemed to be a real member of our family, a sort of very little sister. When she had puppies under the house, we children would crawl on our hands and knees the entire length of the piazza, while she trotted before us, whining with mingled pride and apprehension. I used to sit under the piazza at night with her in my arms, and it was under this same place that she was found dead not long after our Father's death. The Negroes said she had died of grief.

The animals on the place were distinct personalities to us. There was the dangerous jackass, kept confined for a time in a log stable outside of the lot fence. Gulie helped me climb up once to the high window to see him. As we appeared he dashed to the wall beneath us, stood up on his hind legs, and pawed the logs, braying with fury. If one of us had fallen in, he would have quickly put an end to us.

Pinke, the bad cow, was our delight and terror. Once Gulie took several of us into the pasture where she was grazing, teased her into a fury, and, as she started for us, cried, "Run for your lives!" It was literally *Sauve qui peut,* as we made for the rail fence, and threw ourselves over it. I knew in my heart I could never stop to rescue one of the little children, while Gulie, dying of laughter, saw that every child was over before she saved herself. She had absolutely no sense of fear, and, when only a little girl and unable to swim, she had jumped into the James River and saved the life of her little cousin, George Harrison.

The pasture in which Pinke grazed was called The Eighty Acres Field. A road crossed it near the top, on each side of which was a small water oak, the age of Gordon and myself. They have grown with our growth, and are now great of girth, with a mighty spread of limb, and I call one of them my Tree of Life. They are quite as fine as the oaks on the coast, and prove that trees can be of equal size and beauty where they have room to spread and unlimited sunshine.

Beyond the garden at The Cliffs was a long orchard, and we children lived in the fruit trees, from cherry, through plum, peach, and apple, to pear time. Indian peaches were the finest fruit that we had. These peaches were very large, the skin striped red and orange, and so delicate it slipped off under your fingers, and the crimson flesh was luscious. We used to pick lapfuls of peaches, take them down to the spring, put them in, then eat them ice cold.

There was one confection made in our family that I have never seen anywhere else. It was called Peach Leather, and could only be made from very soft, freestone peaches. These were rubbed through a sieve, then boiled with a little sugar. A thin layer of this would be poured into tin plates, and these would be placed out of doors on trestles in the sun. It took three days of sunning to perfect them, and dozens of plates would have to be taken out in the morning and brought in at night. If it ever threatened to rain, there would be a wild rush for the peach leather, children as well as servants helping to save it. Sometimes birds pecked at it, sometimes bees hovered over it, but oftenest there were little finger prints in its golden transparency. When it was ready to put up, each delicate layer was rolled from the plate like a wafer, covered with powdered sugar, and laid away in a tin box. We children never tasted anything but the scraps, for it was always kept to be sent to the Lows in England for Christmas. It was some compensation to hear from Willie Low in after years that he considered it the best sweet they ever had.

In the fall we used to climb on top of the two long scuppernong arbors in the garden, lie at full length, and eat our fill of the ripe brown grapes. This, by the way, is the only way in which scuppernongs should ever be eaten.

The first frost ripened the persimmons, which we considered only better than nothing, though on one or two of the trees which Grandfather had planted, the persimmons were very large, of a rosy color, golden, velvety and delicious.

In the winter we had nuts from hickory, walnut, and chestnut trees. The boys made a business of gathering walnuts, spreading them in the sun to dry, then hulling them, and putting them up in bags for winter use. At a certain season their hands and arms would be stained almost black. We knew every hickory nut tree in the grove and park and disdained any but the largest and thinnest shelled nuts. As for scarly barks—!

The boys used to make wigwams of small pine trees in the grove and line them with layers of leaves. At the opening there would be a large flat stone around which we sat and on which we cracked our nuts.

In the summertime there were often as many as twenty children at The Cliffs, for the three Gordon girls came up from Savannah, and the three Gordon boys came down from Huntsville, and there were fourteen Stiles children already there.

The Savannah Gordons were Nellie, Daisy, and Alice, and the Huntsville Gordons were Willie, Percy, and Cuyler. The boys and girls did not have much to do with each other until they grew older, and their plays were entirely different.

The first play I ever remember was *Playing Ladies*. I do not know that we did much more than tell what our names were, and describe our looks and clothes to one another. It never seemed to go any farther than that, but we vied with each other in describing our charms. Gulie and I were sitting on a rail fence once, and I tried to think of a delineation of beauty that would surpass anything we had ever described. At that age what we admired most were small waists and big legs, so I said, "My waist is as little as a bed post, and my legs are as fat as Grannie Gordon's." And then, even I, realized that I had *overdone it.*

Nellie, the oldest of the Gordon sisters was very clever, with all the self-assurance of a city girl and it was easy enough for her to get the better of me, as I was undoubtedly "dumb." She sprang this on me once, "What is your favorite thing to eat?" I thought desperately of something that might impress her, and then I said, "Hot sponge cake and wine sauce." "Mine is chocolate eclairs," she said superbly, and never having heard of one, I was crushed.

Once when the Warings drove down to visit us, we children were out on the piazza. Mr. Waring kissed us all as a matter of course, and started to kiss Nellie, whereupon she drew herself up and said, "My mother does not allow me to kiss promiscuously," to his intense amusement.

Nellie was Henry's age, and Gulie and herself were inseparable. Daisy was two years older than myself, but, having the same tastes, we spent most of our time together. She was the talented member of her family and could draw and paint, write poetry, recite and act. She had a keen sense of humor and was very witty. Alice, being younger, belonged with Mary to the limbo of between-ages.

The Gordon boys were all musical and had been trained by their father, and, after his death, by their oldest half-brother, George. They formed a little band and used to play for us out on the piazza in the evenings. The instrument that Cuyler used was his own voice, which was like a silver trumpet, and so remarkable that later on we expected him to become a second Campanini.

The plays of the boys were full of tiresome violence, as they were always either Indians or Soldiers. They made bows and arrows with sharp tin points that stuck in trees, and they lived on the War Path in the park. Once when they had laid out an encampment there and were playing Soldiers, we girls attempted to join them. We were far from welcome. They had named themselves Lee, Stonewall Jackson, Ashby, Stuart, and so on, and none of the heroes were left for us, so they named me Sherman and snickered every time they addressed me. This ruse did not work, as I was quite unaware of the indignity, so they then declared that Daisy was a Yankee spy and must be imprisoned. She was small and thin, and they poked her through a hole in a hollow tree, which was so deep that only the tip of her sharp little nose was visible. She was game though and never "surrendered," and they finally hauled her out. And this experience cured us of any further desire to join in their manly sports.

I was never fond of playing dolls, but as soon as I could draw and paint, I developed a passion for paper dolls, and for years Daisy and I painted them, and all of us played with them. Our masterpiece was The Eight Cousins, which I drew and Daisy painted, and some of which are still in existence in 1932! My beauty, however, was Lily Langtry, with an elaborate trousseau, which changed with the changing fashions. When Margie was old enough to paint, she added to our collection, many of our acquaintances, her best likenesses being of Mr. John Postell and Llewellyn Aubrey.

Daisy once wrote a poem in twelve verses called "The Months." At this time Addie Ledyard was our favorite artist, and I illustrated this after

Addie Ledyard. A long way after. We had the audacity to send this effort to *St. Nicholas*, and needless to say it was returned, with, however, a very kind letter from the editress.

It was Daisy who suggested the Reynard the Fox Dinner. Both of us drew on large sheets of cardboard, the dinner table at Etowah. We were ahead of our time, for it was a distinctly Cezanne table seen on end. Around it were seated all of the Henry Stiles family and their guests, each one represented by an animal. We selected these from the large volumes of *Reineke Fuchs*, which had been brought from Germany, choosing those which we thought looked like each person. Uncle Henry was naturally the fierce lion king at the head of the table. Why our elders never knew of this piece of impudence I cannot imagine, as it was freely circulated among the children.

The little girls were never allowed to play with us; though, when we played paper dolls, they might sit on the outskirts and look on. In spite of this selfishness I was devoted to my little sisters. I once heard Bessie crying out on the grass. The little girls were stringing four-o'clocks on grass stems, and Alice Gordon had put a live grasshopper down Bessie's back. I saw flaming red. I started for her, and Alice, who was called "Skinny," flew. Around the whole garden we tore, and I caught her under the mealy pear tree, and put my whole soul into a stinging slap on her face. And all of my anger went out of my fingertips and left me miserable. All afternoon I suffered, and when night came, I could stand it no longer. I walked along the upper piazza to the big middle room, in which the Gordon girls always slept, and, glancing in, saw the three sitting moodily on the bed. I hesitated, and then I went in, and begged them to forgive me for having done what was exactly right. Nellie forgave me grandly, and I was happy once more.

The four-o'clocks, which the little children were stringing on grass blades, were made into cool and fragrant ruches to wear around their necks. To this day, if I want to feel four years old again, all that I have to do is shut my eyes and smell a four-o'clock.

We girls had what we called a "Circus Trunk" at Etowah Cliffs in which we kept all the old finery we could collect. Our greatest treasure was a yellow tarlatan ballet skirt. Whenever we started to dress up, Nellie, being the most quick witted, would call out, "I claim the yellow tarlatan!" I can see her now, perched up in a catalpa tree near the mound in front of the house, wearing the yellow ballet skirt, while a buggy full of visitors drove under it to the front steps. Never but once did I have the bliss of wearing this gorgeous costume, and that was when we played Circus and allowed the boys to be the wild beasts. Nellie Gordon must have been in Savannah.

I never thought much about clothes, though I admired pretty dresses on others, and I have ever forgotten two which my little sisters had. Aunt Kate went to England one summer to visit the Lows, and brought these back from Amy and Hattie, who were the godmothers of Bessie and Margie. Bessie's was a Scotch costume, with plaited plaid skirt, and a black velvet jacket; and Margie's was almost too lovely to be true, a pale blue Cashmere trimmed with swansdown! I do not suppose that those English girls, who had everything in the world they wanted, ever realized what joy they had given those Southern children, who had never seen anything so beautiful in all their lives.

Nellie Gordon, being older than any of us, was naturally our leader, and she invented many delightful plays, her finest being, *The Castle of Red Cliff.* Next to Termination was another high cliff, which rose directly from the water, with many ledges on different levels for rooms, winding flight of steps and a tower. Here we played the story of Miss Young's *Heir of Red Cliff,* Nellie being "Guy" and Gulie "Amy." I was only a minor character, but I had the nicest room of all on top of the tower, with the water far beneath.

Our most exciting play, however, was *Nuns.* Nuns had always fascinated me, and I could never quite make up my mind which I would rather be: a nun or a circus girl. We played *Nuns* at The Monastery, a great, square gray rock, surrounded by dark trees, which was farther up the river. Nellie Gordon was the mother superior, and the rest of us were the nuns, and as we walked in single file around the cliff to our chapel at its base, we intoned,

Ah - bé - cé - derian.
Sac - ré - men - tarian.
Ben - e - di - cite.
Ah - ah - ah - men.

Of course we had many stirring experiences and were frequently confined in dungeons by the mother superior.

The highest and finest of our cliffs was Termination, which was directly below the house, and from the top of which there was a pretty view of the river as far south as the Shoals. The path leading down to its base was almost perpendicular, but, even as children, we managed to scramble down to the flat rock at its foot, where our boat was always fastened.

On the top of Termination the name "Hattie" is deeply cut, though it is now hidden by the ivy that has covered the rock. Hattie Low was a great beauty and had many admirers in Savannah, when her father brought her there as a young lady. I remember seeing her once on the steps of the Mackay house, a superb English blonde, in an elaborate costume of dark green silk, piped with pale blue. Someone of the many who loved her vainly must have cut her name on Termination Rock.

The only boy, as for as I know, who ever climbed up the face of Termination was George Fitzsimmons, who was in love with Margie, and performed this desperate feat to win her favor. Fortunately he was not dashed to pieces on the ledge at its foot but lived to marry very happily someone else.

All children love acting instinctively, and we were crazy about it. The first performance in which I ever took part was a tableau representing *Pocahontas Saving the Life of Captain Smith*. I was Pocahontas, and I can still recall the rapture I felt when I realized that the eyes of the world were upon me. Our stage was a bed, and John Smith's head rested comfortably on a pillow instead of a stone.

Daisy and I always got up our plays, which were at first very primitive, as we made them up as we went along, in the old Italian style. Daisy was once again a Yankee spy and was dragged from under the bed by the hair of her head. Her eyes were filled with tears, but she sang pluckily "Hang Old Jeff Davis to a Sour Apple Tree," until she herself was hung to the bedpost. Another play ended more seriously, when Gulie was a giant, mounted on the shoulders of their dear Irish nurse-girl, Maria. A long cloak concealed Maria, and the giant came out groaning and slashing bout with a carving knife and slashed one of Maria's hands.

Our costumes were of the simplest, and Daisy once wore, as a boy, a pair of panties, with gold paper stripes down the sides, while, on another occasion, Mary was shoved out on the stage, weeping, clad in a chemise, with a blue sash across her shoulder.

Aunt Eliza's younger sister, Mrs. George Harrison, had been a great beauty, and was still, as I remember her, a very handsome woman. She often visited Etowah Cliffs, and was very good to the children, painting the most fascinating paper dolls for one thing, for us. To amuse us she once decided to get up some tableaux. One of them was to be *The*

Daughter of Herodias, and we were wildly excited, for Salome was to carry the head of John the Baptist on a charger! I, as Salome, was to wear a voluminous silk skirt, behind the fold of which Gordon was to kneel, as the Baptist. Only his head was to show, a pasteboard platter being placed around his neck. His eyes were to be closed, his face whitened, and streams of blood were to flow out on the charger. Never had we acted anything so dramatic in our lives, and our disappointment can be imagined, when Aunt Eliza hear about it, said it would be sacrilegious, and would not allow the performance to take place.

As we grew older I wrote the plays, and we acted them in Savannah as well as up the country. We formed a regular company, which we called the Habstigorell Troupe: Habershams, Stiles, Gordons, and Elliotts being among its members. Lotta was the actress I worshipped, and I was fired with the ambition to write her play *Musette* from memory, and have our troupe act it. But that was one time when I bit off more than I could chew.

Though Daisy and I had the same tastes, we were as different as it was possible to be. When she made up her mind to do a thing, she never announced it beforehand, but went quietly to work, and whatever she decided to do she *did*. She never seemed to experience the awful sinking spells that I invariably had. I would undertake anything, and begin with the greatest enthusiasm, and always there came the sickening moment when I would give anything on earth to get out of it. That I generally managed to pull through was owing entirely to the fact that my plans were known to many others, and I could not face their scorn.

The most elaborate play we ever got up was *Anne of Austria*. I had seen the name of a story in *Appleton's*, with a picture of a most lovely queen, and my ambition was fired. It was at The Cliffs and the house as usual was filled with children. I announced that I was going to write a play, and all of the girls were enchanted. The days that followed were hectic, as I tried in vain to think of something to write about. Not for worlds would I have exposed my ignorance by asking the grown people who Anne of Austria was, and I hadn't time to read the story. Besides it was a continued one.

It is easy enough to write a play if you have a story, but I have no talent for making up stories. I remember sitting on the floor of the upstairs piazza, chewing a pencil, with a blank sheet of paper in my hand, and a blank mind in my head, when Daisy passed by, and asked maddeningly how far I had got. "Nellie's going to be an executioner," she remarked, "And Gulie's decided to be a king. They've started on their costumes."

An executioner! Someone must obviously lose a head. A king and a beautiful queen. I had an idea to start with, and I sashed off a three-act play.

I was Anne of Austria, naturally, and Daisy, being the most versatile of all of us, took several parts. Even Mary was allowed in on this, as we needed a large cast. It was in this play that she wore the chemise. I had the bliss of wearing a brown silk belonging to Nellie's mother, who was there at the time. It was made with tight basque, a bunchy overskirt, and a long train. The basque was so much too large it gave me a humped back, but I could not see my back, and I felt perfectly gorgeous.

We had the play in the big old harness room, and the boys were allowed to pull the curtains, which were made of sheets. We charged twenty-five cents admission, the proceeds to go to the Missionaries, of course. Never in our lives did we make any money for ourselves. We would have considered it disgraceful.

In the play I was imprisoned in a tower, and to reveal my presence, I sang a song, of which I had only composed the words. The tune I improvised as I went along, and the result sent Aunt Sarah into such hysterics that she had to leave the room.

The climax of the play was the beheading of Anne of Austria. Why she was beheaded I have no idea. Probably because Nellie Gordon wanted to be an executioner. On top of my own head I held an artificial one, my face being concealed by a cloak. I had to walk the length of the stage, and by the time I reached the block, the head had become so heavy that it rolled off before the executioner could even lift his axe. Instantly Nellie, the quick witted, brought down the axe, and dashed pokeberry juice—for blood—over the headless corpse, and the curtains were jerked together amidst shrieks of applause. It was days before the unfortunate queen could get the sticky juice out of her hair.

The first play that I ever saw in a real theatre was simply heaven to me. It was in the old Savannah Theatre on Chippewa Square, and the play was called *Mazeppa*. I can still see Mazeppa lashed to the back of the coal black horse, which dashed away, going higher and higher into the distant mountains as the curtain fell.

It was in this same old theatre that I had the inestimable privilege of seeing Edwin Booth act. Cousin Leila Habersham, knowing how I adored the theatre, often took me to it when I went down to Savannah in the winter, and on three unforgettable days, I saw Booth act in *Hamlet, The Merchant of Venice*, and *The Taming of the Shrew*, and I have never seen another actor who could touch him.

To me those characters of Shakespeare live as Booth portrayed them. Hamlet, a slender youth, dark and melancholy, whose deep-set eyes seemed trying to penetrate the mystery of the Beyond. Shylock, a powerful old Jew, swathe in rich clothing, a strong, belligerent character, who could only be bludgeoned down. And Petruchio, young and inconceivably graceful, a whip-cracking, leg-slapping gallant, carrying everything before him.

In afterday, not even Irving's poignant interpretation of Shylock could efface the powerful impression that Booth created in my mind.

I realized however, even at that age, the weakness of Booth's productions. He had so small and inadequate a troupe that I think of the other members of the cast as mere shadows in the background. Even his wife, a pretty little young thing who took the parts of his heroines, aroused not the slightest interest. Without the glamour of beautiful scenery, above all with no adorable Ellen Terry to play opposite him, his performances stand out in my memory as no others I have ever seen, and, even as a child, I appreciated Booth's incomparable acting.

After the matinee, we children were so carried away that we rushed around to the stage entrance to see Booth in person. To avoid us, the actor and his wife slipped out of a back door, crossed to the Old Cemetery, and started up Abercorn Street. Lizzie Owens, who was leading us, evidently had scouts out, and we pelted after them, the line growing longer and longer as we followed. By the time the wretched actor reached the house opposite Christ Church, where they were boarding, we were on his very heels, and little Clifford Owens had darted in front of him and was staring up into his tragic face. How horrible he must have thought that Southern children were! It was pure mob contagion, for we were not ordinarily so badly behaved.

Our elders must have thought at last that so long a playtime as all summer and fall should be curtailed, and about the time that I was nine, it was decided that we should have a governess.

The cottage in the grove, where we used to play church, had been for some time unoccupied. Mr. Videy, a one-legged German carpenter, had formerly lived there. He must have been a very good carpenter for he made all of the massive furniture for the Sproulls, whose place was next to our own. He made it so well that even the Yankees could not utterly destroy it, though they did such things as using the piano as a feedbox for their horses. After he left our place, Mr. Videy came to a tragic end, driving his wagon and team into the river one night, as he drove them off the flat.

It was decided to use this cottage for a schoolhouse, and a poor little governess from Cartersville was engaged to teach us. Her name was Miss Atterway, and she was quite young and sweet looking and very quiet and timid. She was to stay at The Cliffs during the week and go home for Saturdays and Sundays. She taught the younger children, and, led by Henry and Nellie Gordon, we spent our time tormenting her. They would think up all sorts of ways in which to harass her, and we thought ourselves quite smart in following their directions. Needless to say, our elders knew nothing of this.

Life ended as tragically for poor Miss Atterway as it did for Mr. Videy, for she lost her mind, and I do not doubt we were partly responsible. It is a black page in my life, which I turn very quickly when I come to it.

8

Malbone

he first time that I knew Etowah Cliffs did not belong to us was at the close of the Franco-Prussian War. Uncle Henry had been on the side of Germany, Father on that of France. Henry and I were seated on the piazza steps, and he was gloating over the German victory. This was bad enough, but suddenly he said, "You think this is your house, don't you? Well, it isn't. It's my father's."

I was struck dumb. Such a thought had never entered my mind. I felt humiliated, outcast, and homeless, but it was not long before that I found out we were going to build a house of our own. The site chosen was about a quarter of a mile south of The Cliffs, in the midst of wide fields, which were bounded by the curve of the river.

The first thing that was done was to build two brick kilns and make our own bricks from our own red clay. The bricks were molded, and laid out in long rows in the sun to harden, and we thought it fun to walk on the soft blocks, and leave the impress of our bare feet on them. Until we were found out! The kilns burned all the time and at night, we could see them glowing across the dark fields.

The house faced north and was square, with double piazzas on the east side, a side porch on the west, and a kitchen wing at the back. The walls, even between the rooms, were of brick, two feet thick, and the roof was of slate. The slate was brought from Rockmart, a little town to the southwest, where there were several quarries, and where every house, large and small, was roofed with dove-gray slate.

The entrance to the house was in the form of a loggia with three arches, which Mother had copied from her old home, Hopeton, and on either side of the loggia was a bay window. From our front steps we could see Etowah Cliffs in the midst of trees, and the grove and park beyond which were the lovely curves of our mountain and the Sproulls', like blue waves against the sky.

Besides the square front hall, there were six large and five smaller rooms in the house, as well as a pantry, storeroom, kitchen, and servants' room, and the total cost was $6,000! Of course Aunt Kate and Aunt Sarah, our blessed aunts, paid for it.

It was decided to name our new home Malbone after Edward Malbone, the miniature painter. He was the first cousin of Robert Mackay, Aunt Kate and Aunt Sarah's father, and had died of consumption in his house on Congress Street in Savannah. Malbone was the one genius in our family, and his name is revered by all of us. Hamilton was the only one who disliked it as the name of our place, which he said should have been called Redlands. Certainly that is what you see when you look at the fields stretching out on every side.

While the house was being built we revelled in walking on the rafters, and when the time came for painting the woodwork, I was simply fascinated. It was painted to represent different wood, and it seemed marvelous to me that the painters could paint the grain and even the knotholes so perfectly. The walls, of course, were all plastered white.

The day that we moved over, we three oldest children felt lost and homeless, as we came together in an upstairs room, in the midst of trunks and unplaced furniture, and realized that we had left Etowah Cliffs forever. It did not take us long to become accustomed to Malbone though, and to love it as our home, but it never came up to The Cliffs, with its splendid rocks and river, its orchard, grove, and park.

All of the furniture in the old house had been divided into two parts, and Mother and Aunt Eliza drew straws for these. We drew the mirror in our lot, and half of the Austrian furniture. When Grandfather was in Vienna he had a beautiful dessert service made of Bohemian glass. An epergne, four tall stands, four candlesticks, decanters, wine glasses, plates and saucers of different sizes. A delicate pattern of vine leaves and grapes was cut white in the ruby glass, and the initials W. H. S. were on every piece. Naturally this set went to Uncle Henry, but we were given two of the candlesticks, as well as the set of china with the apple green borders, and a different flower painted in every plate.

At Malbone the drawing room was on the east side of the hall and opened into the dining room, back of it. There was a bay window in front, and two French windows on the piazza. Opposite this was Mother and Father's bedroom, with a dressing room on the side. Back of this was the staircase, and an entry leading to the side porch, and opening on the entry was a small room which was used as a schoolroom. Its windows, which looked out on the yard, were frosted, and these in time were covered with spirited little sketches scratched by Johnnie, of sportsmen shooting, of birds falling, and of knights in armor on horseback, running full tilt at each other.

Aunt Sarah's bedroom was over the drawing room, but it was entirely too large and comfortable a room for her to keep, and she soon moved into the horrid hot little room at the top of the stairs, over the school room. Aunt Kate's room was above the dining room, with a dressing room attached to it. The boys' room was above Mother's, and there was a small bedroom over the front hall.

A winding stair led from the upstairs hall to the garret, and the first thing we children did was to climb out of the garret windows on to the slate roof. The boys dragged their bags of walnuts across it and spread them to dry on the flat tin roof of the upstairs piazza. I do not think we did much damage to the slates however, as Malbone has only been re-roofed once in sixty years.

I slept on a little bed at the foot of Aunt Kate's, and took my bath in the morning in a tin tub in her dressing room. On very cold mornings Aunt Kate warmed a small copper kettle of water for me on the wood fire but it hardly did more than temper the "water," and I can still recall the shivery shock I felt when I stepped into it.

Bessie and Margie were bathed by Aunt Sarah at night, and after they were put to bed, I used to go upstairs to sing "God that madest earth and heaven," with them before they went to sleep. I remember Father's coming up to hear us once. By the end of the second verse the little girls' voices always died away, and I say this hymn now—and I say it almost every night without getting slower and slower, and almost always it puts me to sleep, as it did the little children so long ago.

It was in the room at the head of the stairs, a kneeling at Aunt Sarah's knee, that we first prayed for Charlie Ross, and for years we prayed every night that he might be returned to his mother. (That a similar crime, and an even more fiendish one, should be committed after sixty years of enlightenment and advancement, would have seemed unbelievable. The Lindbergh kidnap case.)

Malbone was a comfortable house, built in bare fields, its surroundings were at first unattractive. Grass and flowers were planted in front and on the eastern side, and a vegetable garden at the back. A well was dug here first, but though it was a very deep one, they never struck water. I asked the diggers to let me down in the bucket one day, and when I reached bottom, I found myself in utter darkness, but for the small hole so far up against the sky. I brought up one or two rocks in my hand, and felt important when veins of gold were found in them. Hammie told me afterwards it was "Fool's Gold," which he had thrown down himself for the purpose of fooling me. A deep cistern was next dug in the yard, and this we used for many years until a fine well was excavated.

The yard was west of the house, with the servants' house on its far side. Beyond were the barn and stables, and the lane leading down to the river. Trees were planted all around the house and down the lane, and, in the course of time, looking across the fields from the public road, Malbone appeared to be in the midst of a grove.

The field in front of the house, which extended to the park, was sometimes planted in wheat, and when this ripened, it looked like a green sea, with its waves rippling under the wind. The cotton fields were much less beautiful, for we only had "Bumble-Bee" cotton in the upcountry, not much over knee high. It is hard to pick where you have to stoop all the time, and one of our renters, a very tall man, always picked kneeling down, wearing pad on his knees. When I went to a Mississippi plantation after I was married, cotton seemed like another plant. The fields would be filled with pickers, but you never saw one of them, and once I saw a man on horseback, lift his hand to touch the top of a cotton plant.

There were a number of lime sinks in the fields surrounding Malbone, one of them so large that tall trees were growing it. We had a little fox terrier named Pickwell, who followed Hammie when he went out shooting once, and disappeared. For days we searched and could not find him, then at last, his feeble bark was heard, and he was discovered at the bottom of a deep sink, all but finished. A broad space, high on one side, scratched by his little feet, showed where he had sprung up over and over again, and he must have barked night and day despairingly. Hammie jumped down into the sink and brought him up in his arms, and in a short while the little dog was himself again.

I used to be afraid the little children might fall in the far away sinks and be lost, but the nightmare that haunted me was the thought that Hammie might fall into the deep cistern and swim around and around in the black night, with no one hearing his cries, until, exhausted, he sank and drowned. It was Hammie I always feared for. I was afraid he might be the first one of us to die. It seemed terrible that there should have to be a first.

Malbone was simply furnished, but we had plenty of books and pictures, Mother's share of her family things. She was very fond of steel engravings, and had a number by Raphael Morghen. I never cared for engravings myself, they seem so mechanical, nor did I like the copies in oil of the Old Masters. To me these darkened cracked pictures of Holy Families, Saints, and Martyrs have always been depressing, and they made Hammie simply hate the Old Masters.

It had been the custom in the South for young married couples to make the Grand Tour of Europe, and bring back copies of the famous paintings, and almost every Southern family imagined that it possessed a genuine Old Master. Ours was a crucifixion by Paul Veronese. Years afterwards I took it to London to be examined, when it was found to be a good painting, but by an unknown artist of the Bolognese School. I would be glad to give it to anyone who wanted it.

The picture that I loved most at Malbone as a child, was a chromo, which Father had bought in Cartersville. It was the picture of a rosy-checked little baby boy, who had fallen asleep in his high chair, while the cat was lapping his porridge.

The first thing that Mother and Father did after moving into Malbone was to give a ball. We had neighbors in the country surrounding Carters-ville, though we saw very little of them as the distances were so great. They all managed to come to the ball however, and it was most exciting for us. I was up in Aunt Kate's room, which was used as a dressing room, and it was like a vision when Clara and Eloise Stovall came in, took off their cloaks, and stood before the mirror. Clara was one of the loveliest girls that ever was. She was a blonde, with the most perfect features, while Eloise was a brunette with glorious eyes. Clara wore a white tarlatan skirt, with a pale blue bodice, low necked and short sleeved. Eloise's skirt was cream color, and her bodice old gold velvet. Never but once had I seen anything lovelier.

I went downstairs to look on in the drawing room where they were dancing, and saw poor Miss Atterway, in a simple white dress, high necked and long sleeved, with a rose in her dark hair, leaning against the piano, and looking as if she would sink through the floor, as no one spoke to her. After we came to Malbone, she spent one week with us, and the next at Etowah Cliffs. Aunt Sarah, out of kindness, had insisted on her coming downstairs, and her suffering must have been intense. The grown people had too much in their hands to think of her, and she evidently was not known by the elite of Cartersville. I might at least have crossed over and talked to her, but I did not think of it, and she soon disappeared and slipped back to her room upstairs. I can imagine her despair, as she heard the voices of the gay revellers below, and felt her utter loneliness.

The guests danced in the drawing room and hall, someone playing for them on the square rosewood piano. It was there that I saw George Aubrey for the first time, and I remember how high he held his head, and how haughty he looked, as he escorted a young lady into the dining room, with a rosebud in the corner of his mouth. The refreshments were substantial in those days, and included roasted turkey and baked ham, as well as salads and sweets. As far as I know there was nothing to drink (perhaps the men had something on the side), but in spite of this the whole affair was a great success, but for one little broken heart, so soon to sink into the deep shadow, from which it never emerged.

I do not doubt that Mother had a bad headache after it all was over. Grown people had terrible headaches in those days, caused by malaria, I suppose, and Mother had them periodically. They always lasted three days. On the first the headache would be coming on; on its second day it reached the greatest intensity; and on the third it gradually died away. It always annoyed me when anyone was sick, and I never went near Mother when she had a headache. My little sisters, on the contrary, and Katie especial did everything in the world they could for her. It was not until I took lessons in home nursing after I was grown, that I really liked to wait on the sick, which makes me realize that we only enjoy doing a thing when we know how to do it.

It served me quite right that, shortly after going to Malbone to live, I began to have chills and had them every summer until I went to Sewanee in 1877. Hammie and Johnnie had them also. We were "chilling," as the Crackers say. Why, I cannot imagine, as I never remember seeing a mosquito at Malbone, and the upcountry is unusually healthy. For several summers we three lived on quinine. Hammie and I took it in coffee and disliked coffee ever after. Johnnie took it in jam and became eventually a coffee fiend. When we complained of its bitterness, Aunt Kate said, "When I was a child, I used to have to take a large tumbler of quinine bark in water," and we wondered how she survived. At that time I had not acquired a faculty that I now possess. I can prevent myself from either smelling or tasting. How I do it I cannot say, though I think it is by lifting my palate, and closing the orifice between the nose and mouth.

There cannot be a much more miserable feeling than the coming on of a chill. That crawly languor, as you freeze internally, while your head is burning hot. I remember having so violent a chill once, that I was shaken from head to foot, while my teeth chattered continuously. I could not even notice the giggles of Margie and Bessie, as they brought everything in the way of covering they could find in the linen closet to pile on top on me.

The Negroes said that if you jump in the river when you had a chill, the chill would float off on the water, and in desperation I determined to try it. I went down to the Shoals where the others were bathing, and told no one how I felt. I was having a numb chill at the time, and I jumped into the river and went entirely under. When I came up the chill was gone. I present this remedy to the medical profession for what it may be worth.

The chills came every other day for a time, then we would have a respite for seven days. After this we would perhaps go for three weeks without a return. Whenever we were sick Mother's devotion to us was unbounded, a devotion I little deserved. Between times we felt pretty well, and our lives were as happy as before, and as full of activity.

We girls were all fond of walking, and usually walked every afternoon in the park. Sometimes we went upon the mountain, and once we were lost. I had taken Bessie and Margie to the top of it and, in returning, carried them down the other side by mistake. We made our way over boulders and through thick underbrush until poor little Margie, utterly exhausted, began to cry. I could have cried myself, for I had no idea where we were, and dark was coming on. At last we heard the sound of wagon wheels. We had reached the Middle Ground Road, and a Negro, sitting on the shaft of his wagon, came driving by. He good-naturedly picked us up, and we reached home safely.

Belle told me in later years that she had once walked alone to the top of the mountain when she was a little girl, and it makes me cold to think of it to this day.

The tenants all cut their firewood on the mountain, and a wood road wound halfway up its side, and once Gulie, Bessie, and I had an adventure there. I was walking ahead and, on turning a curve, I saw a long snake scalloping across the road. An all along its back was diamonds. "A rattlesnake!" I cried, though I had never seen one, and Gulie ran up just as its tail whisked in the underbrush. Picking up a stone, she followed it, and then we heard its warning rattle. Not the loud locust whir I had expected, making the air ring, but only a slight vibration, like the rustle of a cricket in dry grass. "Come back" I cried, and Gulie, laughing, came back for more stones. Bessie followed her into the underbrush, while I stood at a distance and implored them to desist. They could not see the snake, but it certainly saw them, as it continued to rattle until it finally drew away.

Being perfectly fearless, Gulie did many courageous things in her life, one, I think, especially so. The men of the family were away from home one day, when she heard the awful sound of horses screaming in the lot. Running down, she found that Frank, the stallion, had broken from his stall, and attacked a younger stallion, which had just been brought to the place. The maddened animals were dashing around the barn in the centre of the lot, Frank tearing strips of flesh with his teeth from the back of the younger horse, which was screaming in pain. One or two terrified tenants were hovering outside, not daring to enter the lot. Without a moment's hesitation, Gulie opened the gate, ran across to the barn, and stood in the door of Frank's stall. As the frantic stallions tore by, she sprang out, and seizing Frank's halter, dragged him into his stall and secured him.

All of our boys were fine riders. As little boys they rode the horses down to water, and I have seen them riding standing upon their backs. Hammie could not understand why I could not keep on without a saddle, but try it yourself sideways on a bare-backed horse.

With saddles it was a different thing, and I enjoyed galloping about the place when we could get the horses. I never was an expert rider, and Gulie was the only real horsewoman among us. She loved and understood horses, and when she went to England years afterward, enjoyed hunting more than anything else.

By this time Gulie and Nellie Gordon had given up leading our plays and were devoting themselves to the care of their little sisters. Ethel Stiles and Mabel Gordon were the same age, and were both lovely children. Ethel had golden brown curling hair, and in her large eyes there were golden lights, and Mable's little face was like a delicately cut cameo. They were both of them sweet and gentle and enjoyed the lavish petting and meticulous care of their eldest sisters. I have never seen such a maternal passion as Nellie's at that age. She took entire charge of

Mabel, pared for her, petted and disciplined her, and was interested in nothing else. I would have predicted at that time, that Nellie Gordon would become an absolutely perfect mother.

At Malbone we had a great many visitors who kept coming and going during the summer. They often brought us presents, and when it proved to be candy, there was the greatest excitement. There would be a fierce cry of "*Pile it,*" as we gathered around the marble-topped center table in the hall, and I would empty the box and divide the candy into seven piles. These I would number to myself and, beginning with the youngest, each would choose a number and rush off with his or her treasure.

I think it was shortly after we went to Malbone that the narrow gauge railroad was built from Cartersville to Van Wert. It was quite exciting hearing the whistle of the train across the river and seeing the plume of white smoke curling back over the trees. Not that it did us much good. There was no bridge across the river nearer than Euharlie, three miles away, so it was a five-mile drive to Stilesboro on the other side, where we could take the Van Wert train.

The railroad crossed the Etowah River near nearer Cartersville on a wooden bridge, and here Johnnie had a great adventure. Cousin Robert Elliott, who at this time had a church in Atlanta, came up to Rockmart on some church business. As a treat he took his son Stephen, Harry Elliott, who was staying with us, and Johnnie with him. They road across the river to Shellman's in the morning to take the Van Wert train, but on their return, decided to go on to Cartersville and drive back to Malbone. The train was a mixed freight and passenger and was one car's length longer than the wooden bridge across the river. Just before the engine touched the farther bank, the bridge collapsed from end to end, and only the passenger remained on the bank. The baggage car hung suspended over the water, and the locomotive and tender settled down into the river. The water rose in the cab, but neither the engineer or fireman were drowned, and the conductor and the two clerks in the baggage car were only jarred. Johnnie was looking out of the window at the time so did not spring up as the others did when the bridge fell. They were all thrown down, but not hurt seriously, and were soon out of the train. Cousin Robert gathered all the survivors together, and they knelt on the riverbank, while he gave thanks to God for their preservation, and all of them felt that a miracle had happened owing to the presence of such a holy man. The wooden bridge was replaced by a fine iron one, which is doing duty to this day.

It was about this time that great flocks of wild pigeons began flying through the country at certain seasons. I remember seeing dark clouds of them across the river, where they settled for the night in a little patch of woods. They came in such numbers that the limbs of the trees broken beneath their weight, and everywhere parties of men and boys went out to slaughter them. It was not long before they were exterminated, and we never saw them again.

Hammie and Johnnie were devoted to shooting and used for this purpose long muzzle-loading shotguns. They would melt lead on shovels held over the fire and pour it into the molds to make bullets, and I remember how they rammed wads of paper down the barrels of their guns.

It was remarkable that in all these years they had only two accidents. Johnnie's gun went off once in the lower hall at Malbone, scorching off his brows and lashes, as the load shot up through the ceiling. It gave him a good fright, but as his brows and lashes came out very dark and thick afterwards, no damage was done. Hammie's accident was more serious, and occurred once when he was out in the field shooting doves. He shot out the palm of his left hand and suffered tortures from the powder burns, though Mother and Aunt Kate did everything they could to relieve him. As we were so far from town and doctors, we had a medicine closet in which everything for first aid was kept.

Hammie thought I ought to learn to shoot and offered to teach me, holding the gun barrel on his shoulder, while I sighted it and pulled the trigger. I tried it once. A fluffy little bird was perched on a limb at a little distance, and when the sight was directly on it, I pulled the trigger. There was a spray of feathers and the little bird flew away, I hoped not mortally wounded. It was enough for me, and I have never shot at anything since.

I had the same experience with fishing. I went fishing for the first time on the Gulf Coast in a back bay. I threw in my line, and, with beginner luck, pulled out, one after another, thirteen croakers. They lay on the wharf and sobbed their lives out, and nothing would ever induce me to go fishing again.

There is no denying the fact that I am not sport. And what is more, I have never wanted to be one.

I think our leaving Etowah Cliffs was a good thing for more than one reason. Before we left Uncle Henry had branched out in business, and was now running an iron-ore furnace, many miles beyond Cartersville. It was a charcoal furnace, and the pig iron had to be hauled to town over rough mountain roads. Uncle Robert Couper had recently come to the up-country for his health, and Uncle Henry had given him a position at the furnace. Without experience or sufficient capitol, Uncle Henry was doom-ed to failure, and with increasing financial worries, life was becoming very hard for him.

In the war Uncle Henry had been a captain in his father's regiment. He was wounded, came home to recuperate, and could hardly wait to get well before he was at the front again. Then he was wounded fearfully, and came near dying, and again he went back to fight. Uncle Henry be-longed to the Viking Age, and he looked like a Viking, tall, broad, pow-erful, and magnificently blonde.

He was, I think, master of the whole countryside, and as a child I was terribly afraid of him. He spent the week up at the furnace, and came home on Saturdays to stay over Sunday, and I remember how my heart sank when I heard the wheels of his buggy flying the mound in front of the house. If I was on the other side of the house, I would rush for our own, and only breathed freely when I reached it.

Not that Uncle Henry was ever cross to one of us. He was on the con-trary very gentle with little children and always deferential and affection-ate to Aunt Kate and Aunt Sarah, who were as devoted to him as they were to Father.

I think however that it was just as well that seven of the Stiles chil-dren were removed from Etowah, for, burdened with financial cares and harassed by countless irritations, it must have been absolutely maddening to Uncle Henry to have such swarms of children about the house.

9

Our Neighbors

W hen we were little children we saw nothing of our neighbors. They were few and far between, and we did not realize that anyone else lived in the upcountry. We lived in a world of our own, and were all sufficient to ourselves.

As the Charlestonians looked down on the Savannahians, the Savannahians looked down on the people of Upper Georgia. In 1846, Grandmama Stiles wrote from Etowah Cliffs, "Quantities of common people have moved here this year, and I am afraid all the places will be sold to South Carolina people who are not even genteel."

As a matter of fact many of the people of North Georgia had quite as good an ancestry as the people on the coast, but, living in a simpler way and among plainer people, their culture did not keep pace with that of the low country. The advantage that the coast people had was that they were more in touch with the world. Many of them went north every summer to Newport or Saratoga. Their daughters were educated at Madame Tonio's in New York, their sons at Yale or Heidelberg. Lecturers like Thackery and singers like Jenny Lind came to the Southern cities, and the best troupes of the day were seen in their theatres.

The people of the upcountry had none of these advantages. Most of them were in modest circumstances, and many of them after the war had as little as ourselves, so there was little or no entertaining. Distances were great in those days of fearful roads, and, as old Mrs. Shelman used to say, "The river is such a barrier." Father and Uncle Henry were friendly with the entire county, but the ladies of the family saw little of their neighbors, and, in my childhood I only remember coming in contact with them on two occasions.

I was taken over to Stilesboro one night to an entertainment given in the schoolhouse there. Stilesboro was an embryo town across the river, which had been named after Grandfather. To this day it is an embryo town, not much more than the station, a store, post office, and a church along the railroad track. The narrow gauge line of the Van Wert Road was succeeded by the broad gauge of the East and West; it took so long a time to build the latter, that it was once described by a witty country boy as "Two streaks of rust and a right-of-way."

The Stilesboro schoolhouse stood at the crossroads a little distance from town, and stands there yet. All that I remember of the entertainment was a tableau representing *Morning, Noon, and Night*. Miss Cleo Shelman was Morning. She was young and fresh with a very white skin and very red hair, and she wore a dress of blue tarlatan. Noon was represented by a brunette who wore yellow tarlatan. And then night! It was the first time I had ever seen Miss Josie Martin, who was destined to become the belle of the county. She was about sixteen, small and graceful, with dark waving hair, finely cut features and marvelous eyes. She wore a spangled black tarlaton with a crescent moon in her hair, and I have never forgotten her starry loveliness.

Tarlaton must have been the only material we could afford in those days, and most party dresses were made of it. When Meta Habersham "came out" in Savannah, she even wore tarlatan to the Germans, and looked just as stunning, as if she had been clad in real silk lace.

The other occasion on which I met our neighbors was when a large community picnic was given on the rocky hillside just across the river from our shoals. The only person who impressed me was a young girl who was so ugly that she sat apart on the rocks looking out over the river. During the afternoon Father took me across the river in a boat and jumped out above the Shoals. He must have done this to startle the picnickers, as our boys used to do later on, when we took visitors out in the flat on moonlight nights, and they fell overboard for their benefit.

The place next to Malbone on the road to Cartersville belonged to the Sproulls, and was called Valley View. Mrs. Sproull had been a Miss Marshall of South Carolina, a descendant of Chief Justice Marshall's family, and had come as a bride to Georgia before the war. The young couple had driven over, and Mrs. Sproull had brought a quantity of box cuttings from her old home to plant in her new. The house they built, which was separated from the public road by a large park, was quite striking looking with tall white columns reaching to the roof in front, and from the wide piazza there was an extended view of the valley and the mountains beyond.

The box cuttings were planted in a formal garden in front of the house. A broad path between high box hedges lead from the front steps to the front gate. On one occasion were geometrical flower beds, on the other a fascinating maze. The garden is there today, though the bush box is now so high it is hard to make your way through the narrowed paths, and the tree box, on either side of the front piazza finally grew as high as the roof of the house. There were two daughters and two sons in the Sproull family, and the former became Mrs. Mitchell of Nashville, Tennessee, and Mrs. Fouche of Rome, Georgia. The old place is still in the family and is now owned by the widow of Sproull Fouche, who was for several years an attache of our Legation in Rumania.

The Rowlands lived directly across the river from the Sproulls. They had been among the earliest settlers in the country, Major Rowland having been the owner of Rowland Springs, which was above Cartersville. Mineral springs were very fine and quite popular before the war.

Across from Malbone, on the other side of the river was the Shellman home, Etowah Heights. It stood on a rise of land and was the most imposing house in the whole neighborhood. Its tall white columns, which supported the roof pediment, being visible for a great distance.

The house was, I think, unfinished when the war began, and was probably not occupied by the family when Sherman's army crossed the Etowah just below it. Sherman himself was not with the wing that came through Etowah Cliffs. Its commanders being Hooker and Schofield, but it is possible that he was with the corps that crossed the Etowah at Big Spring farther down the river, as he wrote from Kingston that morning, "I expect to ride across the Rubicon to-day." In that case he might have followed the river to Raccoon Creek and joined the wing that crossed below the Shellmans' house. But it is more probable that, on account of telegraphic facilities, he went with the main part of his army, which followed the railroad down to Kennesaw Mountain.

Mrs. Shellman, who had been Cecelia Stovall of Augusta, Georgia, had known Sherman personally at West Point, where she had been a great belle as a girl. There were three sons and three daughters in the

Shellman family, with whom we were very friendly after we were grown. Etowah Heights is now no more, the fine old house having been burned down to the ground in the nineties.

A few miles south of Etowah Heights was Clarendon, the home of Miss Josie Martin, who was a cousin of the Shellmans. Miss Josie was very well off, and not very pretty but very fascinating, and for years she was the reining belle of the county. There must have been an unusual amount of beauty in Miss Josie's family, for they were always having lovely visitors at Clarendon. I recall particularly the handsome Cassian sisters from Augusta, and that marvelous Odalisque, Sophie Halinquest, from Montgomery.

When Henry grew up, he and his visitors, Willie Gordon of Huntsville and little Willie Owens of Savannah, all but lived at Clarendon, wading their horses across the river above our place. The one attention a young man could show a girl in the upcountry in our day was to take her to drive, and this Henry did frequently. Whether the city belles enjoyed it I do not know, as they were occasionally spilled out, but, at least, it must have been exciting.

Henry was as fine a driver as his father, but he always seemed to have wild horses to drive. I have driven into Cartersville with him, with one of the pair of horses kicking viciously at intervals. The one on my side. One afternoon he took Marie Huger, Percy Gordon, and myself out to drive. Percy had to jump out to open the gates, and, as there was no one holding the horses in, he had to run after us and climb in over the back of the buggy. The drive ended in an overturn in a ditch on Creswell Hill, but none of us were hurt, and none of us seemed to mind it.

The only other large place on the road to Cartersville on our side of the river was Walnut Grove, the home of General P. M. B. Young, who was a great friend of Father's and Uncle Henry's. He had been the youngest general in the Confederate army and was said to be the handsomest. Tall, stout and striking-looking, dark and distinguished, his features were on the order of Napoleon III. His manners were courtly, and I am sure he had the kindest of hearts. As a matter of fact he represented his district in Congress for many years after the war, and no one was more surprised than himself when he was finally ousted by a poor and obscure school teacher and Baptist minister named Felton. This miracle could never have occurred but for the fact that Felton's campaign was conducted by his wife, a very clever and determined woman, who lived to be herself the first female senator of the United States.

General Young was afterwards sent as consul to Russia, and, under Cleveland, became minister to Guatemala, so he did not lose out altogether.

The General was a great beau in his day, and went every summer to the Old Sweet Springs of Virginia. There he became engaged to Mattie Ould, the beauty and wit of Richmond, and we girls enjoyed a story that was told of them. Someone came into the room where they were sitting once and found Mattie Ould with her head on General Young's shoulder. Glancing up at the embarrassed intruder, Mattie Ould said coolly, "Is it the first time you ever saw an Ould head on Young shoulders?"

Why Mattie Ould has never been written up I cannot imagine, for she was absolutely brilliant as well as very handsome and fascinating. For some reason she did not marry General Young, and, in the end, made a very poor match, and died not long afterward.

Walnut Grove is a comfortable square brick house set back from the main road in a grove of trees, and the lands behind it border Pettis Creek. Between this place and Cartersville, on one side of the Tumlins' farms, the five Indian mounds of De Soto's day still stand on the banks of the Etowah, surrounded by the deep ditch, which the Indians used not only for protection but as a fishery. There are one large and four smaller mounds, and before they were excavated, they were very picturesque, the smaller ones being garlanded with Virginia creeper. The summit of the largest one, which is still reached by the inclined road, has been used for years as a corn field, and tall trees are growing on its sides. Fragments of pottery and arrowheads have been found in profusion in the surrounding fields, and when the mounds were opened, in addition to the seated skeletons, decorated with their bead and shell ornaments and enclosed in matting, there were found a metal embossed plaque and a carved stone idol, evidently of Aztec origin.

The idol was sent down to the Atlanta Exposition, and I saw it there, with a sheet of paper pinned beneath it, on which was scrawled. "Idle from the Tumlin Mounds." Someone had drawn a line through the first word, and written "Idol" above it, but had not taken the trouble to use another sheet of paper.

Far be it from me to jeer at poor spelling, however. I realize that these words may reach the eyes of Mr. Edward Weeks of *The Atlantic Monthly*. As a family we have nothing to boast of in that line, and I have a brother and sister who have a positive genius of misspelling. We should have been good spellers, for Mother was a fine one. When she was in doubt as to how a word should be spelled, she wrote it, and could tell at a glance whether it was right or wrong. A delightful friend of ours, Mr. Henry Underwood had a simpler method. "If I'm not sure whether there should be an *e* or an *i* on a word," he said, "I write an *e* and *dot it*."

Living in Cartersville were one or two families from South Carolina, the Calhouns and Youngs among them, and later on the Izard Heywards bought the old Baxter place on the Middle Ground Road nearby.

The Aubreys lived twelve miles beyond Cartersville and must have come to Bartow County about the time we moved to Malbone, for George Aubrey was at our ball. Their grandfather Forsyth has been one of Georgia's most distinguished men, having been congressman, senator, secretary of state, and ambassador to Spain, as well as governor of his own state. The beautiful park in Savannah was named after him, and the golden-belled flowering shrub that blossoms so early in the spring, was named for him—Forsythia.

There were four sons and a younger daughter named Katie, in the Aubrey family. They were all intellectual and ambitious. In spite of limited means, the three oldest sons became lawyers; Llewellyn, the third, educated himself entirely at home.

Between Cartersville and the Aubreys farm was the home of Colonel Charles H. Smith, our Georgia humorist, who was known as Bill Arp. His oldest daughter Hattie, who was very pretty, married George Aubrey. The second daughter, Marianne, was unusually talented and interesting, and when we grew older, we saw a great deal of her younger sister Stella, of Katie Aubrey, and herself.

On the other side of Etowah Cliffs and Summerland, the public road, going north and west, crossed the Etowah on a high iron bridge, which had been destroyed during the war. A little farther on, the road entered the town of Euharlie, through an old roofed bridge over a stream. This stream formerly turned the wheel of an old mill, now abandoned, but still was picturesque. The road forms the main street of the village, and on it there are a general store, two churches, a schoolhouse on a hill, and a number of cottages, gray with age, and half buried in vine and flowers. This road, which is now one leg of the Dixie Highway, goes on up to Rome, which is eighteen miles away.

Mr. Nathan Sayre, whom I remember as a small, dried-up, gentlemanly beau, lived on this road, and across the river from his place was the Lyons family at Fontenelle. I remember hearing the grown people talking about the Lyons runaway match. Mrs. Lyons was an heiress of the Tumlin family and looked like a lovely bisque doll. Mr. Tom Lyons was a dashing, handsome brunette. He had known Father and Uncle Henry during the war, and it was probably on their account that he came afterwards to live in Bartow County. One night Mr. Lyons drove out to the Tumlin place, below Cartersville, assisted the pretty girl out of the window, drove away, and married her secretly in the properly romantic style.

I never remember going to Fontenelle but once, and then I was struck with the wonderful wax flowers which I saw in the drawing room under a glass dome. The fuchsias seemed to me absolutely perfect.

In our early years, the old intimate friends of our family in the up-country were the George Warings. They came from the coast, so our caste was the same, and they had been friends of our family in Savannah before the war. Mrs. Warings had been a Miss Howard, and Spring Bank, the old Howard place, was just outside Kingston, twelve miles to the north of us. The Western and Atlantic Railway ran along of the place, which was entirely surrounded by a low stone wall, which seemed to me to express real wealth. The Howard House stood on a terrace, and just below it a splendid spring gushed beneath a wall of rock, pouring its sparkling icy waters into a stream that meandered all over the place, forming picturesque pools here and there, surrounded by cattails and water plants.

The old wooden house, one and a half stories high, was gray with age, but very comfortable and homelike, and in this the four Howard sisters, who were spinsters, lived. Along side of it Mr. Waring had built a house of his own, were Mrs. Waring, himself, and their five children lived, and it was in their home that we always stayed. The first night I ever slept there, I was startled by the booming of bullfrogs in the pond nearest the house, and thought it was the bellowing of bulls.

Mr. Waring had a cement plant across the railroad, which was doing well at that time so they were comfortably off. The five Waring children were Fred, who was my age, Jean, Mai, Nellie, and George. Between Frank and Hammie, Jean and Bessie, and Mai and myself, lifelong friendships were formed.

I have never known anything to equal the interest Mr. and Mrs. Waring took in their children's lives. They did everything they could think of to make them happy, and we were frequently invited up to Spring Bank, where they spared no pains to make us have a delightful time.

As we grew older they often had dances for us, and I remember a masque ball to which we once took all of our visitors. The Warings always had an abundant table, so the feast following the dance was notable. The next morning all of the boys took a plunge in the pool before breakfast. The first visitors who jumped into the icy water felt as if he had been cut in half at the waistline. He said nothing and let all the others come in, each keeping mum in turn, until the last one made the plunge, and, with the war whoop of an Indian, dashed for shore.

Barnsley's Gardens was about five miles beyond the Warings, but it was not until I read *St. Elmo* that I was ever interested in that place. It was suppose to be the scene of this melodramatic novel, so evidently inspired by *Jane Eyre*.

Ole Mr. Barnsley, an Englishman, had bought the land there before the war and made a fortune from the mines on the place. He planned a great English estate with a handsome house and elaborate gardens on a high plateau, and substantial brick outhouses were erected on the hillside back of it, at the foot of which was a fine spring. The garden was laid out in a formal pattern, with box bordering the beds, and in the centre was a white marble fountain. Trees were imported from abroad and the Orient, some of which are still sweeping the terrace, but the three-storied brick mansion, with a cupola, was never completed, for the war put an end to his plans.

Mr. Barnsley's only daughter, Mrs. Baltzelle, had married in New Orleans and was a widow with one daughter when we knew them. They were living in the two one-storied wings at the back of the unfinished house. These wings were very comfortable, having large high-ceiled rooms, and were furnished at that time with wonderful old French furniture, which had been brought up from New Orleans. Mrs. Baltzelle's daughter Addie was about Bessie and Jean Waring's age, and we looked up on her as an heiress. On account of her wealth, she always kept herself slightly aloof, though she did come down to visit the Warings now and then.

A few years ago we drove up once more to Barnsley's Gardens. The road that used to seem so interminable was comparatively short by automobile, and the place seemed to be deserted when we reached it. The great house was a ghostly ruin. Roof and floors had fallen in, and tall trees were growing with the walls. The marble fountain was shattered, and the bow borders had grown so dense it was impossible to make one's way through the garden paths.

Someone opened a door in one of the wings, and when I addressed the sad, broken, middle-aged woman as Addie, she looked at me with no light in her eyes, and said, "I did not know anybody in the world remembered Addie Baltzelle."

All the magnificent furniture had been sold to the owner of an estate on Long Island, and only two beautifully carved sofas remained in the large room which served as bedroom and living room combined.

On the way up to the Warings was a deep cave, from which salt petre had been dug during the war for making gunpowder. It was known as Salt Petre's Cave, and we often had picnics there, stumbling and sliding down the rocky slopes, out of the sunlight into the darkness below. And then by the light of the pine torches, wandering through an endless succession of vaulted rooms, with stalactites dripping above like icicles. The walls were cold and damp to the touch and sometimes a rush of bats, disturbed by the light, would flitter past. On our return, clambering up the slope to the entrance, it grew warmer and warmer, until we reached the blaze of sunshine above, when the heat seemed almost overpowering.

Then we would drive to Big Spring nearby—where part of Sherman's army had crossed the Etowah—and eat our lunch and then drive home at dusk. Sometimes we went in wagons filled with straw, and in spite of the hideous discomfort of sitting on your own or someone else's feet, we thought it lots of fun, and always as we drove we sang.

Singing was our favorite diversion, and whenever we had company we gathered around the piano at night and sang. Old fashioned songs such as "Juanita," "Annabelle Lee," and "My Bonnie Lies over the Ocean," and all of the new ones as they came out. All girls were taught music in those days. An awful waste of money and time. I was even taught to sing, and later on achieved the role of "Josephine" in *Pinafore.* This performance took place in Brunswick, and Uncle Charlie always said it was the epochal date in the history of the town, everything being classified since then as "Before or After *Pinafore*." I do know that the setting could not have been improved on, for the captains of the ships then in the harbor, brought up the ships carpenters and built the deck of the good ship *Pinafore* for us.

Not near neighbors in the upcountry, but still the dearest of friends, the Hugers had moved to North Georgia, and were at this time living in Greensborough, and one summer Aunt Kate took me to visit them.

Greensborough was a small town and I remember little of it beyond the Huger's house, which was a plain wooden one, with a large side yard on the main street. Just opposite was the fine house of the place, where the Poulains, the most important family in Greensborough, lived.

Having left the plantation, Mrs. Huger was here with her three daughters and youngest son, John Welles. He had, I remember, a spring board in the yard, and his friends and himself would spring from this, turn one and sometimes two somersaults in the air, and land on their feet. Hagee and I watched them sometimes, but we were too much absorbed in our own affairs to be interested in boys. Our only outside acquaintance was Hallie Poulain, a very handsome girl, who was however entirely too sophisticated to take much interest in two such crude little country girls as Hagee and myself.

The Joseph Huger family was a very unusual one, all of its members being talented and interesting. They were of the blood royal of South Carolina, as were attested by the names in the family, Middleton, Kinloch, Prioleau, and Pinckney being among them. Most of the six sons had magnificent physiques, and they always looked to me as though they owned the earth. Arthur, the oldest, was the most gifted, being very original and full of puns and quips. He signed himself, on the title page of a book of poems he published, "A Mug, Son of a Jug," as his initials were A. M. Huger, and his father's J. A. Huger. Arthur Huger loved the woods and ended by becoming a hermit like Uncle Aleck, living for years alone in the mountains of North Carolina. "A Wood Rat," he called himself.

The oldest daughter, Lucy, had married a son of the old Bishop, Dr. John B. Elliott, who was then professor of Chemistry at Sewanee. Katie, the second daughter, who had been named after Aunt Kate, was one of the most talented people I have ever known. In fact, she had too many talents to make the most of any of them. She painted beautifully, landscapes especially. She was very musical, played and had naturally a lovely voice. She wrote poetry gracefully and easily, was very original and a most interesting talker. She told me once that all people reminded her of something else in nature. That a tall, fair young woman in Savannah looked to her like a lily, and that Aunt Rebecca looked like a bird, and she herself like a cat.

Katie was full of life and energy, and kept things stirring wherever she was. One summer when she came to Malbone she got up a most entertaining shadowgraph for us to act. The play took place silhouetted behind a suspended sheet, and she cut out the most amusing profiles for us to wear as the characters. As we acted the pantomime she read aloud the absurd poem describing the play. It was during this same visit that she painted the floors of our hall, drawing and dining rooms to represent inlaid wood. There was nothing that Katie Huger could not do. I remember a stunning dress that she made for herself out of cream-colored homespun, piped with turkey red, which was quite as effective as anything a Worth could have created.

When Katie Huger grew up, one of her Charleston uncles, who was a man of means, lent her one thousand dollars to go to Europe to study art, and she stayed for years in London, Paris, and Italy. She made the mistake of trying to make money to repay her uncle while she was studying. She succeeded, but it was at the price of her health as well as that of her art, for she never reached the heights to which her great talent entitled her, and she died comparatively young.

Marie, the second sister, was also artistic, and drew and painted well, but her greatest gift was for music. She not only played with a soft and lovely touch, but she composed music, and when later on she came to Malbone as our governess, she often sat at the piano in the twilight and improvised. Marie had none of Katie's self-confidence and could never have gone out in to the world alone. She was of the clinging kind, and craved above everything love and sympathy.

Hagee was the youngest, and she and I were about the same age. Her full name was Harriet Harry Huger, so she had the dashing initials H. H. H. She was very high spirited, very cheerful, and always in for everything. She too played well on the piano, and was fond of writing poetry. She and I had always been friends, and simple as the life was in Greensborough, we both enjoyed it thoroughly.

Mrs. Huger was herself very clever, perhaps cleverer than any of her children. She was inclined to be sarcastic, and the stupidity of most people in the world amused her exceedingly. At heart she was one of the kindest, most generous and charitable people I have ever known, and this was, I am sure, the bond between Aunt Kate and herself.

The Hugers had very little to live on at this time, but you would never have known it, they were all so buoyantly light-hearted and full of life. Someone said of them once, "The Hugers can live without necessities, but they can not live without luxuries." At any rate they had the luxury of culture, of books and music and art, and were a most delightful and interesting family.

Other Days

1a. Mackay House on Broughton Street, Savannah, back view

1b. Andrew Low House on Abercorn Street, Savannah

REBEL WOMEN LEAVING SAVANNAH.—[Sketched by Theodore R. Davis.]

2a. Women of Savannah leaving the city because of Sherman's advance

2b. Joseph E. Johnson and
Robert E. Lee in Savannah, 1870

2c. Andrew Low of Savannah, 1866

3a. William Henry Stiles, Sr.,
portrait as U.S. minister to Austria, 1849

3b. Elizabeth Anne Mackay,
wife of William Henry Stiles, Sr., 1849

Etowah Cliffs, at Stilesboro, is one of the Etowah River mansions Sherman spared on his march to the sea, when he learned that a sweetheart of his West Point days lived in this vicinity.

4a. Photograph of Etowah Cliffs, Bartow County,
home of the William Henry Stiles, Jr., family

4b. Drawing of Etowah Cliffs by Caroline Couper Stiles Lovell

5a. William Henry Stiles, Jr. (Uncle Henry), 1872

5b. Eliza C. Stiles, wife of Henry Stiles, Jr.
(Aunt Eliza), 1881

6. Stiles and Gordon family members on rocks in front of Etowah cliffs, 1886. *(Lf. to rt.)* Elizabeth Chadwick Stiles (Mrs. W. H. III), Jessie Low, Mabel Gordon, Johnnie Stiles, Katie Stiles, W. H. Stiles IV, Eliza C. Stiles, Mary Low, Belle Stiles, Guilie Stiles, Marge Stiles, and Mary C. Stiles.

7a. Malbone House, Bartow County, home of the Robert Mackay Stiles family

7b. Robert Mackay Stiles, Caroline's father,
military school portrait in Marietta, 1855

8a. William Gordon Stiles
(Gordon) in Sewanee uniform, late 1870s

8b. William Henry Stiles III (Henry)
and Gulielma Stiles (Gulie), late 1870s

9a. James Hamilton Couper Stiles
(Hammie), Caroline's brother

9b. Elizabeth Mackay Stiles
(Bessie), Caroline's sister

10a. Margie Stiles, a miniature
by Caroline Couper Stiles Lovell

10b. Bishop Stephen Elliott

11. Drawing of Katie Low, Jessie Low Graham, Hugh Graham,
by Caroline Lovell

12. Mary Low with her step-daughters Amy and Hatie, Brighton, England, 1861

13a. Ethel Gordon Stiles, 1888

13b. Ethel Gordon Stiles
by Margie Stiles, 1891

14a. Eleanor (Nellie), Juliette (Daisy), and William (Willie) Gordon, early 1870s

14b. Katie Low

15a. Mary Low

15b. Jessie Low

16. Caroline and Tod Lovell, 1887

10

In The Shadow

 essie, Margie, and myself spent the winter and spring of 1874 in Savannah with Aunt Kate and Aunt Sarah. The boys and the two little girls had stayed up at Malbone with our father and mother.

I was now going to Oglethorpe Academy, having finished at the Massie School. If I did any studying I do not remember it, and my time seemed to be spent drawing in the autograph albums of my friends, and writing what I thought was poetry. I was even asked to recite a poem of my own on some occasion when the public was invited.

Aunt Rebecca had come up from Brunswick to pay us a visit, and I remember she had the little company room next to Aunt Kate's. Two days after my twelfth birthday on May 7th, a telegram was received saying that my father had been killed in a runaway accident. Aunt Rebecca told me when I came home from school, and I threw myself on the floor beside her chair, buried my face in her lap, and wept passionately. I felt that I could not stand so frightful a tragedy.

We packed up immediately and went to Malbone. I did not see Mother when we entered the house, but Hammie and Johnnie were in the hall and I was left with them. We felt very self-conscious and unnatural, and had nothing to say to each other. I thought perhaps Father would be in the drawing room, but the door was open and the room was empty. Nothing was said about his funeral, but I found out afterwards that he had already been buried in the little graveyard at The Cliffs by the side of his mother.

Father had left Cartersville late in the afternoon of the 8th, driving two spirited black horses. In the single buggy with him was Mr. Tinsley, the principle renter on Uncle Henry's place. They had just left a group of congenial friends, and Father, in high spirits, had waved farewell, touched up the horses, and dashed up Main Street. Turning abruptly into the country road as they left town, a front wheel struck a large rock, the buggy was overturned, and Father and Mr. Tinsley were thrown out, Father's head striking the curbing as he fell.

He was carried into the Wallaces' house nearby, unconscious, and Uncle Robert, who happened to be in town, was notified. As soon as possible he drove out to Malbone for Mother, and she took that long drive back to Cartersville after dark.

All night long she sat beside the one she cared for most on earth and watched him dying. He never regained consciousness, and before morning he died of concussion of the brain. He was thirty-eight years old.

The Cartersville Grange, of which he was a member, published the following tribute of respect:

> The entire community is filled with sadness and sorrow. One of the most useful, most honored and best beloved of our number has been suddenly stricken down by the remorseless hand of death in his manly prime, while in the enjoyment of vigorous health, full of high hopes, manly purpose and noblest promise. Few men had so large a circle of warmly attached friends, and no man better deserved them.
>
> A large concourse of his neighbors followed his remains to their final resting place, beneath a magnolia on the banks of the Etowah, its soft and solemn flow lending sweet and mournful cadence to the beautiful burial service. And as they gazed upon the features whose beauty as of chiseled marble, the pallor of death could not mask, and that manly frame habited in his dragoon uniform, tears stood in the eyes of bearded men, and they felt that there was not left behind a braver, a truer, or a noble man to die.

These friends of Father's testified that "his charities to the destitute and deserving were only limited by his means," so the training of Aunt Kate and Aunt Sarah had not been in vain. It was however a deep sorrow to both of them that their beloved nephew had never joined the church.

A deathbed repentance would have been the greatest comfort to them, and Great-Uncle Joseph Stiles, the noted divine, wrote Mother a long letter of consolation, in which he said that, while Father was apparently unconscious, his mind might have been in communication with God.

To be convinced of his salvation all that I would want to know was that he had been kind and generous, and loved by everyone.

Since I have been grown I realize that the greatest sorrow on earth must be the loss of a beloved husband or wife, and I agree with one who said, "How good it would be had the law of our being ordained that to happily married couples death should be simultaneous."

Although the light had gone out of Mother's life, she bore this almost fatal blow with silent fortitude. I have never known anyone who had such perfect faith in God, and it sustained her throughout her life. From that time on she devoted herself to her children, and that they were a comfort and pleasure to her was proved, when death came to her at fifty-seven, and she did not want to leave them. I suppose everyone who has been blessed with a good mother thinks that she is the best mother on earth. Well, if our mother was not the best, there never was a better one.

To Aunt Kate and Aunt Sarah, Father's death was almost as great a blow as it was to Mother, and Aunt Sarah did not long survive it.

I was sitting on the front steps one day reading, when Aunt Sarah came out and said, "Oh, Caroline, is not the whole house changed?" And I had to think what it was that she meant!

My godmother, Miss Louisa Nightengale, wrote me a beautiful letter of sympathy from Brunswick. She was deeply religious, and I am sure that her letter would have been comforting to an older and more spiritual person, but it was very long, and *it tired me*. I seemed to have no feeling at all about Father's death, after that first outburst of passionate grief.

It may have been at this time that Aunt Sarah suggested my taking for my guide every day, a sentence from the thirteenth chapter of First Corinthians. "Charity suffereth long and is kind." "Charity seeketh not her own." "Is not easily provoked," and so on. It was an inspiration as well as a check to one so self-absorbed, so willful and passionate as myself, and it is a plan that has helped me all of my life, though I have not confined myself to the chapter of First Corinthians.

The summer that Father died, a terrible epidemic of diphtheria swept through Bartow County. It spared neither high nor low, and, utterly helpless to conquer it, agonized parents saw their little children strangled by death before their eyes.

Robbie, a dear little boy who was Belle's age, was the first of Aunt Eliza's children to go. A short time before we had celebrated his second birthday, having a party for him on the grass at Etowah. Daisy Gordon had named him The Little Dauphin, and we had seated him in a box bush for a throne, crowned him with vine leaves, and given him a scepter to hold.

He was desperately ill from the first, and, going over to The Cliffs one morning, I was told that he was dead. Rushing home in a passion of grief, I wrote a poem about his death, and the words seemed to come more fluently than in any other I had ever composed. Just as I finished it, someone came from the other house and said that Robbie was still alive. I was horribly mortified, and told no one about the poem, but I held on to it, and felt that it was justified when the dear little boy died before night. Gulie made a cross for his little grave of Queen Anne's lace, the most etherial and lovely funeral design that I have ever seen.

Then in three days Ellen Beirne was smitten. She had been all of her life a quiet sainted child. Whether they told her she was going to die, in the awful way they did at that time, I do not know, but she told her mother that she was perfectly willing to die—at seven!

Our Katie's turn came next. Always a delicate child, she had a dreadful case of diphtheria, and would undoubtedly have died, had not Uncle Henry saved her. He came over every day, and she almost had a convulsion when he entered the room. He would hold her and force an instrument made of tin filings down her throat and drag out the deadly membrane which had formed. He had seen two of his children suffocate, and had realized too late the cause.

Katie's was the last in our family. She recovered, and gradually the awful epidemic subsided. There were few doctors in Cartersville at that time, and it took hours even to reach them, for often, when sent for, they would be miles out in the country on the other side of town. I remember once later on, when it meant life or death, the agony of waiting until the next day, when the doctor came—too late.

The winter after this we all went down to Savannah, and there Hammie had typhoid fever, and was ill for five weeks. When he was well enough he was sent down to Brunswick to recuperate, and Uncle Aleck, who was his godfather, had him out to his hermitage and saw that he had some fine shooting, which he liked more than anything else.

Aunt Sarah had been failing ever since Father's death, and, when the next winter came, Aunt Kate and herself went down to Savannah alone, and there Aunt Sarah died in her garret room and was buried in the family lot in Laurel Grove Cemetery.

I think that it often happens that all the troubles of a family come at one time, and it had been so with us. We had shared them equally, and I felt that so closely were our two families connected that, from that time on, a death in one family would be followed by one in the other, a strange coincidence that has never failed.

The one who missed Aunt Sarah most was poor little Bessie, but when Aunt Kate returned to Malbone she took personal charge of her. After this Margie and herself slept together, and their own close bond of loving companionship has never since been severed.

This was the end of our winters in Savannah. The Mackay furniture was brought up the country, the house on Broughton Street was rented, and when Aunt Kate went down to Savannah after this, she stayed with Aunt Elliott.

Mr. Tinsley, who was with Father when he was killed, lived at the end of the lane beyond Etowah Cliffs, in the old trader's cabin which had been moved from its original site in 1850. This cabin had two stories and must have been very well built, for it lasted until recent years. Mr. and Mrs. Tinsley had a large family, and Lilla, the second girl, was my age, and we were good friends. The Tinsleys' house stood on a high bluff above the ferry, and one day one of their little boys went down to the river with a little friend. They went out on the flat to play, and the Tinsley child fell into the water. His companion, terrified, ran up to the house and told what had happened, but by that time it was too late to save the child. Men gathered from far and near, and Uncle Henry and others dove into the river to search for the little body. Three days later it was found near Burtons Spring, caught in the vines and surrounded by yellow scum.

We should never have been allowed to go over to see the child but we probably went on our own accord, and I will never forget how shocked I was at the sight of the swollen face, an almost iridescent blue. I have never wanted to see a drowned person since.

Whether the child's death influenced the Tinsleys or not I do not know, but they moved soon after this to the Sproulls' place, where Mr. Tinsley took charge of the farm.

The upcountry places, no matter how large, were always called farms, never plantations, and as a rule they were much smaller than the places on the coast.

As our winters in Savannah were now over, it meant that we children must spend them after this at Malbone, and this made a governess necessary. Miss Clelia Gibbes, of a fine old South Carolina family, was secured and arrived in the fall. She was very large and stout, and quite dressy, wearing, I remember, a chignon. As she was over thirty, we thought her middle-aged, thirty being with us the Rubicon.

Miss Gibbes had the little room over the hall, and she kept it simply sealed, the windows and doors tightly shut. It reeked with Pond's Extract, for she had periodic headaches and drenched her forehead with bottles of it, when I am sure a little fresh air would have done her much more good.

The little room downstairs, opening off the cross entry, was fitted up for a schoolroom, and here Miss Gibbes taught us conscientiously, if not inspiringly—French being one of her specialties, which she pronounced exactly as it was spelt. This was strange, as the Charlestonians, with their flat *a*'s, pronounce French naturally and beautifully.

Miss Gibbes was a perfect lady and very kind, and we all liked her. I do not know why she left, unless her headaches did not improve in the close little room, but the next winter she was succeeded by a Miss Tayloe from Virginia, an F. F. V. *She* had certainly passed the Rubicon, and we looked upon her as an old maid. She was small and slight and plain and very pathetic, and I think was very poor, her family having probably been ruined by the war. She was very earnest and did her level best to train our minds. Why she gave me the slightest encouragement to write rhymes I did not know, but she sent one of my effusions to her old father in Virginia, and he wrote her that I was "certainly precocious." I did know whether to be pleased or taken down, as I had no idea what he meant.

Uncle Robert Couper used to come down from the furnace at this time for what we would now call weekend visits. It was nice for Miss Tayloe to have a beau of sorts, and she was quite taken with him. With a man's perversity, he did not appreciate her and preferred to pay attention to young girls, who did not appreciate him. He made a great mistake, for he might have had a happy home life, instead of living, as he did, to a lonely old age.

Uncle Robert, like all his brothers, had been well educated. He was a Greek and Latin scholar and scientific in his tastes, being especially interested in botany and geology. They were all artistic, and Uncle Robert drew and painted with delicate accuracy. His moths, butterflies, and wild flowers were especially well done, and he could have illustrated botanical books beautifully. Unfortunately Uncle Robert lacked practical sense, and in business matters was as helpless as a child. He never spoke of it, but he was deeply religious, and, one of the best of men, his epitaph should have been "The End of the Upright Man is Peace."

Epitaphs have always interested me, and it seems a pity that they are no longer used. The large pagans tombs inscribed simply with the family name seem to me rather blank, and I have seen them when they were even ludicrous, as in Nuremburg, where we read on the tombs, "The Family Rat," and "The Family Pickle." Uncle Charlie had an aversion to epitaphs, as he thought most of them insincere, and he said to me once, "Don't let them put any lies over me when I'm dead. The inscription over every cemetery gate should be 'Here Lie The Dead, and Here The Living Lie.' "

Though I did not study much when I was a child, I read everything I could put my hands on. I remember when I was very little curling up in a big armchair, dead to the world, while I read Grimm's *Fairy Tales.* Mother thought Grimm utterly stupid, and it was a pity that we did not have Hans Anderson's *Fairy Tales*, for they might have stimulated my imagination. I also poured over *The Arabian Nights*. Then came the days of *St. Nicholas*, and no one who has not spent a childhood in the country can realize the delight that this magazine gave us. As soon as it came we devoured it, beginning always with the continued story. At this time Louisa Alcott was my favorite author, and we simply revelled in *Eight Cousins.*

I had read *Little Women, Little Men,* and *An Old Fashioned Girl*, and did not think Louisa Alcott had a peer. When I heard Mother say once that there were very few fine authors living, I defended her as one of the greatest writers in the world!

I longed with all my heart to write like Miss Alcott, and I would try desperately to think of something original to write about. I never thought of an original thing, and it never occurred to me to write about what I really knew.

We children once came, across a dreadful book in our house, *The History of Spanish Inquisition*, filled with lurid illustrations. Where it came from I had no idea. I read it through, and Bessie dipped into it, but when I found that Harry Elliott, who was visiting us, had got hold of it, I felt it my duty to hide it on top of a wardrobe. I thought Harry would go crazy trying to find it, and he reproached me so violently, that at last I relented and let him have it.

After Father's death, Mother used to read aloud to us at night in the dining room. We would sit around the fire, and she read, I remember, *Ivanhoe* and *David Copperfield*. We all liked Rebecca better than Rowena and felt that she was very badly treated. In *David Copperfield*, Hammie particularly disliked Agnes, because she had a "shining forehead"—I have never liked bald foreheads myself—and he could hardly stand it when Dora died.

I do not think sad stories should ever be read to children. I suffered for years over a Russian story that I read once, in which the devoted servant threw himself out of the sleigh to be devoured by wolves, so that his master's family might escape. And when my husband was a little boy, and his mother read *Enoch Arden* out loud, he had to slip behind her armchair, so that the other children should not see him cry.

If I ever tell the story of "The Babes in the Wood" to a child I always have the little boy and girl discovered in time to save their lives, and live happy ever after, which is the proper ending for every child's story.

When I was ten I came across *Jane Eyre*. I had only read a few pages when Aunt Kate discovered it. She took the book away and made me promise that I would not read it until I was fourteen. It was in the house all of that time, and for four years I did not look at it. The morning I was fourteen, I took the book up to my room, and but for eating and sleeping, I did not stop until I had finished it.

It did me no harm that I know of, and would have done me no harm at ten. It started the deep interest that I have always taken in the Brontë family, which culminated when I read by accident *Wuthering Heights*, to me the most marvelous book that has ever been written by a woman.

The grown people in our family always read aloud, one reading while the others sewed, and I remember how interested they were in Mrs. Gaskell's *Life of Charlotte Brontë* and in *Off the Skelligs* by Jean Ingelow. I do not think they cared much for George Eliot, and Mother said Adam Bede was no man at all, not to have at least knocked Arthur Donnithorne down! She had no use for a man who was not manly.

The summer following Aunt Sarah's death was the summer of the Centennial, that important epoch of art stimulation in our country. I longed desperately to go to it, but of course it was as out of the question as flying to the moon. Several of our relatives stopped at Malbone on their return from Philadelphia and told us of its marvels. Cousin Carrie Elliott described an immense painting, in three compartments, of *The Prodigal Son*, which I have never forgotten. And Aunt Rebecca gave an amusing account of meeting Fanny Kemble at the home of her daughter Mrs. Wister. Fanny Kemble had never returned to the South after writing her blasting book on Slavery, so it was the first time that Aunt Rebecca had ever seen her. As she entered the room, the great actress rose, stretched out her arm, and greeted her as dramatically as though she were saying, "Give *me* the daggers!" And how Aunt Rebecca laughed when she described it! One thing seemed especially to impress everyone who went to the Centennial. The delicious Vienna rolls, the first I think we ever had in this country.

Eighteen Seventy-Six was not only the year of the Centennial, it was the year of one of the worst yellow fever epidemics in Savannah. A great many of the coast people refuged in North Georgia, and, in addition to the four Gordon girls, their two little brothers, Willie and Arthur, were sent up to Etowah Cliffs.

Mr. Willie Gordon of course stayed in Savannah, and Mrs. Gordon insisted on staying with him. She showed the utmost courage, visiting the sick and dying, and doing everything that she could to keep up the spirits of those who were obliged to remain in the stricken city. She wrote Aunt Eliza cheerful and witty letters, and only once did she write in a fury, when she described a relative as being "as pig-headed as a mule." I have never forgotten the simile.

There were hundreds of victims, but the only deaths that concerned us nearly were those which took place in the Anderson family. Mr. Edward Anderson was Aunt Eliza's first cousin. He was not afraid of fever, and his family stayed in the city. His oldest daughter, Elise, then a girl about ten, was a perfect beauty. One day he drove her out to his rice plantation, and a few day afterward she was smitten with yellow fever and died, and it was not long before he followed her. Mrs. Anderson, with the remaining children, then came up to North Georgia. The boys, Randolph and George, and Meta, their little sister, came on to stay at The Cliffs.

As the Savannah and Huntsville Gordons were already there, that house was even more crowded than usual with children, and in spite of all the tragedies we had experienced, I remember that on the whole we had a very happy summer.

11.

The Malbone Bouquet

he first thing that I ever drew was the profile of a girl with a full-faced eye and corkscrew curls. A genuine Egyptian head, typical of the childhood of art. I drew it on my slate at school and was enraptured by its beauty. And from that day on until I finally painted miniatures, the head of a beautiful girl was what I loved most to draw and paint.

Father and Mother both drew very well, and we inherited a talent for art from both sides of the family. All my brothers and sisters could draw, but the only two besides myself who kept it up were Margie and Belle, both of whom do lovely things, especially in landscaping.

To be a genius was the longing of my life. I once heard Katie Huger say, "I know that I have talent, but I am not a genius," and I wondered how she could bear being only talented. Until I was middle-aged, the fire of ambition burned in my soul like a flame, and then, when I knew that I would never reach my goal, I hoped with all my heart there would yet be a genius in the family. And he came. The son of my sister Katie, Mrs. Robert Lee Mercer. But he valued his superlative talent for art *not at all,* cast it aside, and devoted his life to other things. Perhaps it is just as well. It may be far from pleasant to have a genius in the family. When I congratulated a friend of mine on the fact that one of her nephews was a genius, she said, with intense feeling, "Give me a healthy stupid boy every time!"

Undoubtedly I valued the wrong things most when I was young. I had no use for anyone who was not "bright." Mother knew how I felt, and she said to me once, "The most important thing in life is to have a good heart." I scorned the idea then, but I have lived to know that she was right.

Miss Louisa Bulloch, Aunt Kate's gay little old friend, told me once of some little girls who edited a paper which they called *The Nosegay*, and later on I learned of the wonderful Brontë children, who wrote one on tiny scraps of paper. My ambition was fired, and the year after we went to Malbone, I decided to edit a monthly magazine, which was called *The Malbone Bouquet.*

Every contributor had, as a nom-de-plume, the name of a flower. In the 1876 volume, the only one left, which was number three in its five years of existence, I find the list of contributors' names, and add it here.

Bachelor's Button . . . W. Gordon Stiles.
Cactus . . . . Phoebe Elliott.
Camelia . . . . Edward Elliott.
Calla Lily . . . . Clara Ellis.
Clover . . . . Caroline C. Stiles.
Coxcomb . . . . Robin Barnwell.
Crocus . . . . Randolph Anderson.
Daisy . . . . Margaret C. Stiles.
Dandelion . . . . Hamilton C. Stiles.
Forget-me Not . . . . Mabel Gordon.
Fuchsia . . . . Katherine M. Stiles.
Heartease . . . . Alice Gordon.
Heliotrope . . . . Mary H. Couper.
Hyacinth . . . . James M. Couper.
Jessamine . . . . Marie E. Huger.
Jonquil . . . . John C. Stiles.
Lady Slipper . . . . Mary C. Stiles.
Larkspur . . . . Arthur B. Elliott.
Lavender . . . . Katherine Aubrey.
Lily . . . . Ethel G. Stiles.
Marguerite . . . . Meta Habersham.
Marigold . . . . Arthur M. Huger.
Menquite . . . . Stephen Elliott.
Migonnette . . . . Meta Anderson.
Oleander . . . . Hamilton Couper.
Poppy . . . . Phoebe Elliott.
Rhynchospermum . . . . . Harry Elliott.
Rose . . . . Gulie C. Stiles.

Rhododendron . . . . . . George S. Gordon.
Shrub . . . . Daisy Gordon.
Sweet Pea . . . . Percy Gordon.
Sweet William . . . . . . William W. Gordon.
Texas Star . . . . Charlotte Elliott.
Tiger Lily . . . . R. Cuyler Gordon.
Tube Rose . . . . Hagee H. Huger.
Tulip . . . . Bessie M. Stiles.
Violet . . . . Clelia Elliott.
Wall Flower . . . . Mrs. R. B. Elliott.

Younger Contributors.

Buttercup . . . . Arthur Gordon.
Heather-bell . . . . Isabel C. Stiles.
Love-in-a-mist . . . . Esther Elliott.
Prickly Pear . . . . Robbie Elliott.
Snowdrop . . . . Georgie Stiles.
Touch-me-not . . . . Mackay Elliott.

The most touching of these flower names was that of Love-in-a-mist, as Esther Elliott, Mrs. Huger's little granddaughter, was deaf, and at the time dumb. Being unusually bright, she afterwards learned the lip language, and had really an advantage over the rest of us. I remember being at a Mardi-Gras ball in New Orleans once, with the Elliotts, when the queen and her maids entered the box above our own. We could not see them and were anxious to know who the queen was. Joe Elliott, Esther's brother, was at the back of the opera house, and they could just see each other's faces. She asked the question without making a sound, he answered in the same way, and at that distance she read his lips and told us.

Mr. Arthur Huger's name of Marry-Gold was amusing, and one of the most appropriate was Touch-me-not for Mackay Elliott, who was so hard to manage as a little boy. All the Bishop Elliott children took the name of Texas flowers, as by this time he had been made the Bishop of Western Texas, and they were living in San Antonio. "We have selected for Robbie," his mother wrote, "the name of Prickly Pear, as being most applicable to his temper." It was Stephen, the oldest son, who said, when asked how he liked a first cousin, "I love him of course because he's my cousin, but *I don't like him a bit.*"

The name of Sweet Pea was bestowed on Percy Gordon, who disliked it extremely, but Little Bill, as we called Nellie and Daisy's little redheaded brother, did not seem to object to being called Sweet William. The Rhynchospermum which Harry Elliott selected, is the fragrant white Confederate jessamine, which grows on the coast. When Uncle Jimmie Couper was planting rice on Broughton Island, he had an old Negro to work around the house, who could be stirred by profanity. To make his language more impressive, Uncle Jimmie used botanical names, his most blasting invective being, "You Rhynchospermum—Jasmineides!", the effect of which was electrical.

The Malbone Bouquet was written by hand on long sheets of ruled paper, and at the top of the first sheet, beneath the title, was a drawing of a bouquet of all the flowers represented by the contributors. The illustrations that I drew myself were drawn directly on the paper, and those that were sent by others were pasted on.

On the first sheet was the news of the day. Then came the continued story, which the editress always wrote. This was followed by short stories and poems, and by an original piece of music, and each number ended with a puzzle page.

As the magazine was written in long hand, there could only be one number, and this had to be passed around to the contributors after it appeared. I certainly wasted a great deal of time doing all this scribbling, which could have been spent to much greater advantage in study.

While others contributed drawings, Daisy and I were the principle illustrators. Daisy's drawings were far better than my own. She had a daintiness of touch, and a correctness unusual in one of her age. Neither of us had ever taken a drawing lesson, and this was quite obvious in my work. I would dash off my drawings without thought or care, while Daisy, I am sure, took the utmost pains, and produced something that was worth while.

In one of the numbers of volume three, Uncle Robert drew a very good picture of Etowah Cliffs to illustrate a history of the old house. Marie Huger made a pretty sketch of Etowah River, from the foot of Termination, and Mary Stiles contributed several studies of flowers. But as a rule our illustrations were confined to drawings of women and children, especially of beautiful little girls. Bessie and Margie's sketches were occasionally accepted, but the number of illustrations that Daisy and I contributed did not leave much room for the work of anyone else.

Every number of *The Bouquet* in the summer and fall of 1876 announced new arrivals and departures at Malbone and the Cliffs. In June Mrs. Huger and Esther came down from Sewanee, Miss Louisa Bulloch came up from Savannah, and Marie Huger arrive from Baltimore, having finished at Madame Lefebvre's School. Her contribution to the June number of *The Bouquet*, was "The Jessamine waltz," a piece of music, which she dedicated "To Clover."

By this time the Ralph Elliotts had stopped coming up to Summerland in the summer, and the place was rented to the Paynes of Atlanta, who lived there for several years. Mrs. Payne, Mr. George, and Master Overton Payne were mentioned as arriving in July, and in the same number of *The Bouquet*, the arrival at Etowah Cliffs of Mr. and Mrs. George Gordon of Huntsville, Alabama, was reported.

George was the oldest of the Huntsville Gordons, being their half brother, and had recently married a pretty, plump, and placid girl of sixteen. He was a lawyer like his father, and also inherited his love for music. He was literary, loving poetry especially, and was deeply interested in young people and their mental activities. He was our star male contributor and sent in an amusing analysis of the rhyme, "Georgie Porgie, Pudding and Pies," and sent in this summer "The Clover Waltz." After surmising that he was named for the four Georges, and commending his good taste in the matter of diet, he wrote, "Now what does Georgie Porgie do? Just what every man has done that ever was born with a grain of sense or a spark of feeling. He kissed the girls. And now comes the question—why did he make them cry? Obviously because he only kissed them once, and did not kiss them all over again."

Mr. Gordon also contributed a page of original puzzles, with this heading, "Rhododendron offers the winner of the following puzzles, any book that he or she may select." Needless to say Shrub won the coveted prize. I remember one of the puzzles. "Why is Gulie like a loaded gun?" The answer being, "Because in each there's a bang impending." "Bangs," I may say, in passing, had just come in. Up to that time all girls' foreheads were as bald as they are at the present day.

Among the news items in *The Bouquet* were advertisements appropriate to the season. In June, "Dewberries, cheap on Creswell Hill." And in August, "Delicious cool melons, to be had on Lane Street." And in fall, "Better get your walnuts now. The stores will soon be closed," and later, "We have had a good frost, and persimmons and foxgrapes are sweet and plentiful."

There were notices of "French Millinery on the Garden walk. Fine and inexpensive." We made hats of leaves and trimmed them with flowers. Of a "Grand Bakery. Operated every Saturday by Tulip and Daisy," and of "Madame Scribble's Drawing School. Opened with reduced terms at Malbone."

In June we read, "The *Esther-Bell* daily makes four passages from Malbone Spring, up through the Straits of Dover and Channel of Gibralta, to Baker's Spring, on the opposite of the river, passing the Peak of Tenneriffe and down again. The boatmen are Masters Hamilton and John Stiles. Delightful accommodations and Free Passage."

This boat was named after Esther Elliott and our little Belle. It had been made by Uncle Robert, for like his father, he had a talent for boat-building. He would draw his design with the greatest care, then set up a frame in the yard beneath a shady tree, and build his boat entirely himself. Pulling on his short cob pipe, which half the time was empty, he would step back, regard his work critically, then adjust another plank with absolute accuracy, and nail it on. It took him a long time, but the boat was perfect when finished, and took like a duck to the water. It must have been rather discouraging to Uncle Robert however to have one after another of his well-built boats swept away in the winter freshets. These we had very often, and the river sometimes rose until it covered all the fields south of our house, and came halfway up our lane. It swept away the soil as well as the boats and did great damage to the place until Hamilton took charge after he was grown and planted all the land along the river in Bermuda grass, which held the soil in place.

Whether he wanted to improve on the *Esther-Belle* or not, I do not know, but during this summer Uncle Robert built another boat, which he named *The Coquette*. It must have been named for Meta Habersham. In these two boats we had an exciting race from the Shoals to Termination, and I can remember to this day the long and painful gasps that racked me as we drew near the cheering crowd. A heartbreaking sport I call it.

The contributions to *The Malbone Bouquet* were not particularly original, though Tulip wrote sketches of the four Georges which were certainly not after Thackery. The First George, taken by his mother to visit an aunt, was told to wash himself for the occasion "as white as milk." To accomplish this he jumped into a pail of milk, which immediately soured and turned into clabber. This was served on the royal table and gobbled up by his five little sisters, when George was discovered fast asleep in the middle of it, "but mercifully he was not killed." George II, having always lived in London, had never seen mud, and when taken to the country for the first time, he thought it was chocolate. To make the town boys envious, he plastered it all over himself, dried it in the sun, and was never able to get it off, and so became the first of the Negro race! George III was to act in some tableaux as a bird so he jumped in a large dish of honey, then through a hole into a feather mattress, and emerging, covered with feathers, terrified everyone so they fled. Finding himself left alone, he ran away and "has never been heard of since. This is true, for you know he was crazy." George IV was so greedy that he ate enough for three hundred and sixty every day, until he finally turned into a ball. A very big ball with arms and legs. When he came near his sister, she saw it was her brother, "George, Thomas, William, John, James, Henry, Prince of England." She was terrified, and realizing this, George IV rolled away, "And, for all we know, he may be rolling yet!"

Daisy's contributions were almost always in the form of rhymes, and in the November number was:

The Fate of the Little Beggar Boy

"Will you give me just one peanut?" said a little Beggar Boy
To a very cross old woman. "If you come here to annoy,"
Said the Woman, "You may go."

"No, Old Woman. No, Old Woman. I will not go just yet.
I only want one peanut, and one peanut I will get."
So he dived at just *one* peanut, but he missed that peanut so,
That he hit his head against a post, and made the blood to flow.

"You will get one—you will get one," said the old woman, "We shall see."
And she caught the little Beggar Boy, and laid his across her knee.
And she spanked him, and she spanked him. She then sent him on his way.
And he never troubled her again to his very dying day.

But Daisy's masterpiece was, I think:

Little Buddie

Little Nannie and her brother
Walked up the street together.
Little Buddie was so neat,
Everybody he did meet,
Said to him, "You look so sweet."
Then made answer little Buddie,
"Huddie, huddie, huddie, huddie."
And he said it with such grace
That they kissed him in the face.

Once a gentleman passed by
And when Buddie he did spy,
One bright tear dropped from his eye.
"You are like the boy I lost
In the time of snow and frost."
Then made answer little Buddie,
"Huddie, huddie, huddie, huddie!"

It was of course only as a record of family news that *The Malbone Bouquet* had any value.

The weather report in July was, "No rain! No rain! Hot as fire! Baking!" And the following items appeared. "Three bathing places on the Etowah River. The Ladies at the foot of Termination Rock. The most fashionable one for the men, at the Ferry—a famous place for diving—and the other at the new Fish Trap, farther down the river." "Croquet is the great game here now, and everyone seems to be going croquet mad. There was a grand match at Malbone the other day." In this number the editress "was sorry to disappoint the vast populace of Malbone and Etowah Cliffs," but the troupe, which had been expected to act in the Drawing Room Theatre, had unfortunately not arrived, and the ballad of "Lord Ullen's Daughter," and "Lochinvar's Ride," could not be presented. She regretted that the entire Habstigorell Troupe was not available.

In August there were heavy rains, and the heat continued. "On Tuesday last there was a dinner party at Malbone, and though it was raining, all the invited guests assembled and had a very nice time."

In September *The Croquette* was launched, and advertised daily trips up the Etowah to an especially fine grape region. And then followed "A Narrow Escape." "Jonquil came near breaking his precious neck the other day, for he fell from a high tree where he was getting grapes—luckily into the soft mud of the riverbank." Johnnie was the reporter of *The Bouquet*, but I do not think that either he or the other boys took much interest in it.

In this month Jonquil reported, "A surprise party at Etowah. A Professor Sheffield arrived with his violin, so the music was quite good. There were a great many beaux, but unfortunately a scarcity of belles, because of a great masquerade ball in Marietta. Many of the young ladies had gone down to it, but the party nevertheless passed off delightfully."

Mother's first cousins, the Frasers, lived in Marietta, a married sister and five old maids, all typically Scotch in appearance. They were the most indulgent people to children I have ever known, and were as kind as possible when any of us went down to visit them.

All summer and fall guests had been arriving and departing, and in September the following notice appeared, "Arrivals at Etowah, Mrs. W. W. Gordon, of Savannah and family." Departures. "Mrs. W. W. Gordon, after a stay of one night." The family remained. By October it was very cold, and there was a description of a picnic upon the mountain, where it was necessary to build a fire, around which the picnickers sat to eat their dinner.

In November it was still colder, but none of the young people seemed to mind it. A dance was given at Malbone, and one at Etowah in honor of Miss Daisy Gordon's sixteenth birthday.

While most of our visitors departed before the bitterest weather came, neither house was entirely deserted. Aunt Rebecca had come up from Brunswick, and before Christmas, Aunt Dora, Mary, and her two brothers arrived. I do not know how we made people comfortable at Malbone, with only wood fires and icy halls, but I think we dressed more warmly for one thing. We wore woolen underwear and flannel petticoats, and we would not have believed it if we had been told that the day would come when women would wear chiffon lingerie in winter.

On Christmas Day there were twenty people at Malbone, and in the December *Bouquet* is the following description. "Christmas Day was spent delightfully. Stocking of course in the morning. The children rose at 2 A.M. in a body and went downstairs to Mother's room to get their stockings but were promptly sent back to bed. In due time they received them, and all day long a constant firing of crackers was kept up by the boys. Services in the morning were followed by a grand dinner, and then at dusk all were surprised by a beautiful tree, given by Mrs. James Couper and Miss Rebecca Couper. It was perfectly splendid." "Splendid" and "awful" were our favorite adjectives.

After we moved to Malbone, we took turns having the Sunday service, which was always held at twelve o'clock on Sunday at Malbone, and the next at The Cliffs. It was evidently our turn on this Christmas Day, which accounts for the twenty people present, and after church, the family from the other house stayed for dinner.

The Christmas tree ended the gaieties of the season, for in the same number of *The Bouquet*, these departures are recorded. "Miss R. I. Couper, for Marietta, Georgia. Mrs. J. M. Couper, Miss Mary, and Master James Couper, for Brunswick." Hammie Couper stayed for the winter.

The December number of *The Bouquet* is the last we have of the magazine, though it was continued for two years longer, filled, I suppose, with the same crude attempt at stories, poems, and illustrations.

It was strange that the older people should have been interested in it, but in one of these numbers is a letter from Cousin Carrie Elliott, written at Sewanee, in which she says, "*The Malbone Bouquet* has been read, and thoroughly enjoyed by your friends at the University. The Bishop of Western Texas desires me to thank you, through the columns of your valued paper, for the very acceptable gift for his mission work. He will find good use for it."

Meta Habersham had stayed on the coast this summer at a resort called Beach Hammock. We did not consider her literary, but the poem she contributed to the November number of *The Bouquet* was by far the best of the rhymes which any of us wrote, and I conclude with the

Lines From Beach Hammock

If I had the gift of eloquent speech
I would tell of the charms of this beautiful beach.
It is firm, it is smooth, it is long and wide,
And its edge is bathed by the restless tide,
Whose surges dash with their crested foam,
And the sea-bird swoops o'er its ocean home.
While embedded deep in the clean white sands
Lies the mast of a ship from distant lands.
It is bolted with iron, and shaped with skill.
But how can that hinder old Ocean's will?
So he cast it on shore like a broken toy,

And there was an end of the mariner's joy.
Now it serves as a seat, our feet to rest,
While we gaze on the clouds in the dazzling west.
Then when the bright colors have turned to gray,
We peacefully turn on our homeward way.

Marguerite

12

Transition

he road between Etowah Cliffs and Malbone curves southward across the fields, the boundary line between the places being just beyond the two great water oaks, my Tree of Life and Gordon's. Near the center of the road on our side there was a low place, which was always muddy after a rain, and Hammie and Johnnie were given the job of bridging it. They drove a one-horse wagon up the mountain, cut down saplings, trimmed them to the proper length, and, bringing them back, laid them side by side across the dip, making a little stretch of corduroy. It was hard work for boys of their age, and for this job they were paid twenty-five cents apiece. We other children thought that perhaps this money would go to the missionaries, but I hope that Hammie and Johnnie were allowed to keep it and spend all of it on themselves.

When we went into Cartersville from Malbone, we always drove over this road to the Other House, as we called The Cliffs, to see if they wanted anything in town. We seldom went oftener than once a week, so there were many things to buy, and something was always forgotten at the last minute. Then a child would run across the field to the park, to intercept the buggy, and we found this shortcut very serviceable.

A footpath was cleared on one side of the road, and Mother planted elms beside it, and every afternoon Aunt Eliza and herself met and walked back and forth along the path until the sun set across the river and dark overtook them. And along this path they walked until the elms grew high enough to shade it. In later years when their children had gone out into the world, and they were left almost alone in the two big houses, it was their only recreation. As they walked they talked of their family affairs, of the letters they had received, and of what was going on in the outside world. To the end of Mother's life—Aunt Eliza survived her by thirty years—they were devoted friends, and though different in many ways, they were alike in being absolutely unselfish and deeply religious.

Aunt Eliza was rigid about the religious training of her children, and I used to think she was too strict with her sons. I have seen her stop them throwing ball to each other on the grass on Sunday. I thought later on there might be a reaction, but a lifetime had passed, and her three sons—the only members of the family living—are still good churchmen and devoted to her memory.

When Henry finished at Sewanee, he went to a business school at Poughkeepsie and then to Savannah to work in his Uncle Willie Gordon's cotton house. He was very handsome at this age, almost as handsome as Huntsville Will Gordon, but so shy that he would walk around an entire block to avoid speaking to a girl. (I do not expect to be believed by anyone who did not know him at that time.)

Gordon followed Henry to Sewanee, and when he arrived, with his bright color and curly golden hair, the boys at once nicknamed him "Susie." For a man to be small in the Stiles family was a disgrace, and up to the time that Gordon was sixteen he was short. He was then told that if he continued to smoke cigarettes he would never grow tall. He gave it up at once and grew to be six feet, not quite reaching Henry's mark of six feet three and a half.

It was during these years that George Gordon of Huntsville came into our lives, and, taking a deep interest in young people, he added much to our pleasure.

The oldest of the family, he devoted his life to his younger half-brothers after their father's death, and their home in Huntsville must have bee a very happy one. George Gordon, like his father, was a lawyer, but I think he was more interested in his avocation. He—also like his father —was a fine musician, and directed the choir of the Episcopal church, in which all of the boys sang. The fact that he was an atheist did not seem to interfere with his church activities. He was an atheist I am sure because of his worship of Shelley. How we knew that he was one I have no idea, for he certainly never mentioned it to us, but the children have a remarkable way of finding out things without being told. We were perfectly aware, for instance, of family skeletons, which our elders thought safely concealed in locked closets.

George Gordon was as fond of Dickens as he was of Shelley and would gather us all around him in the drawing room at The Cliffs and read Dickens aloud, stopping now and then to laugh heartily. Whenever he started to read, his pretty girl-wife would slip out of the room. This made us think she was not "intellectual," but what was of more importance, she was practical, with a real talent for housekeeping, and I am sure she made the Gordon home an even more pleasant one than it had been before.

Daisy and I were George Gordon's favorites, and I suppose he was as demonstrative to her as he was to me. I must confess that this made me uncomfortable, and I think that our intense friendship was rather an artificial one on my part. With Daisy, it was genuine, however, and they remained devoted friends to the end.

About this time we girls began to keep Mental Photograph Albums, in which we asked all of our friends to write. On each page was printed a list of questions, such as, "What is your favorite time of the day?" "Season?" "Color?" "Flowers?" and so on. "What trait of character do you like or dislike most in man?" "What is your motto?" The last and most important question being, "If not yourself, who would you rather be?"

We took the greatest pains with our answers, feeling that they were of the utmost importance as a revelation of our characters. We were at the age of intense self-consciousness, and felt things more deeply perhaps than we would ever feel them again.

Our visitors took them seriously, too, and I remember Llewellyn Aubrey pondering for hours before he wrote his answers. But then he expected to become president of the United States, and his Mental Photograph would some day be of the greatest value.

I wish that I could find some of those albums, but they have all disappeared, and I only remember a few of the answers in my own. As I recall it, all of the boys said that blue was their favorite color. Mine was yellow. The color of sunshine. That glorious color had not then been degraded to represent cowardice. Nor had the splendid color of red come to stand for Bolshevism and Blood.

My favorite tree was the pine, because of the tall dark pines in our park: and my favorite time of the year was Autumn. Only the young can like autumn best, with the sharpness of winter beyond it. As you grow old, it is spring above all that you love.

Marie Huger was full of sentiment, and she wrote, in answer to the question, "What is your favorite time of the day?" "When Evening draws her curtain down, and pins it with a star."

The boys took the question more lightly than the girls, and Fred Waring wrote that his favorite flower was "Mint." But Margie was passionately in earnest, when in answer to the question, "What aspect of character do you dislike most in man?", she wrote, "A black beard." After all these years, she says that it is still! I think her aversion came from the fact that her Savannah godfather had a black beard. He was a friend of our elders, and we didn't think much of him, as he had only given Margie a spoon and fork when she was christened, when everybody knew that a silver cup was the proper thing! This dislike of beards, however, may have been a family trait, for we all have it, and Belle acknowledged, after she grew up, that the horror of her life had been marrying a black-bearded widower!

The trait of character that I disliked most in man was cruelty, and, needless to say, it is still. My motto, I remember, was "Hope on, hope ever."

To the important question, "If not yourself, who would you rather be?", the answers varied from "Nobody," to "Most Anybody." One scorbutic Cartersville youth wrote, and underscored, "*Napoleon at Austerlitz*", and the answer of the Reverend Mr. Patterson of Memphis was "A little Nigger."

There was only one sister in the Huntsville Gordon family, Lina. (Fortunate girl not to have been called by her given name.) She came next to George and was a young lady when we were children. Like all of her family, she was very amiable, and she too read aloud to us when she came to Etowah Cliffs. I remember hearing her read Miss Muhlbach's *Henry VIII* as we girls sat around the fire in Aunt Eliza's nursery. She read at breakneck speed, and at first we were stunned, but we soon became accustomed to it, and did not miss a word, and, to this day, the names of Seymore, Dudley, and Essex still have power to move me.

Lina Gordon started my cult of Miss Muhlbach, and I read almost everything she had written, my favorite novel being *Mohamed Ali*. I once said to Percy Gordon—vain gloriously, I suppose—"I am as ambitious as Mohamed Ali." He rebuked me gently, "Our ambition should be to be a good wife," he said. "The perfect idea!" I thought disdainfully.

Aunt Sarah did not approve of my reading these novels, and when I tried to defend Miss Muhlbach by saying that she had written them by the bedside of her invalid husband, she said, "She would have been much better employed reading her Bible." Well—I don't know. She probably had to support her husband.

Lina Gordon was quite pretty. She had large round brown eyes, a complexion like a magnolia leaf, and very white teeth. In those days no decent girl painted, and her coral lips and the faint rose in her cheeks were much admired. Annie Owens of Savannah and herself were great friends, and when they came out society together, were the belles of their day. Annie Owens, who afterwards became Mrs. Daniels, was a vivid brunette beauty, animated and attractive.

I remember being in Lina's bedroom once in Grannie Gordon's house, when she was dressing to go to an entertainment with Annie Owens, who was standing by. Gulie and I were looking on, when Gulie said rather bitterly, "Some people have everything in the way of looks, and others have *nothing*." Lina turned and said warmly, "I would change my looks with you any day." Then she glanced in the mirror. "All except my eyes," she said, "*I could not give up my eyes!*"

Gulie knew all about Lina's career and told me once of a romantic experience she had when visiting her aunt Gulie Harrision at Lower Brandon. She was at a house party, and one afternoon, being alone, she had fallen asleep in the drawing room. She was waked, in delicious agitation, by one of the young men kissing her. I suppose I looked shocked, for Gulie hastened to explain, "You know a man has the right to kiss you if he finds you asleep."

Beirne was the brother next to Lina, but we saw little of him as he seldom came to The Cliffs, and nothing after he went to Savannah to work in his Uncle Willie's countinghouse.

Willie was the third brother, and by far the handsomest of the family. He had dark sparkling eyes and dark wavy hair with a very white skin and very white teeth. I think he was the handsomest boy I ever saw. He had a sweet disposition and was very attractive and deserved a better fate than the one that befell him.

Percy, the next brother was more conscientious and took life more seriously than Willie, but he was not so bright and not nearly so winning. He was in love with me for two summers, and then a misunderstanding turned him to Daisy. At that time and in the country, if a boy fell in love with you, the only attentions he could pay were to ask you to go to walk or to ride on horseback, and the only words of endearment he ever uttered were a few shy compliments. Not even a touch of his hand took place. That a girl would let a boy kiss her was unbelievable.

We saw little of Percy after he grew up, for when he finished college, he decided to enter the ministry. This must have been a blow to his brother George, who probably felt about it is his classmate, Dudley Du-Bose, did. Dudley met me soon after and said, "Did you know that Percy Gordon had gone to the bad?"

George Gordon lost his young wife in childbirth, and almost lost his mind in consequence, and he did not survive her many years. When he was dying, Percy came to him and I feel sure that he was his greatest comfort. I seriously doubt if anyone *dies* an atheist.

What a mercy it is that none of us can look along the vista of our lives and see the end! Percy grew up to be very handsome and attractive, and, as a minister, was adored by the members of his congregations in Geneva and at the North, where he had most of his charges, and, in the end, he met the saddest fate that comes to a man. (Committed suicide.)

Lina Gordon's was the first romance that came into our lives. Her suitor, a wealthy young man from New Orleans, named Richardson, came to The Cliffs to address her. Gulie knew exactly where he proposed. It was in the wild grape arbor in the park, at the foot of the long hill. She accepted him, and the next time that she came to Etowah was just before she was to be married.

Mr. Richardson had presented her with five velvet, satin-lined cases of diamonds, and she brought them to show the family. There was a necklace, bracelets, pins, and so on, the most beautiful of all being a butterfly of rubies, sapphires, and diamonds mounted on a quivering spiral to wear in her hair. We were breathless when she told us that she had almost thrown the box containing the butterfly in the fire, thinking that it was empty.

We saw no more of Lina Gordon after she was married, for she went to New Orleans to live. Most of the young people who spent their summers at The Cliffs came no more after they were grown. Not many were loyal like Daisy, who continued to come to the end of her life to see her beloved Aunt Eliza.

But then persistence was the keynote of Daisy Gordon's character. While you never knew what she would do next, for she was maddeningly erratic, she always did what she made up her mind to do, and we might have known that some day, as Mrs. Juliette Low, she would found the Girl Scouts of America.

By this time the Gordons had become very well off, as Mr. Gordon had made a fortune as a cotton broker. Nellie had said years before, "When Mummer is forty, she's going to have a brown velvety dress." And I have no doubt that she had it.

"Mummer" had been Eleanor Kinzie, the first white child born in Chicago, and she was one of the wittiest, most entertaining people I have ever known. As her son, Arthur, describes her, "She was small, quick as a flash, with snapping eyes and tireless energy, and she kept everyone in roars of laughter by her witty and unexpected remarks."

Mr. and Mrs. Gordon had made the Grand Tour of Europe, and, on their return, Aunt Nellie stopped at The Cliffs to distribute the gifts she had brought to her family. Nellie was presented with a Swiss watch and chain, which set the seal on her superiority. For some time however, she had been drawing apart from us, and soon she was to be sent to an expensive French boarding school in New York, and after this she was to be called "Eleanor."

Later on Daisy and Alice went to the same French school, and there poor little "Skinny" died of typhoid fever, and died heroically.

I believe, however, that young people are more willing to die than the old, and less afraid of death. They face it almost always with sublime resignation, while in middle age, body and soul rebel against it bitterly. Uncle Charlie always said that the more religious people were, the more they dreaded death.

In the fall of '76, Gulie too went off to boardingschool, going to Edgehill, a country school near Charlottesville, Virginia, which was kept by the Misses Randolph, descendants of Thomas Jefferson. From all accounts it must have been a delightful school, and I am sure that the winter she spent there was one of the happiest of dear Gulie's life.

This winter we had a new governess. Miss Tayloe had decided not to return, and a Miss Hill of Baltimore took her place. She was a tall, gaunt, tragic-looking woman, silent and reserved, and she stayed by herself most of the time. She was kind to us as all of our governesses were, but I do not think she taught us any more than the others did. Perhaps it was our own fault. I am sure it was mine, as I only studied what I wanted to. Mother did not understand Miss Hill, nor did she care for her, and I am sure it was a relief to Aunt Kate and herself, when she announced in the spring that she could stay no longer. When she was leaving, she held out her hand to Mother, and said tragically, "We shall never meet again. I shall pass out of your life like a leaf floating away on the Stream of Time." Mother thought this nonsense, but we realized what she meant, when we heard the next year that she was dying of cancer. I went to see her in Baltimore when I was there at boarding-school, and she seemed glad to see me, but she would not allow me to kiss her when I said goodbye. Poor soul! She had probably had that fatal trouble all the time that she was with us.

Aunt Eliza went down to Savannah this winter to visit her mother, taking the little children with her, and Mary come over to Malbone to stay with us. She and I slept together, and I remember on a bitterly cold night how delicious it was to jump into the feather mattress and have it almost close over you, you went down so deep. The wind used to howl around the northeast corner of the house like the wailing of banshees, and Mary, who was always a little strange, said to me one night, "Do you know what that sound is? It is the Dead, moaning in their graves."

Poor girl! She's in hers now, in the little graveyard at Etowah. She knew the heights and depths of life, but now, at last, her life's fitful fever is over, and she rests in peace.

That winter, I remember, was dark and raw and rainy, and sometimes when the sun did not shine for days, it was piercingly cold. Every after-noon Mary and I walked down in the park, and the wind roared so in the trees above us, it was like walking under Niagara Falls.

It made me strangely restless, and for the first time in my life I felt shut in by the mountains and longed wildly to escape. For the first time in my life I felt lonely.

We had heard by chance of an offer that had been made to Southern girls, and we longed to take advantage of it. A wealthy Baltimore lady, named Mrs. Buckler, feeling deeply for the Southern families who had lost everything after the war, offered to educate a certain number of Southern girls in Europe, and the offer had come to Aunt Kate, who was an old friend.

I would have given anything on earth to accept it, for it would have meant not only going to Europe, but having an art education, and I felt perfectly desperate when I found that Aunt Kate would not even consider it.

Perhaps she was right. I would have been separated from my family for years, and been under a lifelong obligation to a stranger. Above all it might have unfitted me for the simple life I was destined to lead.

Years later I met a little old maid from South Carolina. She was refined, cultured, and a perfect French scholar, and I found that she had been one of the Southern girls whom Mrs. Buckler had educated. She had spent eighteen years in Europe, and became almost one of the Buckler family. To me she seemed cheerful and happy, but when I told her nieces that I might have gone to Europe with her in my youth, they said, "You are fortunate not to have gone. She has never been perfectly satisfied with her life since she returned."

What I minded most was missing the opportunity of becoming a painter. What I wanted was to be a portrait painter. The greatest woman painter in the world! If that had been possible, would it have compensated for missing the happiest life on earth?

While we had to stand this bitter disappointment, Mary and I had a great pleasure this winter in the first visit that the Lows ever paid to us.

Katie and Mary had finished school in London, and their father had decided to bring them out to The States to see their American relatives. Aunt Kate, as usual, went down to Savannah to visit Aunt Elliott, and on her return brought the two girls back.

When they arrived at Malbone they came first into the dining room, where there was a bright fire, and we all sat around it for a little while, before the girls went up to their room, where their maid had preceded them.

Katie was small, with a trim figure, a pretty piquant face, dark eyes and hair, and the most brilliant color we had ever seen. Mary was tall and graceful, with irregular features, amber eyes, a lovely mouth, with the enchanting smile that now and then appears in the Stiles family, and you felt at once her unusual personal charm. Both girls wore perfectly fitted tweed suits, with tailored hats to match, and, *as they crossed their legs*, we could see that they wore silk petticoats, silk stockings, and Oxfords. Both girls were very sweet and friendly, though it was a little hard at first to understand their melodious broad *a-d* language. They pronounced Mary, Mair-y, which made it a pretty instead of an ugly name. Neither Mary Stiles nor I could utter a word!

When the Lows had gone up to their rooms, Aunt Kate took us sharply to task. It was the first and only time she had ever scolded me. She was incensed that we had been so tongue-tied, and appeared to such disadvantage. Mary and I flew out of the dining room, to the loggia in front of the house. There we seized each other by the arms, jumped up and down, and *squealed*.

It did not take us long to find tongues after that and to become devoted to our English cousins, and we had the most delightful visit of two weeks from them. Everything they said, everything they did, everything they wore interested us deeply. We had never seen beautiful underclothes before, or sheer lacy nightgowns, folded into embroidered cases, which were laid on their pillows each day. Or black silk openwork and clocked stockings. Or dozens of different kinds of boots and slippers, some of them paten leather, with dull or cut-steel buckles. I had never had but one pair of shoes at a time in my life, and I had never yet had a pair of slippers.

While the Lows did not wear evening dresses at night, they always dressed up in pretty gowns, which, to our amazement, were put on by their maid, a nice cheerful white girl, who also did their hair and buttoned their boots. She was called by her surname, I remember.

The girls brought up their own claret and port, and, to my surprise, drank tumblers of it at dinner, which perhaps helped them to enjoy our simple fare. Whatever we had was always well seasoned, however, as Mother was a fine housekeeper. They especially enjoyed the sweet potatoes they had never tasted before, and the ground nuts, which we used to parch and eat at night, as we sat around the fire.

Katie was a fine horsewoman and went out riding with Uncle Henry several times. The first time that she mounted at our side steps, I was shocked by catching a glimpse of pant and boots beneath her short riding habit. I had always ridden in Mother's old habit, which hung at least a yard below my feet. It was made of dark blue lady's cloth and was so heavy that I could hardly lift it to put it on.

Katie had already come out in London society, and Mair-y was to come out the following June, and be presented at court. She pinned a tablecloth on to her dress as a train and showed us how she would approach Queen Victoria, make a deep curtsey, kiss her hand, and back gracefully out her presence. When this event did take place, she wore a train of cornflower blue brocade, and must have looked very lovely, with the three feathers in her hair, and a long filmy veil.

Both Katie and Mary admired our Mary's looks, and thought her like an English girl, with her long face, deep-set eyes, aquiline nose, and decided chin, and we found afterwards that she was rather like their youngest sister, Jessie, who was a very handsome girl. The only thing that was said of my looks was that bangs would improve me, and, to my delight, I was allowed to have them. Katie tied a ribbon around my head, and cut my hair straight off across my forehead, and I wore it that way for many years.

When Katie and Mary returned to Savannah they sent us a trunk full of clothes, and I had, for the first time in my life, a beautiful dress. There were three silks. A gray one was sent to Gulie at boarding school. I have forgotten the color of Mary's, but mine was a royal blue. The deep blue that you see in a peacock's feather, that turns to purple in certain lights. It was a heavy lustrous silk that lasted for years and was beautiful to the end.

From that time on the Lows came often to see us in winter, and what rapture they brought into our quiet lives! I suppose they had no idea of what their visits meant to us, and of how exciting it was to hear of house parties, hunts and balls, of theatres and operas, and of travels on the Continent. To us they seemed to be rolling in wealth. Wealth which they shared so generously and lovingly with us from that day on. I could not, if I tried, recall all of the wonderful things they have done for our two families all of their lives.

Never, in spite of the many sorrows that have come to them, as they come to all, have they forgotten their American cousins, or ceased to care for them. Dear Katie, most wonderful of all, whose entire life was spent in unselfish service for others; lovely, sweet, charming Mary; and later on, Willie and Jessie, so handsome and attractive; they came into our lives at the time when we first felt the glamour of romance, and in memory they will always remain young and beautiful, loving and generous.

13.

Sewanee

hen I was fifteen I left the state of Georgia for the first time. This was an exciting event in the lives of each one of us, and when it was Margie's turn to experience it, she wrote on a postcard, "I am out of Georgia at last. We came up Lookout Mountain to-day. There are ten of us in the party, the Warings and ourselves. We travel in a carriage and a white covered Cracker wagon, stopping every night at some house. We girls have a room and the boys sleep in the wagon." The party spent a week on Lookout Mountain, where the Warings' cousins, the Howards, lived, and tramped to Little River Falls. In the woods above the fall a triple line of embankments is still to be seen, where De Soto is thought to have defended himself for several months against the Indians, and where many arrowheads are still to be found. The little party return- ed as it went, taking days for the journey, which now takes hours, and, because they were young and strong and happy, they enjoyed even the hideous discomforts of the trip.

My own exodus was less adventurous. I had continued to have chills every summer, and Mother and Aunt Kate decided that I would have to take a change. None of us dreamed that it would be the change of my entire life.

Mrs. Huger and Hagee were living at this time in Sewanee, Tennes- see, with Dr. and Mrs. Elliott, and as "Miss Lucy" was willing to have me, I was sent up to board for the summer. Miss Katie Huger and I traveled up together from Malbone, and when we reached Cowan, at the foot of the mountain, we boarded one of a long train of flat cars that was going up to the coal mines at Tracey City. As I remember it, we sat on chairs, while two cadets, the only other passengers, sat on boxes at the forward end of our car.

The track wound higher and higher around the spurs of the mountain, and the long train in front of us looked so like a gigantic serpent, we named it Scorpio. Now and then billows of black smoke enveloped us, and cinders splintered against our eyelids. Opening my eyes after one such experience, I saw one of the boys up in the front, looking back at me and grinning sympathetically. He was Ed Quintard, the son of a bishop of Tennessee, and I thought him most attractive. He was evidently not similarly impressed, for I never saw him again.

At Slope Wall, near the top of the mountain, Scorpio came to a stand still; far up in front, we could him panting after his long climb. Below us the valley stretched out like a vast crazy quilt, little irregular fields of varied colors, fitted together like patches, joined by a brier-stitching of rail fences. Far off to the west a misty ridge of mountains was ruled against the sky.

Once on top we reached the Sewanee depot, where our trunks and ourselves were deposited on the ground, while Scorpio grated on the track for the coal mines at Tracy City.

Hagee was there to meet us in the crowd assembled to see the train come in, and we drove in a hack up the broad and rocky road, through the deadly little village, and on to Dr. Elliott's house, about half a mile away.

When the University of the South was planned before the war, by the Episcopal Church, ample means were assured for its building and maintenance. Only its cornerstone was laid however, when the war came on and left the South in ruins. Even the cornerstone, dedicated with such ceremony, had been blown up by the Yankees.

The spirit of the South had survived the cataclysm however, and six years after the war a few buildings were erected at Sewanee, and, with only a handful of students, the University of the South was established.

When I went to Sewanee in 1877, the school buildings, as well as the residences, were all of wood of the simplest construction, and it was many years later before they began using the fair, creamy-pink "Sewanee Stone" and the Oxford style of architecture.

The broad road from the depot led northward up a gentle slope, and directly in the middle of it a little church was planted to define the limits of the village. The road skirted around this, and at the back of the church, Sewanee proper began.

The first house on the left, with the straight path leading to it, bordered by box hedges, belonged to Monsieur Pillet, the French tailor, who made the most perfectly fitting of uniforms. Trousers at that time followed the beautiful curves of a man's leg and were not the disfiguring bags of modern days. A college ad of that period reads, "Pillet feels sure that he will triumph in contest with ready-made clothing, believing in the survival of the fittest." When he did not approve of a fit, he would say, "Your suit makes me think of two French cities—Toulon and Toulouse." Though collections were probably difficult at times, Monsieur Pillet remained always the good friend of the students.

Next to Monsieur Pillets was the studio of Mr. Judd, who, for many years, took very fine photographs of the Sewanee celebrities. Mr. Judd was said to photograph the soul of Sewanee, and he was always the loyal supporter of its traditions and ideals. A great lover of nature, his grounds were filled with rare beautiful flowers, and the birds were his personal friends. He once succeeded in taming a hummingbird and taking a perfect picture of the tiny creature on his hand. The professors and Mr. Judd were warm friends, and he was a member of their literary society, the E. Q. B.

Beyond these two establishments the Sewanee houses began, standing on either side of the road, each surrounded by its fenced-in lawn or garden. Dr. Elliott's was halfway up, a two-storied house set back on a large lawn, shaded by fine white oaks.

The Sewanee sidewalks were unpaved, but, packed hard by constant use, were high and dry. Along some of them maples were planted, and when in autumn their star-shaped leaved changed to every shade from rose to crimson, their beauty took your breath away.

About three quarters of a mile from the depot, the broad road branched to east and west, directly in front of the pleasant gabled home of Bishop Elliott. On one corner stood the Inn, on the other there was a dip of woods named Manigault Park, but called by the boys Nanny Goat Park. Beyond this, on the road leading east, were the university buildings enclosed in a whitewashed fence. It was on the boards of this fence that the *graffiti* of the students were scribbled at commencement time, when they indulged in open insults to the professors, without fear of punishment. The chapel stood in the middle of this enclosure with the Grammar School on one side, and Forest Hall on the other.

Directly across the road was the home of the vice-chancellor, General Gorgas, where, in an adjoining building, a number of boys had the inestimable privilege of being under the supervision of Mrs. Gorgas, one of the finest women I have ever known.

One of Sewanee's greatest assets in its early days was the fact that the students all stayed in the private homes of ladies, most of them widows of Confederate officers. Their individual influence on the boys was so fine that Sewanee gained the reputation of turning out only gentlemen. When I first went there, every Sewanee cadet touched his cap when he met a lady, whether he knew her or not.

Willie Gorgas, the son of the General, was a student at Sewanee at this time, but, being myself only of grammar-school age, I never remember meeting him. He was noted for two things at Sewanee, pluck and perseverance. Determined to become an expert boxer, he practiced boxing every afternoon with the proctor, Mr. Van Hoose, who was a large and powerful man. Despite the awful punishment he received—when his battered nose would be swollen, it looked like a polished red apple—Willie Gorgas persisted until he mastered the art. He was once dragged the entire length of the baseball field by his hair but never let go of his opponent. Such a little thing as a *aëdes aegypti* (yellow fever mosquito) was not going to down William Crawford Gorgas in later life.

Next to the Gorgas house was Fulford Hall, the home of Bishop Quintard, who was known in England as My Lord Bishop Tennessee. The Fairbanks home, on the other side of this, was the most attractive house in Sewanee. Built of logs, with many gables, it was completely covered by a magnificent wisteria vine, and the wide, deep lawn in front was shaded by fine old trees. It was here that Rene Fairbanks, one of Hagee's best and finest friends, lived.

The Kirby-Smiths were beyond the Fairbanks, a swarm of curly headed, happy children. The old General, as incorruptible as he was courageous, was a notable figure in the chapel on Sundays, in his Confederate uniform with his long flowing beard. He was the professor of mathematics at Sewanee, and, with his plump, warm-hearted wife at the head of it, theirs was a home of happiness and hospitality. Like all the professors, he was devoted to Sewanee, and used to say, "It's a good place to live in, and a good place to die in." And he lived and died there.

Most of the professors at Sewanee were ex-Confederate officers for all the gentlemen of the South had fought in the war. General Shoup, who had married Miss Hessie Elliott, was the professor of metaphysics, and Dr. DuBose, who had been, like Bishop Quintard, a chaplain in the army, was dean of the theological department.

As the highest salary of a Sewanee professor at this time was fifteen hundred dollars, no one was wealthy. It was a place of high thinking and low living, or as one of the professors put it, "A place where people of eminent respectability dwelt together in cheerful poverty."

In those days the school term at Sewanee was from March until December. This plan, which differed from that of any other American university, had been adopted by the trustees for a very good reason. Most of the Southern boys lived where it was very hot in summer, and in this way they could have the advantage of a cool and bracing climate at this season and return to their homes for the pleasures of Christmas, and the winter shooting. Of late years this plan has been changed, so that Sewanee may conform to the scholastic year of other universities, and the students now stay on the mountain during the bitter and lonely winters and return to their homes for the intense heat of Southern summers.

Conditions were very primitive when I first went to Sewanee, but I did not even notice that there was neither plumbing nor lighting in the houses. In fact, I went for so long a time in my life without these luxuries, that I am hardly yet over the excitement of having a bathroom and electricity in my own home. As there were not street lamps, the inhabitants had to carry lanterns when they went out at night, and I remember, even years later, seeing little Frank Gailor, coming through Nancy Goat Park to see us, looking, with his little lantern, like a firefly out for a call.

Dr. John Elliott was the second of the great Bishop of Georgia's sons. Cousin Robert, the oldest, was now a bishop himself, and, Habersham, the youngest, was a noted civil engineer. Dr. Elliott was a very handsome man with the beautiful manners of the Old South, which it is now the fashion to deride. He had been educated in Europe and was now the Professor of chemistry and geology at Sewanee, practicing medicine also in a limited way. In later years his field expanded, when he left Sewanee to become a noted physician and dean of the medical school at Tulane University in New Orleans.

I remember how striking looking Dr. Elliott was when he mounted his horse in the afternoon and started for the woods, his two Irish setters, Romp and Hab, bounding on either side. He was fond of botany and a great woodsman, and he once laid out a picturesque winding road through the woods, which he called "The Curleyqueu."

At this time the John Elliott family consisted of "Miss Lucy," Mrs. Huger's oldest daughter, and five children. Mrs. Huger and Hagee lived with them, and Miss Katie frequently spent her summers there. The two dogs, Romp and Hab, were members of the household, Hab being a surly animal, while Romp was everybody's friend. This dear red dog was absolutely trustworthy, as was proved on one occasion when he was accidently locked up overnight in the storeroom. In the morning he was found, seated just below a joint of meat, which was hanging within his reach, his eyes were fixed on it longingly, and a pool of saliva on the floor, showing how much his mouth had watered for it all night long.

Romp was finally given to Joe Lovell, and the affectionate, sensitive boy loved him so devotedly, that his death, though only from old age, was a tragedy to him. That is the trouble with having pets. You always suffer in the end. I gave up having them long ago, for I went through experiences I cannot bear to think of to this day.

As Sewanee was a church school, services were held every morning and twice on Sunday in the chapel, and Hagee and I attended them all religiously. Though she was probably right, I remember how uncomfortable it made me when Mrs. Huger remarked, with an amused smile, that we only went to chapel to see the cadets.

Mrs. Huger had no idea of having us spend our entire time in idle pleasure, and she insisted on our studying French and Egyptian history every morning with her. She was intensely amused by my French pronunciation, her own being perfect, and enjoyed taking me down. Why she chose Egyptian history for us to study, I have no idea. Miss Sada Elliott lent us volumes of it from her dusty shelves, and we found the inside as dry as the out, and, as we dragged through one deadly dynasty after another, we were longing to be out in the bracing air and brilliant sunshine with our friends.

Miss Sada was at this time Sewanee's literary celebrity. I think she was now writing *Jerry* out in a log cabin at the back of their lot, a quiet and undisturbed sanctuary. Years after, when a favored gownsman would be taken there, he would say impressively, as the door was opened, "So *this* is where *Jerry* was written!"

Miss Sada had been so great a belle among the students and professors at Sewanee, that it was said a hopeless love affair with her was one of the required courses at the university! Now, if she had only written her memoirs—!

Miss Sada Elliott and Miss Katie Huger, as the two outstanding young women at Sewanee, were, in a way, rivals. Miss Katie had just returned from Europe, where she had been studying art for years, and was now painting very lovely landscapes.

Almost everyone has a rival I think. Someone who continually annoys you, and whom you distinctively dislike. A rival of your own so about your own age, and one in your own sphere of life.

I think Mrs. Huger must have found that Egyptian history did us little good, for after a while we dropped it and had time to enjoy the pleasures of Sewanee. Through its surrounding woods, winding roads led in every direction to beautiful views on the brink of the mountain. Where the view is at the head of a cove, the spurs of the mountains beyond dovetail into another, or lie, like giant camels kneeling on the sand, their necks outstretched and gray humps rising behind. Where the view is clear over the valley, you can see to the edge of the world.

Some of the rocks are of fantastic shapes. There is a perfect Natural Bridge spanning a cove on the mountain side, a small replica of the Natural Bridge of Virginia. Proctor's Hall, on the edge of the mountain, is like a cyclops's tomb hewn out of the rock, and covered with a great slab of stone. Point Disappointment, like a gigantic gargoyle, stretches out from the edge of a precipice, high above the tree tops in the woods below. This rock was named by one of Miss Sada's discarded suitors, but, as he did not throw himself from it, and lived to marry three wives afterward, he survived the disappointment. In a remote place in the woods, three cascades fall over the rocks to a stream below, and when they were discovered by one of Hagee's discarded suitors, he announced that he had found the Indian Ka-Ma-Ha Falls. He had named them after Katie, Marie, and Hagee Huger!

Walking out to these views was one of the greatest pleasures we girls had, and we usually went in parties. I remember once hearing a cadet practicing on his bugle, and, we neared the view, seeing his figure outline against the sky. And once when I was alone, I heard around a curve beyond, the dramatic delivery of a commencement oration and I turned and slipped away.

The woods were the happy hunting of the Sewanee boys, and when my brothers went there later on, they roamed them like wild Indians.

One of Hagee's very nicest friends was Annie Lovell. The Lovells lived just across the street from the Elliotts. They were quite well off and owned in the family five cotton plantations on Palmyra Island, in the

Mississippi below Vicksburg, another in the Yazoo Delta, and a sugar plantation below New Orleans. All of these places were managed by Colonel Lovell, who spent most of his time down there and only came up to Sewanee for a short visit during the summer.

The Lovell family spent their winters in New Orleans or on Palmyra and their summers at Sewanee where the boys were at school. John and Tod were the oldest sons, then came Annie and Rose, the youngest child being a little boy named Joe. Mrs. Duncan, Mrs. Lovell's widowed sister, and her son Pat lived with them.

I realized from the first that the Lovells were a very exclusive family, and, compared to my own, a very rich one. I was especially impressed by the fact that they had olives in their pantry. I had never seen, much less tasted one, and it seemed to me indicative of wealth.

Mrs. Lovell was not a person who cared for general society, and her deepest interests were in her own household. Her mind to her kingdom was, literally, for she had a powerful intellect and a rare imagination, inherited from her German ancestors. The most gifted of General John Anthony Quiltman's children, she was the one most like himself and had been appropriately named for her father, Johanna Antonio.

Mrs. Duncan, the beloved "Aunt Rose" of the family, had lived with them ever since the death of her young husband, which occurred before the birth of her only son, William Patterson. At this time she was in her prime, a large and handsome woman, with jet-black curling hair, a high color and deep violet eyes. She was very fond of dress, and, having just returned from a year in Europe with her boy, had brought back from Paris many handsome costumes. I remember especially a shiny black satin, which fitted her like a glove, and in which she was very striking-looking with a red rose pinned on her breast.

In those days dresses fitted you, and a wrinkle on a sleeve or basque was unforgivable. I doubt if even a poor white girl would have been seen in the shapeless garments we wear today. However being vastly more comfortable, I am entirely on the side of modern clothes, and I thoroughly approve of discarding corsets. I only draw the line at pajamas for women in public and backless evening gowns, as I have never admired pantalettes or shoulder blades.

Colonel Lovell came up once to Sewanee while I was there, and I remember seeing him, but I always cleared out when he was around. Stout and of medium height, he was a fine-looking old gentleman, of the coloring called sanguine. A blond, originally redheaded, he had that school-girl complexion, sharp blue eyes and an aquiline nose, and he wore a fierce white mustache and imperial.

He had been in the United States navy before the war and was the young commandant of the president's yacht, the *Water Witch*, when he met and married the daughter of General Quitman of Natchez, Mississippi, who was then in Congress. When the Civil War came on, Colonel Lovell joined the Confederate Navy, and, after it was over, remained in the South to take charge of his wife's property.

The Colonel was a blustering, fiery old gentleman, a born martinet, and it was just as well that at that time I did not know he would some day be my father-in-law!

Annie Lovell was a little younger than Hagee and myself, and at this age, a really lovely girl with a perfect complexion, very pretty features, and dark eyes and hair. Hagee and I said once in her presence we would give anything to be pretty. To our amazement Annie said, "So would I," *and meant it.* For some reason we thought it would be indelicate to tell her that she was, and it might have given her such pleasure. Annie had a very fine character, was very warm-hearted and loyal and always did what she thought it her duty to do.

Rose, who was a slender little blonde with waving golden hair, a peach-blown skin, and shining gray eyes, was four years younger than ourselves, and so belonged to the "little girl" class and did not enter into our exciting lives. Most of her time was spent with her double first cousin, Allie Lovell, who was her own age, and who lived farther down the street on the road to the depot. Being equally affluent, they went every Saturday afternoon down to "Bishop" Wadham's bakery store at the top of the hill from the village station, where they bought bags of pink sugar mice and were served ice cream and cake in the entrancing little arbor in the garden outside. Ice cream in that arbor was my idea of delectation, but of course Hagee and I were never able to afford such a luxury.

Mrs. Joseph Lovell, a widow, was the oldest sister of Mrs. Storrow Lovell and Aunt Rose. She also was comfortably off and in her pleasant house had many of the beautiful things she had brought up from Monmouth, the old Quitman home in Natchez. I remember especially the heavy crimson brocaded curtains and the great mirrors reaching to the ceiling, in one of which were reflected two nautilus vases borne aloft by silver mermaids.

"Aunt Ludie" had been married twice, and had two daughters, Eva and Allie, who were half sisters. Much older than the rest of us Eva was now a grown young lady. With the kindest of hearts, she was mannish in character, original and independent, and probably very shocking to her elders. She took not the least interest in society and cared nothing about the handsome clothes her mother so carefully selected for her. Returning one night very late from a dance at Forensic Hall, she put her feet, high white kid boots and all, into a tub of cold water because they hurt her after hours of dancing.

Of the boys in the Storrow Lovell family, John was the eldest. A cadet at V.M.I., he had just returned for the holidays. He was much older than Hagee and myself, at least two years, and he noticed us no more than if we had been the dust beneath his feet. He was a fine-looking blonde and wore a grand uniform, holding himself rearingly erect. Our only encounter was once at the corner of the Inn, when he looked haughtily over our heads as Hagee and I were passing. Hagee, who had the keenest sense of humor, burst into a smothered laugh. "General Pif Paf Pouf!" She whispered.

Not having the privilege of meeting the fine gentleman at this time, I do not know whether John Lovell gave promise of being the brilliant conversationalist he afterward became. Later on he went into the navy, and when he came on leave to visit us in the summers at Malbone, all of the young people would gather around him on the grass, and he would talk far into the night, enthralling us with tales of his experiences in the Arctic and along the Western coast down to the roaring straits of Magellan, and I have never forgotten his description of the entrance to Rio Harbor and have longed to see it ever since.

Tod Lovell was the second son. The old gentleman had been called "Star" in his younger days, and it may have been that in trying to call his little brother Star, John had arrived at "Tod," the name by which he has been known ever since.

Both Lovell boys were loyal to their younger cousin, Pat Duncan. When John mistreated Pat, Tod fought John. When Tod bullied Pat, John fought Tod. So the younger boy, though he had anything but a peaceful life between them, had two protectors and was devoted to both.

There were never three more different characters than those of the three boys in the Lovell home. John was gay, light-hearted, careless and pleasure-loving, without an unkind instinct, and, while never aggressive, he was fearless and could not be put upon. Tod was both fearless and aggressive, masterful, and, like his father, high tempered. However, he had, like Siegfried, one vulnerable spot, which in his case was his heart. Pat was a quiet, thoughtful, sensitive boy, with a touch of melancholy and a tendency to brooding. It must have been an effort to him to keep up with Tod's strenuous life, but he was game to the core and never flinched when the test came.

I do not know whether Pat's life would have been a happy one for he died on its threshold.

When Tod Lovell was first sent up to Sewanee at the age of eleven, he stayed with John, who had gone before him, at Gorgas Hall. Crossing the street next day, he joined a group of boys who were in the Grammar School yard. Ed Quintard, the son of the bishop, had been up to this time the cock of the walk at Sewanee. Approaching the group, he put a chip on his shoulder, walked around them, and dared anyone to knock it off. When he reached Tod Lovell, Tod knocked it off. Ed was so astonished, he did not attempt to fight, and, from that time on, the two were good friends.

In those early days Sewanee had two baseball teams, the Sewanees and the Hardies, and all Sewanee was on one side or the other and was divided by the fiercest rivalry. The Sewanee color was blue, Hardies was red, and at one time Tod Lovell and Ed Quintard were captains of the opposing teams.

Ed was the first boy that pitched a curved ball at Sewanee, having gone to the North one winter and learned how to do it. The professor of physics declared that it could not be done, when Ed proved it by stationing the catcher behind a tree and pitching the ball to him.

Even in those early days the fine spirit, for which Sewanee is famous, showed itself. One of smallest universities, its football team continues to this day to compete year after year with colleges that have thousands of students to draw from, and, though often defeated, Sewanee has never been downed.

Hagee, Annie, and myself always went to the baseball games where a few rough benches on the grass constituted the grand stand. Of course we all three were ardent Sewanees.

Now and then we were allowed to go to the dances at Forensic hall, escorted usually by embryo theologs, as Hagee always attracted them, and finally married one. Robin Barnwell was our friend among them. There was one tall, conceited theolog, who condescended to pay Hagee some slight attention and who infuriated us by writing in her autograph album, "Be good, sweet maid, and let who can be clever."

Although our party clothes were of the simplest description, we always had a good time, and I do not remember ever having to sit out any dances. Of course we were never the belles that Kate Thompson of Memphis was—young, lovely, and very well off. She was only sixteen, but a real young lady, dressed in grownup clothes of silk or satin, made square-necked and elbow-sleeved, with bouffant overskirts and short trains. The university "men" were daft about her, and among her most ardent admirers was Leroy Percy of Greenville, Mississippi, one of the handsomest, most fascinating and brilliant men I have ever known. I feel that no greater honor could have been paid to any girl, and yet Kate Thompson married another man!

Outside of the windows of Forensic Hall there were always crowds of boys looking in, and I suppose making jeering remarks. They were the boys who could not dance, and I think Tod Lovell was among them, for unlike his brother John, he did not shine in society.

I did not meet Tod Lovell for some time after going to Sewanee, but, late one afternoon as Hagee and I were walking home and neared the corner of the Lovells' fence, a tall boy came striding toward us, his head held high, and his military cap cocked over one eye. As he came on, his eyes, like blue flame, caught and held my own.

The next morning at chapel, as I looked up toward the benches placed lengthwise against the wall, on which the cadets sat, I saw the same bold blue eyes fastened on me, and, as far as I know, they never left my face during the service.

Not long after this a crowd of us went on a picnic to Natural Bridge, and Tod and I were thrown for the first time together. We were sitting in a group under the trees below the bridge, when he dared me to eat a honey-leaf. I suppose it was the same instinct that prompts a small boy to knock off the hat of the little girl he admires. It was like eating red pepper, and while I would not even exclaim, the tears started to my eyes, and Tod's remorse was extreme. From that time on he could not do too much for me.

I do not know why we imagined that no one knew of our feeling for one another, but it was a real shock to me when I heard a remark that Dr. Elliott made. The most reserved and considerate of men, when someone said at the end of summer, "How wonderfully Caroline's health has improved," he remarked with his charming smile, "I think little Toddy has had something to do with it!"

The wonderful summer came to an end at last—77 has always rhymed with Heaven in my memory—and I returned to Malbone: Tod, Pat, Hagee, and Annie coming down as far as Cowan to see me off.

I will never forget my dreary homecoming. When, very downhearted, I reached Cartersville just before dark, I found that Uncle Henry, who had come to town, had been asked to drive me out. He was in an irascible humor, probably tormented by financial worries, and when I tried to make conversation, he turned on me so fiercely, though it was only to ask me what I was saying, that I never ventured another word, and we tore in perfect silence from the lime kiln home.

My welcome at Malbone however was all that could have been desired. I felt the deep though speechless devotion of Mother and Aunt Kate, and the passionate loyalty of my brothers and little sisters who hung on every word I said and immediately adopted my new and unknown friends as their own.

When I left Sewanee, Tod and I were engaged. We were both fifteen, though he was six months older than myself. It was our secret and I did not want another soul to know it, so I was terribly upset when my first letters from Annie and Hagee came. Tod had confided in Annie, so that he might send messages through her to me, and Annie and Hagee, deeply concerned, had consulted earnestly and decided that it was my duty to tell Mother. I hated to do it, but, having all my life been afflicted with a conscience, I finally made up my mind that I had to.

Annie and Hagee had continued to write and urge me to do my duty, so I gave Mother their letters to read and left it at that. Mother was as embarrassed over the situation as I was myself, and for days I heard no word on the subject. Then one afternoon when I was helping Aunt Kate weed the grass under the dining-room window, she spoke.

I am sure that all along Mrs. Huger had kept Aunt Kate informed by letter, and her opinion of Tod could not have been a favorable one, for I could feel Aunt Kate's deep disapproval as she spoke. She said that Mother and herself had talked the matter over and thought we were entirely too young to be engaged. They had decided that we were not to see each other for three years. If at the end of that time we still cared for one another, we might become engaged. Of course they both thought that by the end of three years we would have forgotten one another.

Aunt Kate had the deepest feeling on the subject and ended her intense and guarded soliloquy by saying that Mother would allow us to write to each other three times a year. On my birthday, May the seventh, on Tod's, October the twentieth, and on Christmas Day.

On the second Christmas Day after we parted, Tod wrote me a letter seventy-two pages long.

14.

Baltimore

ammie was the first of our family to go off to school and when he left for Sewanee in March 1878, it was an exciting event for us as well as himself. Bishop Robert Elliott had obtained a church scholarship for him, and Johnnie was afterwards sent in the same way.

Hammie stayed with Gordon, Arthur Elliott, and several other boys in a cottage next to the old Bishop Elliott's house, where Miss Sada had charge of the establishment. I do not think Miss Sada cared much for younger boys, and Hammie was not very happy there and the year after went to another hall.

Miss Sada had one favorite among these boys however, and this was Arthur Elliott. This was natural as Arthur had grown to be one of the dearest boys that ever was, gentle but manly, and with a charming sense of humor. His mother had by this time married Mr. Joe Huger, and Arthur lived at Murray Hill, his stepfather's plantation just across the Savannah River from the city. Here he learned from the Darkies to speak the coast Gullah so perfectly, that his Negro stories were inimitable. Later on, his four little stepsisters and brother followed in his footsteps, and their "shouting" and singing of the Negro spirituals was marvelous. It was of the Huger children that Margie said, "Every one with glorious eyes, and not a nose between them."

The greatest pleasure that we had was receiving Hammie's letters for, thought he hated writing, he wrote to Mother—as we all did when we went away—every week. In his first letter he wrote, "I like it up here pretty well, though would rather be at home . . . Mr. Puckett, our proctor, is just as nice as can be. He does not talk of religion much. Last Sunday he heard the first chapter of Genesis read for the first time. He says he is going to take the Bible and make a study of it. He had two examinations not long ago, and made Three on both of them. This is the highest thing you can get."

Charles McD Puckett was one of the most brilliant students who ever went to Sewanee. He married Miss Charlotte, the youngest of Bishop Elliott's daughters, and afterwards became a prominent newspaperman in Louisiana.

In another letter, Hammie wrote: "We go over to the Hugers nearly every Sunday night, and Mrs. Huger shows us pictures. She says she will show us more when we come again. She has a crowd of them. . . . I think the views up here are splendid. Last week we had a choir holiday, and Gordon, Arthur and I went to Poised Rock. It is higher than the trees, and right on the edge of the mountain. We climbed on top of it, and threw rocks down into the valley, and cut the top of a tree clean off. . . . We do not wear our uniforms every day, but have to when we march to chapel on Sundays. . . . In the holiday in August, we are going to make up a party of boys, and are going down to Elk River, about ten miles off, and camp out. We will take a tent to sleep in, and hooks and lines to fish with."

Short as the distances were in the South, there was no coming home on intervening holidays for Sewanee students, and I look with amazement on the modern boys, who seem to think it only their due to come from Harvard, Princeton, and Yale back to the South, not only at Christmas time, but for the Easter holidays as well.

Hammie enjoyed more than anything else roaming through the woods. In the fall there was nutting, and when cold weather came he was occasionally allowed to go shooting in the valley. Once he wrote, "I killed a wild duck on a pond, a thrush, and two sparrows and two sapsuckers. Coming up the mountain we got so hungry, we stopped and built a fire and ate all but two of the birds." Hammie was on one of the younger baseball teams and was of course a Sewanee. But the sport he most enjoyed was swimming. They had dismal-looking old tank down in a dark dip shaded by trees, and Hammie wrote, "It takes three lengths of the tank to make the width of our river, and I dove the length of it. Only two other boys have done it."

Of his studies he did not have much to say, though he wrote, "We have head and foot in our Latin class, and I stayed head two days. Gordon stays head more than anybody else."

These were the days when table-tapping became the vogue, and in one of Hammie's letters, he said, "Every moment we boys have, we make the table tap, and we make it answer all kinds of questions. It answers by tapping the letters that spell the words." He gave several proofs of its mysterious power, and ended, "The other night we told the table to walk to the bed and get up on it. It would raise up one foot, and wheel around on the other, and kept on that way until it got to the bed. Then it raised up on side and tried to get up, but it could not. So we asked it if the bed was too high, and it tapped three times for 'Yes.' " Poor thing! Utterly exhausted evidently.

It was at this time three poverty-stricken old maid cousins of Mother's, who lived in what was then the God-forsaken state of Florida, spent an entire winter writing a book which was revealed to them by means of table tapping. What the book was like I do not know, but its title was certainly spirited enough, for it was "Rapped Out by the Table."

Marie Huger was at this time our governess, having succeeded poor Miss Hill. We were all devoted to her, Hammie especially, and she and I called each other "Better Half," and do this day, though we have been separated for many years. She stayed with us for a long time, and I think that, on the whole, her life at Malbone was a happy one.

Meta Habersham, having finished at Madame Lefebvre's, was spending the summer with us, and Gulie, Marie, and herself had a very pleasant time, as the young men of the neighborhood began to call, and they sometimes went to dances at the hotel in Cartersville. There was a rather fascinating man named Leutze, a son of the German artist who had painted *Washington Crossing The Delaware.* He was with Uncle Henry at the furnace, and he came down now and then with Uncle Robert for the weekends. Then there were Robert and Charlie Shelman just across the river, and Jimmie Sproull nearby, and in town were the Youngs and Harrises, while Llewellyn Aubrey was a constant visitor.

All was grist that came to Meta's mill, for she was the greatest flirt I have ever known, and quite irresistible to men. We thought her worldly, and yet, in no time, we ourselves were thinking how romantic it would be to marry a Northern man of immense wealth, and live in a castle on the Hudson. We thought of all Northerners as immensely wealthy and had not the slightest feeling against them.

This year there was another wonderful event in our family, for in the fall Aunt Kate sent me to school in Baltimore, Hagee Huger and Mary Couper going with me.

When I left Malbone I told Aunt Kate goodbye in the hall. She stepped back behind the door in the dining room, and I realized that she was crying. It was the first time I had ever seen her cry. She loved me dearly, little as I deserved it, and I know that she felt she would never see me again. Little I thought of such a thing. I was wild with excitement.

In one of her first letters to me, Aunt Kate wrote: "We have not gotten used to being without you. . . . You are a dear good child to write to us so often. We always rejoice when a letter comes." And Mother added, "Your nice long letter came this morning. You need never be afraid of writing too much. We are deeply interested in every particular, and every child wants to hear every word you write."

Mrs. Lefebvre's was one of the two fashionable boarding schools for girls in Baltimore at this time, the other one being Mrs. Pegram's. Our school was on Franklin Street just two blocks from Cahlres, in what must have been a fine old mansion. It stood directly on the sidewalk and was four stories high. On the ground floor two drawing rooms opened into the front hall, and at the foot of a broad flight of steps, a mirror reached from the floor to the ceiling. As I entered, I turned towards this thinking it another hall and saw someone coming towards me. "I have seen that person before," I thought, and realized it was myself.

Mrs. Lefebvre's drawing rooms, which were rather low ceilinged and dark, were always *sacrosanct* to the girls. Occasionally we might enter one when we had a visitor, but we never felt at ease in them. These were the days of so-called aestheticism, when decorative art was the rage, and it gave me positive thrill when I first went into the front drawing room, and saw on the seat of a deep velvet armchair, a china teapot and set of cups and saucers!

My sister Mrs. Snowden Marshall has had one or two exhibits of "Inferior Art" in her New York apartment, and I think Mrs. Lefebvre's armchair would have taken one of her prizes, though the first prize of all, I feel sure, would have been awarded a gilded turkey foot tied with pink ribbon which I once saw standing on a mantlepiece in a country town.

In those days we had no use for anything old fashioned. We cared for neither Colonial nor Empire houses, but admired the style that was called Queen Anne. Rounded bays with pepper-pot turrets and any amount of machine grillwork we thought perfectly beautiful. We ourselves lived in a substantial old house that would be defaced, but we did our best to live inside of it. We filled umbrella stands with cattails, draped chairs and mantlepieces, pinned opened fans on the walls and stuck peacock feathers everywhere, and it was not many years before Katie and Belle were painting old mahogany furniture with thick brown paint.

On the second floor of Mrs. Lefebvre's were the schoolrooms, huge double rooms across the front and back, divided by a transverse hall, which had probably been the drawing room and dining room of the old mansion. They were handsome rooms with high ceilings and great mirrors and white marble mantlepieces supported by Canova's dancing figures.

On the third floor was Mrs. Lefebvre's large front bedroom, and back of this the individual rooms for especially favored girls. On the top floor were little cubicles where most of us stayed, three or four in a room. The large dining room and kitchen were on the ground floor at the back of the lot and were reached by a covered passage on one side of an open court.

There were about thirty boarders and twice as many day scholars when I was at Mrs. Lefebvre's. Mrs. Johnstone the matron, Miss Mary the housekeeper, Mademoiselle, and Miss Chandler, who taught us French and English, lived in the school, while Professor Daves and Dr. Barto came in to teach us literature and chemistry, and the girls went out for music and singing lessons.

Mrs. Lefebvre was a fine-looking woman, tall, stout and very dressy. Her white hair was arranged in perfect waterwaves beneath a gauzy cap, and all of her clothes were in the latest style. I remember how excited we were when she first put on her black watered silk circular, lined with fur, and drove out in her carriage. We looked upon her as a sort of Queen Victoria, and, kind as I now realize she was to me, I would be afraid of her if I met her today.

Mrs. Johnston had been one of the beautiful Elliott sisters of Beaufort, South Carolina, who "never put foot to the ground." A widow who had seen her husband killed by the enemy on her own doorstep and had been left penniless, she had been obliged to support herself and daughters in middle age. One of them, Emma, had been adopted by the wealthy Wyman family of Baltimore. She was such a beauty that when she went to a fancy ball once as Mary Queen of Scots, she was said to be the duplicate of her portrait. One of Mrs. Johnston's nieces, Gertrude Gonzales, was at school at this time, and she too was a very handsome girl as well as a fine student.

Miss Mary, the housekeeper, was so neutral a character that we did not even know her surname. Her only distinction was that she was a friend of Madame Jerome Bonaparte and took the girls to visit that famous lady once a year. She died before I had a chance to meet her, and all that I ever saw of her was the Stuart portrait, with three views of her lovely face on one canvas. It is one of the pictures I have seen in my life which I have always longed to possess.

Madame Laminar was French to her tapering fingertips, good-natured and kind to us all, but I think it was just as well I was not adept in the French language at that time. Miss Chandler was an F. F. V., intense but self-controlled, a pathetic person who had never had her share of the joys of life.

Almost all of the boarders were from the South, and several like Hagee and myself, were taken at reduced rates. We were never made to feel this however, nor do I think it was known to the other girls. Some of them were very well-off, and one—Julia Sanchez of Cuba—was an heiress. The large bedroom back of Mrs. Lefebvre's was shared by her mother and herself. Mrs. Sanchez was a dark, handsome, languorous woman, who wore diaphanous white sacques, and spent her days sewing dreamily. Julia, a stout and swarthy little creature with a hooked nose, was passionate and spoiled, and none of the girls cared for her. After she left school, she went abroad and eventually married a Russian prince, to the great amusement of her schoolmates. It is hoped that she died long ago, and so escaped the hideous fate of most Russian princesses.

Several of the girls were from Charleston, but if they felt superior, they were too ladylike to show it, and I had some good friends among them, particularly Susie Heyward and Rita Pinckney. The Virginia girls were the most interesting of all, as Virginians always are, and one of them, Josephine Venable, was our most brilliant student.

Many of the girls had ideas that were different from my own, and it shocked me to hear one of them say she was engaged to two men at the same time. I kept my own engagement a secret, but in some way Camille DuBose found it out, and I have never forgotten a remark she made. When I said, as a matter of course, that I had never kissed another boy, she laughed and said, *"Fool who?"* To this day the fact that she did not believe me is painful to me, for Camille was the girl I adored.

Camille was one of the girls who were well-off, and the selection of whose clothes Mrs. Lefebvre personally supervised. This stylish set sat in Mrs. Lefebvre's pew at St. Paul's, while the rest of us sat on the other side of the church, where I am sure we had a more interesting time. An old gentleman sat in the pew in front of us and growled comments on the sermons, aloud and contemptuously, to our great amusement.

After I had been at Mrs. Lefebvre's a few weeks, I had one ghastly spell of homesickness, and I have never known a more desolate feeling. That was the last of it however, and from then on I had as good a time at boarding school as I could have had, disliking discipline as I do.

Hagee, Mary Couper, and Susie Heyward of Charleston were my roommates in the little back room on the fourth floor, where we slept on four little white cots against the wall, on mattresses as hard as boards, and slept as soundly as we ever did on feather beds.

We had our lessons in the different classrooms in the mornings, and in the afternoons all of us had to take a walk. We went two together always and were not allowed to walk on Charles or any of the shopping streets. After supper we studied in the large back schoolroom, and when we went to bed each took an apple from a bowl as we passed out of the door. I am sure it was the "apple a day" which kept us in such fine health, for during the three years I was at school, there was only one cases of serious sickness.

Perhaps the Baltimore climate had something to do with it, bitter as it was in the winter. The Baltimore girls have always been noted for their beauty, and I am sure it is because the climate—like that of England—gives them their "peaches and cream" complexions. Even we girls from the far South had cheeks like damask roses while we were there.

Mrs. Lefebvre's school had been beautifully equipped. For the study of botany there were large papier-mâché specimens of flowers which could be taken apart from sepal to seed. For astronomy there a set of lantern slides which showed the movements of the whole solar system, including eclipse of the sun and moon. And for the study of physiology, there was a wonderful little manikin about three feet tall which could be taken apart from his skin to his skeleton. It was one of the studies I was really interested in, and I enjoyed nothing more than unpacking his neat little organs and putting them in place again. I have ever forgotten how beautifully his heart and lungs and diaphragm fitted into his little box of a chest. If there was one thing I knew when I left boarding school it was the construction of the human body. Mrs. Lefebvre herself taught us physiology, and I remember on one occasion she had a calf's heart brought up on a plate, and, in silent dignity, cut it in half, severing the heart strings. Then she put the knife and fork down and looked at us.

"There!" she seemed to say, "You see!"

Words were quite unnecessary, and we were properly impressed.

Mrs. Lefebvre was nothing if not impressive. Everything she did was majestic and awe-inspiring. On Wednesday nights we assembled in the back schoolroom where she read aloud to us. One book which she read was *Westward, Ho.* I used to sketch while she read, but I think most of the girls did sewing of some kind, and when she had finished, Miss Mary brought us in hunks of dry sponge cake and very tart lemonade, not made with lemons.

The only class that I really enjoyed was that of English literature. Professor Daves was a wonderful teacher, though how he could retain his enthusiasm teaching such a set of dull and unresponsive girls, I cannot imagine. Because I was interested and at last summoned up courage to answer his questions, he took a fancy to me and formally invited me to his home.

This was an adventure in Bohemia that was almost painfully exciting, for I always went on Sunday night, when Bessie Daves and her men friends gathered around the piano and sang the jazz songs of that day. The men all smoked and were free and easy, and, though I enjoyed it in a way, I never felt easy myself. It was a far cry from singing hymns on Sunday night at Etowah Cliffs and Malbone.

The hero of these carousals was a great society man named George May. At that time they had a genuine Little Theatre in Baltimore, and the Daves took me one night to see George May act, which he did very well. When he asked me to act in their next performance, I felt as if I could die of joy. Fortunately Providence, in the form of Mrs. Lefebvre, intervened, for while I might be one of the star performers in a boarding-school play, I could hardly have shown among semi-professionals.

Our French plays at the end of the school term were the great events of the day or rather year. A stage was built in one of the large school-rooms on the second floor, and all of the day scholars as well as their families and our personal friends were invited. We acted the tragedies of Racine and Corneille chiefly, and the comedies of Moliere.

I adored acting and was given many delightful parts, the only one I did not enjoy being that of Louis XI, though I did my best to make it convincing. I wore a long heavy cloak, and the flat hat with the leaden images in its band. At the end of the play, when I was down on my knees, trying to pray with all my soul, I suddenly remembered that I had forgotten to makeup, and the thought of that old devil with the face of a pink-cheeked school girl, all but undid me. What I thoroughly enjoyed was taking the part of a boy in one of Moliere's plays, when I could wear knee breeches and a white wig.

After the play we could go downstairs and mingle with our guests in the drawing rooms and receive their kindly encomiums, and a word of praise from Mr. Daves would send me into a seventh heaven of delight.

Mrs. Lefebvre herself saw that the girls had the opportunity of going to all the fine concerts, lectures, plays, and operas that came to Baltimore. I could not afford to go to many, but, while at boarding school I had the inestimable privilege of hearing Gorstaer sing and seeing Sara Bernhardt act. I have heard all of the great singers of our day, and, with the exception of Patti, whose voice was like liquid honey, I have never heard one who could touch that nineteen-year-old German girl. Only the angels of heaven could have a more beautiful voice that Gorsta's. She sang in *Lucia de Lammermoors* and in the flute song, her voice was even more beautiful than the flute itself. When she returned to America two years later, she had been married and had a child, and the angelic voice was no more.

Of course we girls simply adored the Divine Sara. Her acting was so superb that we even thought her beautiful! And the tones of her voice were almost as lovely as Gorsta's.

Another great privilege that I enjoyed at Mrs. Lefebvre's was taking my first drawing lessons. Mrs. Cuyler of Savannah, who was then living in Baltimore, gave them to me. She had not wanted me to know that she gave them, and it was a mistake telling me, for I felt miserable until she died because I could never repay her as I longed to do. If I only could have gone on studying after this first good start, I might have become a real artist.

Among the friends that I was allowed to visit outside of the school was the family of Sidney Lanier. I used to go there occasionally to supper on Sunday nights, and, after our very simple little meal, we would walk around to the Peabody, where Mr. Lanier played the flute in those marvelous concerts.

I think he was an ill man even at this time. He was very tall and thin and stooping, and he wore a long beard, I think as a protection to his chest. His features were aquiline and very refined, and his expression most kind and sympathetic, while his manners were always generous and courteous. Mrs. Lanier I can best describe by saying that she looked like the ideal poet's wife, and there were three bright, interesting little boys, who told me they were "half past" so and so, when I asked their ages.

I had never read anything of Sidney Lanier's at that time, and I realize now that I was utterly unworthy of the honour conferred on me in meeting that great poet so intimately.

15

Fledged Out

he greatest pleasure that I had when I was at school was receiving letters from home. Mother, Aunt Kate, my brothers and little sisters wrote to me regularly, and I have every word of the children's letters still, bound in a volume entitled, "We Are Seven."

In Johnnie's first letter he wrote, "We all miss you a heap. Mother is reading *Anne of Geirstein* out loud at nights. . . . I have another battle in my sketchbook. It is between the Swiss and Austrians and is a very spirited action."

And Bessie wrote, "Margie and I go down every evening to the river." The evening meant the afternoon with us. "We climbed foxgrape trees and get just piles of them. We get sugar berries, persimmons, haws and walnuts. Hammie Couper has the most walnuts. He has about eight thousand. . . . Harriet has gone to Atlanta. She was so afraid of being left that she got up at two in the night. The train that she was to go on left at ten o'clock, so she waited seven hours in the depot in Cartersville. Fanny Mann is cooking for us." Harriet Whittaker was the fat middle-aged cook, who never came back, as she had run away to get married.

And Margie adds, "I am writing in the schoolroom, and Bessie is making paper dolls. She makes lovely ones now, most as pretty as you. The boys are playing marbles out in the yard. Mother and Aunty are lying down. Miss Marie, Meta and Aunt Rebecca are in their rooms, and Katie and Belle are playing in the garden."

Hammie continued his Sunday letters to Mother, and about this time he wrote, "I cut this piece of paper little, as I did not have anything to say, and I wanted to write four pages. . . . I haven't heard from Caroline this week, but I guess she has been too busy to write. You see how it is. Girls take up Latin and a whole lot of other studies, and when they finish their education, they know a little of all these, and it does not do them any good. A boy takes about four studies, and when he has done his education he knows them. . . . Please somebody send me a knife for my birthday. There is but one knife in the hall, and that belongs to Ponder and he hardly will ever lend it, he is so afraid somebody will break it. Yesterday Thompson got a box from home, and he gave us a little, and he has not given anybody else any except Ponder and Puckett. I know this looks just like a hen had scratched all over the paper, but I have an awful pen, and it is after ten, and my light ought to be put out."

It is pleasant to know that Hammie received the knife, and I am sure that he was generous with his birthday box in October the 20th. "It had a bundle of walnut candy in it," Bessie wrote, "And one of caramels, one of town candy, a bag of raisins and a cake. Aunt Kate sent him a dollar, Aunt Rebecca, a knife, Miss Marie, a box of paper, Aunt Eliza, some money, and Johnnie, a cravat."

Aunt Eliza always gave us a dollar on our birthdays, and she must have been a wonderful manager, for in spite of her very slender income, she never went in debt and always had money on hand. Thrift must have been a Gordon inheritance. Whatever good points the Stiles may have had, the ability to make money or to keep it was not among them.

In a later letter Johnnie wrote, "Bishop Beckwith preached in Cartersville, and we went in to hear him, and when we came home in the evening, Mr. Reese had church again, so we had two churches a day. Miss Bessie Beckwith is staying at the other house." Bessie Beckwith, the bishop's second daughter, was a dear friend of Gulie's. "This week," Johnnie continue, "is the time they are going to have the fair in Atlanta, and there is going to be a grand ball. Miss Marie, Aunt Rebecca and Meta have received invitations, but they are not going. We had compositions the other day in school. I wrote about Trenck. Bessie wrote about Milton, and Hammie Couper on sheep. . . . Mr. Leutze has gone away for good to Savannah. . . . Dr. Memler was baptized in the Baptist Church the other day, and was nearly drowned."

Dr. Memler was a little hunchback German who spoke with an atrocious accent. There was something shady about him, *and I am certain now that he was a quack*, but as he was the only doctor in Cartersville at this time, we were obliged to have him when it was necessary. In Johnnie's next letter he said, "Dr. Memler was not hurt by being baptized. He has opened his hospital, and it is a kind of hotel, and lots of Cartersville young men take their meals there. I would not like it. . . . Uncle Henry and Uncle Robert went to the Atlanta Fair last week, and the car ran off the track, but nobody was hurt. . . . There is going to be a barbecue in Cartersville, and you can ride upon the Van-Wert Railroad free."

Two political barbecues were given in Cartersville this fall, and Johnnie wrote later on, "They had two grand barbecues in Cartersville last week, one for Felton and one for Lester, and today is election day. I will draw you a picture of how the cars looked when they passed our house across the river." In his spirited sketch, people swarmed like black ants, not only inside and on the roofs of the cars, but on the couplings between and on the cowcatcher, and I have no doubt that, with the quick eye of a boy, he saw just what he drew. "You could go free to Lester's barbecue," Johnnie continued, "but, if you went to Felton's the day after, you had to pay half-price. So a heap more went to Lester's than to Felton's."

Election day was a grand day for the Negroes in Bartow County. They were for once of some consequence and could get at least a dollar for their votes, and they all crowded in to Cartersville to sell them.

In his next letter, Johnnie wrote, "I forgot to tell you that a man ate himself to death at the barbecue." It must have been at Lester's! "He came home that night and died the next morning."

Old man Felton won the election in spite of Lester's munificence, for he remained in Congress for many years.

Cousin Mary Huger and her little girls had come up to Malbone for a visit this fall, and now Mr. Joe had arrived to take Meta and his family back to Savannah, and Aunt Rebecca was leaving at the same time for Brunswick.

Meta was to come out in society this winter and was glowing with health and happiness. She was now very handsome with her fine erect figure, glorious hair, and one real beauty in her perfect Cupid's bow mouth and pearly teeth.

Meta's social career was a great success, and was enjoyed as much by her mother as herself. Cousin Leila went to every German in the Guards' hall, where she sat in the gallery, swathed in the deep mourning of a war widow and never took her eyes off of her adored daughter. Meta was a decided belle both in Savannah and at "The Old Sweet," where she went in summer, and three years later she married our second cousin, King Couper, then a successful young cotton weigher, and made him a fine wife. She had one little girl, named Leila, to whom she was devoted, who died in a year's time. She herself, poor girl, soon after developed consumption, and died at twenty-four. Her death was intensely sad, for she did not want to die, but she accepted her fate without a complaint and died with the utmost courage. It is always tragic when the young die first, and it was sad that Cousin Leila should have had to outlive her beloved daughter for almost a quarter of a century.

Meta had a kind heart and bore no malice to anyone, and in spite of her love of the world, she turned out quite as well, or better than the rest of us, with the exception of Gulie, whom none of us could touch. In spite of all she had to bear—poverty, suffering, disappointment, and sorrow— she never lost her spirit or bowed her head. Her entire life was sacrificed for others, and she died, as she lived, a thoroughbred.

After the summer visitors left Malbone this year, the family settled down to its regular routine, the children to their school duties, and the grownups to their family affairs. Johnnie wrote to me every week, and in a November letter, he said, "Miss Marie, Bessie, Margie, Hammie Couper and myself are picking cotton for Uncle Henry. We pick an hour a day at recess, and we pick a basketful every time. Miss Marie takes a chair with her, and moves it as she picks. . . . Miss Marie, Hammie and I row down the river to get cedar trees to plant along the lane. We have planted twelve trees already and they are growing nicely. . . . We are nearly through *The Conquest of Peru*, in school, and are reading *Waverly* out loud at nights. While Mother reads, Hammie and I pick the seeds out of the cotton. . . . We do not sing hymns any more on Sunday nights, because there is nobody but Miss Marie and us children."

To this letter of Johnnie's, Aunt Kate added, "Your Mother is trying to get a nap as she has a strong threat of headache, and Marie has neuralgia through going about, so we are not a very lively household. We miss Mary Huger very much. She is delightful company, and the little ones too. It seems very strange to be quite by ourselves. The weather is perfectly lovely, though it has been so cold, your Mother has put the flowers in the pit. We have not gotten used to being without you. Good - bye Darling."

The children were sometimes satirical at each other's expense. Bessie wrote, "The line above Johnnie's mouth had gotten a quarter of a shade darker, and he will soon have to buy himself a razor." And Margie, after praising Katie as "the most beautiful girl in the family" went on, "Belle goes to her manners and singing. Her favorite new song is 'Darling, I

Am Growing Old.' " Positively. Johnnie too had something to say of Belle. "She is developing into a genius," he wrote. "She makes up lots of poetry. I will give you one of her pieces. This is it. 'Mother, Mother, don't you hear me calling? Give, oh, give me, a piece of Brother Spalding.' She is more spoilt than ever, and she eats a heap. She is the first to the table, and the last to get up."

Belle was one of the dearest of little children. Always sweet tempered and happy, and always singing like a bird. In her first letter which was written for her, she asked: "Dear Tannie: My hands are all stained up with walnuts, and my little bottom tooth is out. All of the grapes at Aunt Eliza's are gone. I did not get any bad marks today. Your dear little sister, Belle."

Katie's letters were almost as brief: "Dear Tannie: I wish that you were here on Christmas. I went up to the meeting. Harriet has the toothache. We make leaves houses and play birds in the evening. Henry and Miss Marie went to ride and Eddie Elliott went on a mule, to find some pigs of Henry's. Bessie sends her love to you and Susy. I have nothing else to say. Goodbye form your loving sister, Kate."

Bessie and Margie were learning to ride horseback at this time, and Bessie wrote, "I wear your riding skirt, and the body just fits me. We ride Mabel and Flora, and we both like Flora best." Mabel and Flora were our two dear horses. As Mother became less well-off they had to be used for ploughing, and I cannot bear to think of Flora's fate for she had to be sold in the end. Bessie's letter continued, "Mother is reading *Guy Mannering* aloud at night, and I make Christmas presents while she reads." And the letter ended, "Mary comes over every morning to practice, and then she goes back to say lessons to her Grannie."

Why Grannie Gordon was staying at The Cliffs this winter, I cannot imagine, as she had never done such a thing before. It was almost as if she had a premonition.

Gordon and Hammie were still at Sewanee as the school did not end until just before Christmas, but in November Gordon received an offer from his Uncle Willie of a position in his countinghouse at $20.00 a month. By this time Uncle Henry was having a struggle to make both ends meet, and the offer was gladly accepted. Gordon came down from Sewanee, and Johnnie and Hammie Couper had holiday on the two days that he was at home.

"We spent two days and nights with Gordon," Johnnie wrote, "And he come over here to dinner. We went shooting, but none of us killed anything but George Paine. He killed a turkey, but I believe it was a tame one."

Gordon stayed in Savannah with Henry at his Grannie's home, and I haven't a doubt that he saved money on his $20.00 salary, for he had plenty of sense and was absolutely self-controlled. From now on life was to be nothing but hard work for him, poor boy, and the days of his happy, carefree youth was over. Two years later, he went out to Western Texas, where on a ranch in Tom Green County, miles from another habitation, he spent years of his life alone. When he came home, as he did now and then, I remember how silent he was. He seemed to have forgotten how to talk. Once he bought a guitar to take back, thinking its music might be "company for him." We were all glad when he made a success of the cattle business, moved up to the Panhandle, married a fine girl, and had the happiness of a home again.

In December Johnnie wrote, "Hammie will soon be coming home, and I wish you were coming too for Christmas. . . . Hammie Couper and I went down to the old gin to get some lead. We got a heap, about two pounds, and I moulded all of mine into bullets. On Thanksgiving Day we went out shooting before breakfast, and I shot a rabbit with the rifle, and the next day killed four larks with the shot-gun. . . . Mrs. Joseph Huger and Esther Elliott, and Mrs. John Elliott and her family are coming down here. Mrs. Huger and Esther will stay with us, and the rest of Aunt Eliza's. . . . Lou Aubrey came down to Miss Josie Martin's, then to the Shelmans, then to Uncle Henry's, and he visited our house before anyone was up. He came to bring Mother some chrysanthemums and to borrow *Jane Eyre*. It could not be found, but after he left, it was found on top of a press. . . . All of us have written our letter to Santa Claus, and I asked for some powder and shot and a knife."

On December the third, Aunt Kate wrote me, "I want you to study hard, and get all the good you can from your opportunities. We may not be able to send you another year, though I hope we shall be. It is my wish to send you five dollars for Christmas. Not very much, but money is none too plenty. We are all in the dining room downstairs, Mother altering a dress for Margaret."

Mother made all our clothes, and our dresses went down through the family as long as they lasted. Margie I am sure never had a new dress in her life as a child, or for that matter, anything new except her toothbrush.

Aunt Kate continued, "Bessie is crocheting a pocket handkerchief case for a Christmas present. She has done it beautifully, and so quickly."

Bessie has rushed all of her life, and it is wonderful how well she does things in spite of it. "Margaret is making a crimson scarf for Clelia, and Marie is winding white wool to make her mother a fascinator before she comes."

We all wore *fascinators* on our heads when we went out in the evenings in summer. A triangle crocheted in shell stitch usually of white, pale pink or pale blue, tied under the chin, and often quite becoming.

"To tell you how much we long to see our Caroline," Aunt Kate concluded, "and half how much she is missed in this house would be impossible." These were her last blessed words to me.

Mother wrote later that she would send me a box either for Christmas or New Year's Day and mentioned that Aunt Kate would go down to Savannah as usual in January, to visit Aunt Elliott.

Soon after Mrs. Huger and little Esther arrived at Malbone, with Mrs. John Elliott and her children, who were to stay at the Other House.

On December the 19th, Mother wrote, "What do you think of Hammie's taking us by surprise, and coming on Saturday night? He looks as sweet as possible, with a nice color, holds himself well, and is very polite."

Hammie and Johnnie were good looking boys, though neither were as handsome as Father.

"We feel quite proud of him," Mother went on, "And Uncle Henry and Aunt Eliza say he is so handsome. He passed in arithmetic and history, but not in French."

And then came a break in Mother's letter.

"Just as I had written so far, dear child, I was interrupted by Janet's running over." Janet was a little colored maid at The Cliffs, one of the Kincaid family. "She came to ask for some sticking plaster, as Baltimore, the Jersey bull, had hurt Uncle Henry. We were much alarmed of course, and poor Mary came over a few minutes after, and said it was very bad."

Baltimore was a ferocious Jersey bull, of whom everyone except Uncle Henry was afraid of. Told that the bull had broken out of his pen and was eating a pile of shucked corn in the lot, Uncle Henry went down and found a number of the renters on the outside of the fence, none of them daring to go in and drive the animal away. Uncle Henry walked into the lot, and struck the bull on its flank with his hand, ordering it off. The animal turned away sullenly, then, as Uncle Henry walked back to the gate, swung around, lowered his head, and, rushing at him, tossed him in the air, then, as he fell, gored him savagely in the thigh. Roused to action, the horrified tenants ran in, and by shouting and throwing stones, finally drove the maddened animal away.

"They brought Uncle Henry up to the house," Mother wrote, "And fortunately Dr. Memler was there, having come to see little George who had an attack of the croup. The wound on his leg had to be sewn up, and Lucy Elliott had the courage to hold the parts together, while the doctor sewed them. It is quite a deep gash, and the main artery came within a hair's breadth of being cut. The doctor is going to stay there to-night, and I trust all will go well. The trouble will be to keep him quiet until the place heals."

On December the 19th, 1878, Uncle Henry died, at the age of forty-five. In Mother's next letter, she told of his death:

I know you will want to hear everything, so I will try and write to you this morning. Mrs. Huger's letter to Hagee, I suppose reaches her to-day, and you know by this time, that it has pleased the Lord to remove your dear Uncle Henry from what was to him, a weary world, and taken him I trust, to an eternal rest. His life for many years had been a struggle in a financial way, that he could know no happiness, and he was weary and almost overwhelmed. I suppose none of you young people realized it, and we did not think it was necessary to tell you. He was always so brave and cheerful that no one knew what he was suffering, except Aunt Eliza, Aunt Kate and myself.

When I wrote you on Tuesday I felt it was a very serious accident, but it was not until Wednesday night that we became really alarmed. Aunt Eliza sent for me about nine o'clock, saying that the doctor wanted more help that night. We had to dress the wound every hour. About three o'clock poor Dr. Memler gave out entirely, and said he would have to go home and send out his partner, Dr. Johnson. I am sure now that he felt there was no hope, and I believe he was so overcome that he could stand it no longer. Dr. Johnson came about seven in the morning, but all hope was gone then, though Uncle Henry was perfectly calm, and tried to make us think it was not so bad. We sent for Aunt Kate about eight o'clock, and about nine, he seemed to realize his condition, and sent the doctor and Mr. Murphy, who had nursed him that night, out of the room and said he wanted to talk to us. Then he told us that he wished his son Henry to come up and take charge of his affairs and he thought he would do well, as he had business training, and would probably manage better than he had done.

He had all his children come and kissed them around in the most cheerful manner, just as though he were going on a journey. He then asked to be left alone with Aunt Kate and myself. We asked him if he was sure of God's mercy, and he said, "Of course. I was so well brought up, and have had the prayers of so many good women, I know He will take care of me." He tried then to tell Aunt Kate something, but his tongue was so paralyzed that he could not make her understand. He then turned his head, and in a very little while, his spirit took flight. I cannot but think that he is safe, and we shall meet again.

We sent a dispatch to Mr. Gordon, and Henry and Gordon left Savannah on Thursday night. The funeral was postponed as late yesterday as possible that they might be present. They did not get out until dark, and the service was performed by lamp-light. It was a fearful night, rain and sleet, and no one but the men could go to the grave.

I stayed with Aunt Eliza. She is overwhelmed, of course, and no one but the good Lord can help her. . . . My dear child, this is a great sorrow to me. I loved your Uncle Henry dearly, for the sake of your own Father, for he was so much like him in many ways. The two were very much to each other. Uncle Henry has been kind and good to us since we have been left alone. We will miss his kindly protection, but the Lord will provide, and I feel sure we will be taken care of.

Gulie has been everything to her Mother through all this trouble. She had arrange so much about the house-keeping, as for days the house has been full of men, coming kindly to give what assistance they could. Miss Lucy has behaved in the most wonderful manner so efficient, so brave and so thoughtful in every way. Mr. and Mrs. Waring came down yesterday, and everybody has shown the greatest sympathy, and proved that Uncle Henry was respected and loved.

It was thought that Uncle Henry's death was caused by the re-opening of the terrible internal wound he had received in the war, as the external wound was healing at the time of his death. Whatever the cause, it was for him only a blessed release.

Christmas Day must have been a sad one in the two houses, though my brothers and little sisters wrote quite cheerfully, giving detailed lists of the presents they had received. Lucy Elliott and her two little sons, John B. and Joe, came over to Malbone for dinner, and Aunt Eliza had all of her children with her, and Henry stayed on to take charge of the farm.

After Uncle Henry's death Aunt Kate began to sink. It was just as it had been when Aunt Sarah was unable to survive our father's death. She had caught a cold going over to The Cliffs in the rain and sleet. This turned into pneumonia, and on January the seventh her precious spirit left this earth.

"You loved her I know dearly," Mother wrote to me, "And she loved you the same, and perhaps it maybe some comfort to you to know that her last words were of you. . . . Your blessed aunt is at rest. She is with all those she loved so dearly, and though you children have brightened life for her, it was sad for her in many ways, and I know she was ready to go."

"It is such comfort to have Mrs. Huger," Mother ended, "I do not know what we should have done without her. She was like a sister to our dear Aunt Kate, and feels so kindly for us. It is really a blessing to us that she is here."

Aunt Kate's dear body was taken to Savannah to rest beside that of Aunt Sarah in Laurel Grove Cemetery. She had given us everything in life, and, in her will, with the exception of a few legacies, she left everything that she had to Mother and her children.

Kind Grannie Gordon died a few years later, and Mother and Aunt Eliza were left alone, with about the same limited incomes on which to raise their large families of growing children.

As far as we were concerned, the day of our youth were as happy as the days of our childhood, and every summer found the two houses filled with our gay young friends.

I realize now that, absorbed in my own entrancing life, I was merciless to Mother, but I trust that she found her happiness in that of her children.

Three years after we parted Tod Lovell came to Malbone and we were formally engaged. He had left Sewanee and gone down to work for his father on Palmyra plantation. Every September he was allowed to come up and spend one month with his own family and ours. We had kept to the letter everything required of us, and seven years after we met at Sewanee, we were married in the drawing room at Malbone.

The end.

Families & Genealogy
by Hugh Stiles Golson

he *Andrew Low family* was Scotch in origin. Andrew Low was born at Criggie in Kincaidshire and came to Savannah as heir to his namesake uncle's Andrew Low and Company on Johnson Square. After the war, Low and his daughters by his second marriage resided primarily in England at Beauchamps Hall near Leamington Spa. Low's Savannah home on Lafayette Square was designed by John Norris and later became the residence of Daisy Gordon Low and the site where she organized the first Girl Scout troop in America. It is now owned by THE NATIONAL SOCIETY OF COLONIAL DAMES OF AMERICA IN THE STATE OF GEORGIA and serves as its headquarters and house museum. Godfrey Barnsley's carved *Meridiennes*, mentioned by Caroline in her "Neighbors" chapter, face one another across the large double parlors of the home.

The *Ralph Emms Elliott family* was presided over by the widow Mrs. Margaret Mackay Elliott, a sister to Mrs. William Henry Stiles, Sr. and the Misses Catherine and Sarah Mackay. Lieutenant Robert E. Lee was a member of her wedding party in 1829 when she wed the Beaufort, South Carolina doctor in the parlor of the Mackay house. The Elliotts always maintained a residence in Oglethorpe Square, but, after the death of Dr. Elliott, Mrs. Elliott sold the summer residence near Pendleton, South Carolina, and built Summerland next to Etowah Cliffs. After Mrs.

Elliott's death, Summerland was sold to the Henry Stiles family. It was dismantled in the 1970s.

The *William Washington Gordon family* was headed by Sarah Anderson Stites Gordon, widow of the founder of the Central of Georgia Railroad. Mrs. Gordon lived in the mansion at Bull and South Broad (Oglethorpe Avenue) that was built for her uncle, James Moore Wayne who served on the U.S. Supreme Court for thirty-five years. Of Mrs. Gordon's seven children, four survived to produce families. George Anderson Gordon and his family lived in Huntsville, Alabama. William Washington Gordon, Jr. and wife Eleanor Kinzie of Chicago lived in Savannah. Eliza C. Gordon was Mrs. William Henry Stiles, Jr. of Etowah Cliffs. Gulielma C. Gordon married George Evelyn Harrison of Virginia and lived at Lower Brandon on the James River. The Wayne-Gordon house in Savannah is now owned by the Girl Scouts of America and maintained as a museum of the period when Daisy was growing up.

The *Stephen Elliott family* was comprised of the Bishop of Georgia and his children by two marriages. Bishop Elliott was a cousin of Dr. Ralph Elliott and a son of the noted naturalist of the same name. Elliott was educated to be a lawyer, but was eventually ordained a minister of the Protestant Episcopal Church. In 1840 he was elected the first bishop of the Diocese of Georgia. Bishop Elliott served as rector of St. John's Church and Christ Church in Savannah, president of the Montpelier Female Institute in Macon, and president of the Georgia Historical Society. He was also a co-founder of the University of the South in Sewanee, Tennessee. One of the bishop's sons, Stephen, was a brigadier general in the Confederate army, and son Robert became bishop of western Texas. After the bishop's death in 1866, his second wife and cousin, Charlotte Bull Barnwell Elliott, and his daughters settled in Sewanee, Tennessee, where their home was called "Saints' Rest" and their guest cottage "Sinners' Retreat."

The *Joseph Alston Huger family* was of South Carolina origin, owning the rice plantation Murray Hill north of Savannah. Mary Esther Huger and her husband, Dr. J. A. Huger, were cousins of the same name. Dr. Huger lost his fortune during the war and shortly thereafter the family broke up. Mrs. Huger lived for a while in Greensboro, Georgia, but finally settled at Sewanee where her daughter Lucy lived with her husband

Professor John Barnwell Elliott, a son of the bishop. Son Thomas Pinckney Huger lived for a while with the Mackay family as Kate Mackay and Mary Esther Huger were close friends. Son Joseph Alston Huger, Jr. married Mary Stiles Elliott, daughter of Margaret Mackay Elliott and widow of Robert Habersham Elliott.

The *Habersham family* was descended from James Habersham of Beverly, Yorkshire, who arrived in Savannah in 1738 to run Bethesda Orphanage for the Reverend George Whitefield. Habersham moved into the commerce merchant business and amassed a fortune, but his loyalist sentiments put him at odds with his Patriot sons. Grandson Robert Habersham maintained the family firm and resided on Orleans Square in the Bulloch-Habersham house designed by William Jay. He reared his nephew Frederic Augustus Habersham who was married to Leila Elliott, daughter of Margaret Mackay Elliott. Fred Habersham served in the artillery during the war and was killed at the Battle of Chancellorsville.

The *George H. Waring family* were, like the Stiles, a Savannah family transplanted to Cass (Bartow) County. Mrs. Ella Susan Waring was the daughter of the Reverend Charles Wallace Howard who, with William Henry Stiles and Godfrey Barnsley, were among the first to settle in the former Cherokee country. Reverend Howard served several Presbyterian churches, operated a school at his home Spring Bank, and managed extensive agricultural enterprises. Daughter Frances Thomas Howard wrote *In and Out of the Lines*, an account of her witnessing General Sherman's invasion of North Georgia. George Waring built a home near Spring Bank and operated a cement manufacturing enterprise.

• • •

Hamilton Stiles remained a bachelor farmer at Malbone and active in the local farming community. In the 1920s Malbone was sold to Henry Stiles's son Robert whose family still lives there.

Johnnie Stiles became Jack Stiles of Brunswick, a prominent businessman in that town. His first wife was Edith May DuBignon and his second wife was Eleanor Burdette.

Bessie Stiles, who was married and widowed twice, was a Savannah resident. Her first husband was Alfred E. Mills and her second was Franklin Buchanan Screven. She was most active in the affairs of Christ Church and the Colonial Dames and served both in many leadership positions.

Margie Stiles never married. She was a serious artist who taught for many years at the Hartridge School in Plainfield, New Jersey, but returned to Savannah and shared a home with Bessie off Monterey Square.

Katie Stiles became Mrs. Robert L. Mercer and made her home in Savannah on Calhoun Square. She was also active in the affairs of Christ Church and the Colonial Dames and was noted for her culinary talents.

Belle Stiles married attorney H. Snowden Marshall, a descendant of the third chief justice. They made their home on Park Avenue in New York City and traveled extensively. After Mr. Marshall's death, she returned to Savannah and lived on Calhoun Square next to Katherine Mercer.

Henry Stiles took over the management of Etowah Cliffs shortly after his father's death and remained in that capacity all his life. His marriage to Lizzie Chadwick bore nine children, but they separated, Lizzie remaining at Summerland and Henry moving in with his mother and Gulie at Etowah Cliffs. Henry and his horse Frank became legendary in the Cartersville area. After his death, Etowah Cliffs was closed up, and it was destroyed by fire in the 1970s.

Gulie Stiles remained unmarried and spent most of her life managing Etowah Cliffs with her brother Henry. She was her mother's constant companion and her nurse during Mrs. Stiles's lengthy infirmity.

Gordon Stiles left Georgia as a young man to try ranching in Texas. He first settled in Reagan County where a ghost town bears his name, but relocated to the Texas panhandle where the Stiles Ranch near Wheeler is still operated by his family.

Mary Couper Stiles married aristocratic Englishman Ted Swann, and they moved to his rustic Quorn Ranch near Calgary. Mary's health and Ted's mink ranching both failed, and they moved back to Etowah Cliffs where Mary died, followed shortly thereafter by Ted.

Ethel Stiles died of typhoid fever at age 23.

George Stiles lived in Rome, Georgia. He married Nell Crumblis, and he trained and raced harness horses.

Katie Low remained unmarried and cared for her father until his death at Leamington Spa. She later lived at Old Dolby Rectory and kept a home in London. She was an accomplished equestrian who enjoyed riding to the hounds.

Mary Low married international businessman David Charles Guthrie. Their estate East Hadden is near Northampton.

Willie Low inherited his father's fortune and moved freely among the Marlborough set, the Prince of Wales among his cronies. Willie made his home at Wellesbourne House in Warwick. His tempestuous marriage to Daisy Gordon ended in separation followed shortly by Willie's death.

Jessie Low married Hugh Graham, a son of the Duke of Somerset and an avid sportsman. In their later years they made their home at Barford Hall near Warwick. Jessie was a patron of the young author Evelyn Waugh, who patterned several fictional characters on her.

THE WILLIAM HENRY STILES, SR. FAMILY

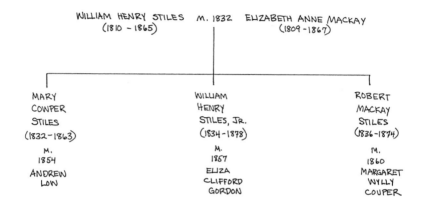

WILLIAM HENRY STILES   M. 1832   ELIZABETH ANNE MACKAY
(1810 - 1865)   (1809 - 1867)

MARY   WILLIAM   ROBERT
COWPER   HENRY   MACKAY
STILES   STILES, JR.   STILES
(1832-1863)   (1834-1878)   (1836-1874)
M.   M.   M.
1854   1857   1860
ANDREW   ELIZA   MARGARET
LOW   CLIFFORD   WYLLY
                        GORDON   COUPER

THE HENRY STILES FAMILY

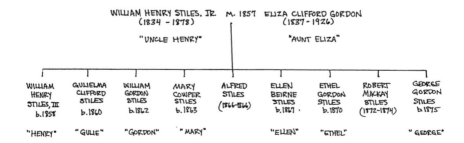

WILLIAM HENRY STILES, JR. M. 1857 ELIZA CLIFFORD GORDON
(1834 - 1878)   (1837 - 1926)
"UNCLE HENRY"   "AUNT ELIZA"

WILLIAM   GULIELMA   WILLIAM   MARY   ALFRED   ELLEN   ETHEL   ROBERT   GEORGE
HENRY   CLIFFORD   GORDON   COWPER   STILES   BEIRNE   GORDON   MACKAY   GORDON
STILES, III STILES   STILES   STILES   (1866-866) STILES   STILES   STILES   STILES
b.1858   b.1860   b.1862   b.1863   b.1867   b.1870   (1872-1874) b.1875

"HENRY"   "GULIE"   "GORDON"   "MARY"   "ELLEN"   "ETHEL"   "GEORGE"

THE ROBERT STILES FAMILY

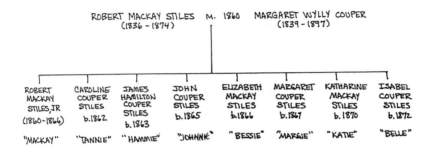

ROBERT MACKAY STILES   M. 1860   MARGARET WYLLY COUPER
(1836 – 1874)   (1839 – (1897)

| ROBERT MACKAY STILES,JR (1860-1866) | CAROLINE COUPER STILES b.1862 | JAMES HAMILTON COUPER STILES b.1863 | JOHN COUPER STILES b.1865 | ELIZABETH MACKAY STILES b.1866 | MARGARET COUPER STILES b.1867 | KATHARINE MACKAY STILES b.1870 | ISABEL COUPER STILES b.1872 |
| "MACKAY" | "TANNIE" | "HAMMIE" | "JOHNNIE" | "BESSIE" | "MARGIE" | "KATIE" | "BELLE" |

THE ANDREW LOW FAMILY

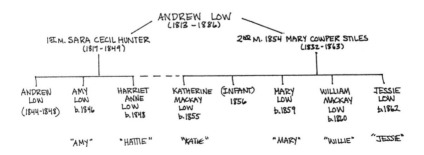

ANDREW LOW
(1813 – 1886)

1ST M. SARA CECIL HUNTER   2ND M. 1854 MARY COWPER STILES
(1817 - 1849)   (1832 - 1863)

| ANDREW LOW (1844-1848) | AMY LOW b.1846 | HARRIET ANNE LOW b.1848 | KATHERINE MACKAY LOW b.1855 | (INFANT) 1856 | MARY LOW b.1859 | WILLIAM MACKAY LOW b.1860 | JESSIE LOW b.1862 |
| | "AMY" | "HATTIE" | "KATIE" | | "MARY" | "WILLIE" | "JESSIE" |

About the Contributors

Caroline Couper Lovell was born at Etowah Cliffs, Bartow County, Georgia in 1862. She was the daughter of Robert Mackay Stiles and the former Margaret Wylly Couper. A talented artist and patron of the arts, Caroline Couper Lovell published *The Golden Isles of Georgia* in 1932, and it has become a regional classic. Lovell's memoir of her childhood in Georgia, *The Light of Other Days*, was written during the late 1920s and early 1930s and is published here for the first time.

Hugh Stiles Golson, a native Savannahian, is a graduate of the University of South Carolina and Armstrong State College. A high school educator for more than twenty years, he has served on various local and state committees for many organizations, including the Georgia Historical Society, the Georgia Department of Education, and the Massie School of Savannah. At present he teaches advanced placement U.S. history in Chatham County and is chairman and founder of the Society for the Preservation of Laurel Grove Cemetery in Savannah.

LeeAnn Whites is associate professor of history at the University of Missouri in Columbia. She was a contributor to the volume of essays *Divided Houses: Gender and the Civil War* and has also published articles in the *Encyclopedia of the Confederacy* and various historical journals. Dr. Whites's *Civil War as a Crisis in Gender: Augusta, Georgia 1860-1890* will be released in the fall of 1995 by the University of Georgia Press.